T0330946

Ethics of Environmental Health

Environmental health encompasses the assessment and control of those environmental factors that can potentially affect human health, such as radiation, toxic chemicals and other hazardous agents. It is often assumed that the assessment part is just a matter of scientific research, and the control part a matter of implementing standards which unambiguously follow from that research. But it is less commonly understood that environmental health also requires addressing questions of an ethical nature.

How can we determine the 'acceptable' risk level for the general population or for certain groups? How should we deal with uneven distributions of risks and benefits? How do we communicate about risks with the stakeholders? This multi-disciplinary collection brings together a number of leading researchers and scholars in order to generate discussion surrounding these key questions, and to bring the ethical implications of science and technology to the forefront of critical thought.

Providing a broad overview of the Ethics of Environmental Health, its philosophical foundations and practical applications, this book offers a significant contribution to ongoing discussions in sustainable development and will be of interest to scholars and practitioners of Environmental Health, urban studies and healthcare.

Friedo Zölzer is Head of the Department of Radiology, Toxicology and Civil Protection at the University of South Bohemia, Czech Republic.

Gaston Meskens works part-time with the Centre for Ethics and Value Inquiry of the Faculty of Arts and Philosophy at the University of Ghent, Belgium and with the Science and Technology Studies group of the Belgian Nuclear Research Centre SCK-CEN, Belgium.

Routledge Studies in Environment and Health

The study of the impact of environmental change on human health has rapidly gained momentum in recent years, and an increasing number of scholars are now turning their attention to this issue. Reflecting the development of this emerging body of work, the *Routledge Studies in Environment and Health* series is dedicated to supporting this growing area with cutting edge interdisciplinary research targeted at a global audience. The books in this series cover key issues such as climate change, urbanisation, waste management, water quality, environmental degradation and pollution, and examine the ways in which these factors impact human health from a social, economic and political perspective.

Comprising edited collections, co-authored volumes and single author monographs, this innovative series provides an invaluable resource for advanced undergraduate and postgraduate students, scholars, policy makers and practitioners with an interest in this new and important field of study.

Ethics of Environmental Health
Edited by Friedo Zölzer and Gaston Meskens

Ethics of Environmental Health

Edited by Friedo Zölzer and
Gaston Meskens

LONDON AND NEW YORK

First published 2017 by Routledge

2 Park Square, Milton Park, Abingdon, Oxfordshire OX14 4RN
52 Vanderbilt Avenue, New York, NY 10017

Routledge is an imprint of the Taylor & Francis Group, an informa business

First issued in paperback 2018

British Library Cataloguing-in-Publication Data
A catalogue record for this book is available from the British Library

Library of Congress Cataloging-in-Publication Data
Names: Zèolzer, Friedo, editor. | Meskens, Gaston, editor.
Title: Ethics of environmental health / edited by Friedo Zolzer and Gaston Meskens.
Description: Abingdon, Oxon ; New York, NY : Routledge, [2017] | Series: Routledge studies in environment and health series | Includes bibliographical references.
Identifiers: LCCN 2016048362| ISBN 9781138186620 (hbk) | ISBN 9781315643724 (ebk)
Subjects: LCSH: Environmental health—Moral and ethical aspects. | Public health—Moral and ethical aspects. | Environmental ethics.
Classification: LCC RA566 .E874 2017 | DDC 615.9/02—dc23
LC record available at https://lccn.loc.gov/2016048362

ISBN: 978-1-138-18662-0 (hbk)
ISBN: 978-0-367-15226-0 (pbk)

Typeset in Bembo
by diacriTech, Chennai

Contents

Contributors

Matteo Andreozzi is a PhD candidate in philosophy at the University of Milan, Italy. His research is mainly on environmental ethics and bioethics. He is particularly interested in the moral status of other-than-human entities.

Robin Attfield is a professor emeritus of philosophy at Cardiff University, UK, and a former member of the Council of the Royal Institute of Philosophy. His recent publications include *Environmental Ethics* (Polity, 2014) and *The Ethics of the Global Environment* (Edinburgh University, 2015).

Marie Claire Cantone is a professor of applied physics in the Department of Biomedical, Surgical and Dental Sciences, University of Milan, Italy. Her specialization is in health physics. She is a member of the ICRP task group on Ethics of Radiological Protection.

Christopher Clement is a health physicist who for many years worked with the Canadian Nuclear Safety Commission. He is currently the Scientific Secretary of the International Commission on Radiological Protection (ICRP), based in Ottawa, Ontario, Canada.

Mark Coeckelbergh is a professor of philosophy of media and technology at the University of Vienna, Austria. He also has an affiliation as a professor of technology and social responsibility at De Montfort University in Leicester, UK. His recent publications include *Human Being @ Risk* (Springer, 2013).

Carl Cranor is a distinguished professor of philosophy and faculty member of the Environmental Toxicology Graduate Program at the University of California, Riverside. His recent publications include *Legally Poisoned: How the Law Puts Us at Risk from Toxicants* (Harvard University, 2011).

Jürgen Kiefer is a retired professor of biophysics and general radiology at Justus-Liebig-University Gießen, Germany. His research interests are the biological effects of different kinds of radiation, as well as radiation protection, but also the relationship between science and philosophy.

Jacques Lochard is a professor at the University of Nagasaki, Japan. Before, he served as director of CEPN, an advisory institution in the field of radiation protection, in Fontenay-aux-Roses, France. He is Vice-Chair of the International Commission on Radiological Protection (ICRP).

Gaston Meskens is a physicist, philosopher and artist. He works part-time with the Centre for Ethics and Value Inquiry of the Faculty of Arts and Philosophy of the University of Ghent, Belgium, and with the Science and Technology Studies group of the Belgian Nuclear Research Centre SCK•CEN.

Michio Miyasaka is a professor of health care ethics at the School of Health Sciences, Niigata University, Japan. His research focuses on Japanese leprosy control policy, the Minamata disease, and the recent disaster at the Fukushima Daiichi Nuclear Power Plant.

Deborah H. Oughton is a professor of environmental/nuclear chemistry and the research director of the Centre for Environmental Radioactivity. She is a member of UNESCO's World Commission for Ethics in Science and Technology, ICRP Committee 4 and its task group on Ethics of Radiological Protection.

Colin L. Soskolne is a professor emeritus at the University of Alberta, Edmonton, Canada. Prior to his retirement, he was a professor of epidemiology in the School of Public Health at that university. He is currently an adjunct professor in the Health Research Institute at the University of Canberra, Australia.

Christian Streffer is a professor emeritus for medical radiobiology at the Faculty of Medicine, University of Duisburg-Essen, Germany, and a board member of the Institute of Science and Ethics, University of Bonn, Germany. He is also an emeritus member of the International Commission on Radiological Protection.

Friedo Zölzer is a professor of environmental sciences at the Faculty of Health and Social Sciences of the University of South Bohemia, Ceske Budejovice, Czech Republic. His specialization is in radiobiology. He is a member of the ICRP task group on Ethics of Radiological Protection.

Preface

Environmental health encompasses the assessment and control of those environmental factors that can potentially affect human health, such as climate change, radiation, toxic chemicals and other hazardous agents. While the tools and methods for assessment and control are generally believed to be well developed, relying as they do on modern science and technology, the ethical frameworks and underpinnings that guide environmental health research and regulations are not always made explicit and, in our view, require greater attention. The reason, we believe, is that an understanding of these frameworks and underpinnings will not only facilitate evaluation of existing regulations, but also unveil the possibilities, limitations and pitfalls of the way science can provide policy advice in general, and in the broad and complex field of environmental health in particular.

If ethics is about questions of right and wrong, then there are certainly different 'levels' of thinking about these questions. 'Meta-ethics' deals with concepts of right and wrong as such (What is rightness? What is goodness?). 'Normative ethics' considers the standards that can be used to evaluate specific practices or ways of conduct. In that sense, normative ethics refers to 'what ought to be' in absence of 'evidence' that would facilitate straightforward consensus and consequent action. 'Applied ethics' gives a perspective on practical cases such as coping with climate change, the use of nuclear technology, or the handling of toxic wastes. It is not so much concerned with passing judgement on the 'morality' of these practices themselves, but rather with finding some common ground for deciding how to deal with them.

How does the environment itself figure in all this? Whether the concern for the integrity of our environment is a means to ensure human well-being, or rather an end in itself is a philosophical question that has 'meta-ethical' as well as a 'normative' aspects. But this book focusses on the influence of environmental factors on human health, and thus discussions on anthropocentric versus biocentric or ecocentric views on our habitat do not play a central role in the texts presented here. Rather, 'ethics of environmental health', in our view, starts from a critical analysis of 'applied' questions. How do we make sense of those complex societal challenges in which science and technology either provoke problems for human well-being or serve as means to deal with them? In this context, the 'health of our environment' comes in either as a norm to guide preventive or restorative action (as in the case of climate change) or as a metaphor that should inspire 'better' policies and 'more responsible' practices that in the long run are in the interest of human well-being on a collective and individual level.

The previous considerations may justify the selection of contributions of scholars and practitioners who come from the whole range of environmental health research and practice as presented in this book, differing not only in their focus on the ethical implications for science and technology but also with respect to the application of research results in the regulatory and policy domains. We hope the reader will find them inspiring in an ethical-philosophical sense as well as useful in their own daily professional practice.

The editors are grateful to the contributing authors not only for their texts, but also for their openness to feedback and suggestions, and to the reviewers for their constructive and insightful comments. This publication is an outcome of the Second International Symposium on Ethics of Environmental Health, held in České Budějovice, Czech Republic, in June 2014. Financial support for the symposium was kindly provided by OPERRA, the 'Open Project for the European Radiation Research Area', which included a subtask aimed at 'identifying issues and relevant institutions in the fields of risk communication, risk perception, and ethics of radiation protection'. While this may sound rather limited in scope, it was recognized by all involved that the ethical issues of radiation protection must be addressed in a multidisciplinary manner, and thus the input of colleagues from public health, ecology, toxicology, bioethics, philosophy and other related fields was all the more appreciated.

Gaston Meskens
Friedo Zölzer
October 2016

Foreword

Medicine saved the life of ethics. This was the message of a famous article of British philosopher Stephen Toulmin in 1982. His argument was that the many challenges facing contemporary healthcare have transformed moral philosophy from a meta-discourse into applied ethics. Dilemmatic cases and problems such as organ donation, futile treatment and prenatal testing demand practical answers rather than theoretical expositions. The emergence of applied ethics shows that philosophy and ethics can successfully integrate with and contribute to healthcare. The field of bioethics especially developed rapidly into a new discipline. After 50 years it is now an established area in universities, research institutions and policy-making at the national and international level.

However, there is reason for a critical review. This book, a collection of essays on the ethics of environmental health, demonstrates that human health is seriously threatened by environmental influences, while ethical reflection of the consequences of environmental deterioration is still rather limited. It is not a major concern in bioethics but a subject within other fields of applied ethics. After decades of examining and discussing ethics in relation to health, ethical analysis of environmental determinants of health (and the same is true for social determinants) is disseminated over various areas of applied ethics, e.g. environmental ethics, food ethics, agricultural ethics, engineering ethics, animal ethics and science ethics. Bioethics continues to be focused primarily on the perspective of the individual patient, based on the moral principle of respect for autonomy.

Perhaps it is time to reverse the message of Toulmin: ethics should save the life of medicine. This would endorse the view of Van Rensselaer Potter who coined the term 'bioethics' in 1971. For Potter, bioethics should have a broad scope. We need to combine our scientific knowledge with value systems in order to address the problems that humanity is facing. The problems he mentions half a century ago (poverty, pollution, politics) are still the same today. But they are now acknowledged as interconnected problems. They can only be addressed from a global perspective, and regarded as shared challenges requesting humanity to cooperate. An individual approach is insufficient. The implication is that bioethics should be global bioethics. For Potter this implies not only that a planetary view should be taken; the ultimate goal of ethics is the survival of humanity and thus the planet. But 'global' also implies an encompassing view that takes into account various theoretical perspectives.

Since global ethical problems nowadays are interconnected, it makes no sense to study them in specialized subareas. The challenge of emerging infectious diseases for example can only be resolved if the animal industry, food industry, loss of biodiversity, microbes behavior and poverty as well as individual hygiene are examined in connection. Bioethical discussion of how to treat or vaccinate individual patients will only look at one piece of the problem. It will never be able to propose effective policies as long as it does not scrutinize the underlying sources of emerging infections. As Potter argued long ago, ethics and health should combine individual, social and environmental perspectives.

Immediately in the first chapter of this book, this point is underlined. More attention should be paid to 'upstream determinants': global ecological changes that impact the conditions of health. It is a similar message to that conveyed by Michael Marmot for social determinants of health. The recognition of these broader contexts for the ethical debate has an important consequence. The question is whether we have the appropriate ethical framework to address these contexts. A broader framework will be necessary if we want to go beyond the individual perspective. Prioritizing the moral principle of respect for autonomy will no longer be enough. We need to extend the framework of mainstream bioethics. This framework (autonomy, beneficence, non-maleficence and justice) was developed because the roots of bioethical problems in the last century were in scientific and technological advances. How to deal with resuscitation or reproductive technology? How should individual patients make decisions? Nowadays, the roots of bioethical problems are in the social and environmental conditions in which we live. Poor people have limited or no choices; they lack healthcare because of lack of insurance or employment, not because of their own choice. People in developing countries are exploited in research projects because it is their only opportunity to ever see a doctor. Global problems such as organ traffic, commercial motherhood or brain drain are not related to individual autonomy but to social and environmental conditions that are often the result of neoliberal policies of globalization that emphasize profits (rather than health) and market approaches (rather than protection of the vulnerable). This economic source of ethical problems requires a new set of ethical principles, not just an extension or adaptation of the current framework. This quest is undertaken elsewhere in this volume. It will not be an easy endeavour. But interest for global bioethics is growing. We can no longer separate biomedical ethics from environmental ethics (as well as other specialized areas). Ethics should be an integrated approach and way of life.

If we are not able to overcome the boundaries of our disciplines, we will learn that global challenges will not respect them.

Henk ten Have
Former Director of the Division of Ethics of Science and Technology, UNESCO
Director of the Center for Healthcare Ethics, Duquesne University, Pittsburgh, USA

Part I

Insights from the discussion of related topics

1 Global, regional and local ecological change

Ethical aspects of public health research and practice

Colin L. Soskolne

Contextualizing this chapter

On a subject that addresses the public health dimensions of global, regional and local ecological change, the unfamiliar reader justifiably may ponder the relevance and, indeed, the appropriate place of ethics in the research and practice domains of public health. Thus, how public health ethics is contextually situated under disruptions to those ecological systems in which humans are embedded – locally, regionally and globally – warrants attention.

The connections between human activity and the disruption of the ecological balance are gaining public attention through real world examples such as climate change, as well as through declines in air, water and soil quality. Ever-widening disparities between the rich and poor continue to grow. These are some of the changes that are already taking a toll on human health and well-being, with the anticipation that, under current trends, catastrophic harms are inevitable (Butler et al. 2015).

As we tamper with the very fabric of life through expansion of the human enterprise, Nature's Services (Daily 1997) are changed; these services we take for granted and assume free of charge in their support of life. The effect is a net negative, with global impacts as noted above. These are contemporary global-scale issues with major human health implications.

While public health is a multi-disciplinary field that exists to protect the population health, epidemiology is the applied science discipline central to public health. It is the science that informs the translation of evidence observed in experimentation, in the real world as the 'natural experiment' or in the laboratory into public policy. As the science for informing health policy, epidemiology can be used correctly or incorrectly, and it also can be abused. Abuse arises when special interests spur us to favour biased as opposed to impartial enquiry.

For a fuller explication of the connections between global ecological change, public health and ethics, the reader is referred to two seminal publications, one by the Canadian Public Health Association (Hancock et al. 2015) and the other by The Rockefeller Foundation–Lancet Commission on planetary health (Whitmee et al. 2015). Their almost simultaneous appearance in mid-2015 demonstrates the escalating attention being devoted to this important, complex and challenging topic.

Objectives

The three objectives of this chapter are to provide a basis for keeping our collective house in order by:

1 Understanding the ethical imperative for epidemiologists to include local, regional and global environmental change under their purview as a legitimate field of enquiry;
2 Exploring the influences that drive global trends in public health in relation to professional values and ethics; and
3 Identifying novel ways forward if humanity is to change from a path destined to the collapse of civilization to a sustainable path of respect and care for the community of life, ecological integrity, social and economic justice, democracy, non-violence and peace.

The epidemiologist and epidemiology

Paraphrased from *A Dictionary of Epidemiology* (Porta 2008), the epidemiologist is a professional who strives to study and control the factors that influence the occurrence of disease or other health-related conditions and events in defined groups of people, has expertise in population thinking and epidemiological methods, and is knowledgeable about public health and causal inference in health. The control of disease in populations is often considered to be a core task for the epidemiologist involved in the provision of public health services.

More specifically, the discipline of epidemiology is defined as the study of the occurrence and distribution of health-related states or events in specified populations, including the study of the determinants influencing such states, and the application of this knowledge to control any health problem. Such *study* includes surveillance, observation, hypothesis testing, analytic research and experiments.

Distribution refers to analysis by time, place and classes or subgroups of persons affected in a population or in a society. *Determinants* are all the physical, biological, social, cultural, economic and behavioural factors that influence health. *Health-related states* and events include diseases, causes of death, behaviours, reactions to preventative programmes and provision and use of health services. *Specified populations* are those with common identifiable characteristics. *Application to control* makes explicit the aim of epidemiology, namely to promote, protect and restore health.

Further to the modern definition of epidemiology that includes the *control* of disease in populations, Sir Austin Bradford Hill (1965) concluded that 'All scientific work is incomplete – whether it be observational or experimental. All scientific work is liable to be upset or modified by advancing knowledge. That does not confer upon us a freedom to ignore the knowledge we already have, or to postpone the action that it appears to demand at a given time'. This comment is often cited as justification for action on the part of epidemiologists in the presence of knowledge, action serving to prevent harms to population health and well-being.

The relevance of these definitions and the above comment by Hill (1965) is that they provide context for the study by epidemiologists of disruptions to global, regional and local ecological system functioning. This contextual framing is directly relevant to community health by virtue of its focus on the prevention of disease, disability and premature death in communities regardless of the determinant.

Some epidemiologists focus on studying the more proximate causes of disease, working more at the micro-level. Others find working at the macro-level, with a focus on the upstream connections between social and/or health policy and disease, worthy of intellectual pursuit. In both areas of focus, equally important, a health problem is studied with a view to informing policy interventions to correct the problem.

Traditional determinants, such as those studied by communicable/infectious and chronic disease epidemiologists, can no longer be seen as the sole focus of epidemiology. Indeed, it is argued in this chapter that the more upstream determinants of, among others, energy, social, political or economic policy falling under the general rubric of 'global ecological change' also can fall under the purview of epidemiology, which sub-specialty would best be termed eco-epidemiology.

The case made in this chapter is that epidemiologists and public health researchers and practitioners need to be concerned with matters of a global nature, specifically to bring their multi-disciplinary skills to prevent harms on a massive scale. They also would wish to preserve the right to life for both present and future generations.

Regardless of whether one focuses on the more proximate or the more distal determinants of health, what health impact could be more significant as an attributable risk than the potential for ecological collapse with its associated massive negative impact on health and well-being locally, regionally and globally? The need to be preventative and invoke the precautionary principle when harms could be so far-reaching becomes all the more significant and deserving of attention (Soskolne 2005). Hence, the focus of this chapter is on the ethical imperative of epidemiologists to see as a legitimate area of investigation the application of their skills to prevent harms from ecological change.

On the challenges of working in this field

One of the single greatest challenges in addressing factors on the scale of global change is that of the classical reaction from very powerful interests determined to maintain the *status quo* through 'denial', the denial of claims of harm caused by business-as-usual practices. To understand this response, an appreciation for the work of Elizabeth Kübler-Ross (1969) provides a useful analogue. She had identified the now classical paradigmatic five stages of grief in her seminal book *On Death and Dying* as human reactions to bad news as follows:

- Denial
- Anger
- Bargaining
- Depression
- Acceptance

This framework was developed for the case of the physician relaying bleak news to the patient. Reactions in the individual patient are not necessarily linear as presented above, and the ultimate goal is 'acceptance'. The same initial response of 'denial' with an ultimate goal of 'acceptance' apply at the global, regional or local levels. Whether speaking to patients with a severe diagnosis, or in speaking truth to power, denial of the facts presented is often an initial response.

More specifically to relaying bad news to any manager, the 'Four D's' are seen to apply. This has been well recognized by many in the field who study that which does not support the *status quo*. Management's reaction is usually a linear, step-wise response where they successively invoke the following reactions to maintain the *status quo*:

- Deny
- Delay
- Divide
- Discredit

Recalling Kübler-Ross' identification of denial as the individual's initial reaction to bad news, we should not be surprised that the person in a management position, on being presented with a problem, will deny it as implausible. Next, delays in the need to take action and maintain the business-as-usual approach will be invoked, often by suggesting that more research be done. Next, division among those arguing in support of the problem will be created by funding other researchers to defend the *status quo,* thus creating division among scientists. If the bearer of bad news persists, then the final stage could well be invoked by discrediting the efforts of the researcher.

Armed with the knowledge of anticipated influence and reactions by powerful interests, the public health researcher and practitioner can be better prepared to rise to the challenges presented in this field of enquiry.

The influence of dominant paradigms

The more upstream the epidemiologist operates in the pursuit of the connections between cause and disease, the more directed and intrusive become the forces of powerful people with interests vested in maintaining the *status quo*. Whether we are speaking of the tobacco or asbestos industries, big pharma, the energy sector, the banking sector or, indeed, our economic system, when challenged, some of those at the helm have a record of responding forcibly, their intent being to silence their critics (Epstein 1978; Davis 2002, 2007, 2010; McCulloch and Tweedale 2008; Michaels 2008; Oreskes and Conway 2010; Hedges 2015). Out of the need to counterbalance such intent lies the more challenging, indeed, vexing, of the ethical dimensions that must be considered by the professions that work in the public interest if the topic of this chapter is to gain traction.

As individuals, we live our lives according to a particular narrative, a script that, for practical purposes, dictates our very actions and reactions as members of society. This script is formulated by the cultural and other influences that surround us.

Thus, we typically find ourselves, as epidemiologists, pursuing avenues of enquiry constrained by our respective narratives. In so doing, we are conforming to the dominant paradigm.

As professionals, we also have different theoretical approaches (also known as paradigms) that we can select from to address a question. We may, for instance, in addressing complexity, opt for a quantitative as opposed to a qualitative approach when, in fact, a post-normal approach, one that combines the two approaches, would be more appropriate for exposing the truth in the study of any complex causal pathway (Funtowicz and Ravetz 1992; Rotmans 1998; Soskolne 2015).

If it is truth that is sought, then scientific enquiry demands impartiality on the part of the scientist. As one from whom objectivity is a *sine qua non,* the scientist has to be able to step outside of her/his paradigmatic constraints to identify that model most appropriate to finding truth regardless of whether or not it will provide answers in conformity with that which is dictated or, indeed, expected to fit the narrative or dominant paradigm (Soskolne 2015).

It is the duty of scientists to uphold the pursuit of truth as a core value in the mission of science. Only through the pursuit of truth can science contribute to the advancement of knowledge that can be relied upon if the public interest is to be both respected and protected, locally, regionally and globally.

Indeed, the scientist is accorded by society a trust to serve its best interests. Any influence that detracts from impartiality thus requires mechanisms of oversight through not only individual self-monitoring, but also through scientific peer assessment and review. This is intended to better ensure that the mission of science is respected. One example of where the mission of science was derailed occurred when one scientific paradigm for use in a health risk assessment was wittingly, or unwittingly, selected to pit industry against regulatory frameworks and the communities that regulation is intended to protect (Soskolne 2015, 198).

Missed opportunities to minimize the risk of partiality in research can have detrimental effects not only on the path that science takes, wasting public funding and resources for research, but more immediately can negatively impact the lives of people directly affected by biased findings. The scientific paradigm selected, for instance in health risk assessment, can pit industry against regulatory frameworks and the communities that regulation is intended to protect. When mechanisms fail, the whole question of both the scientific and moral integrity of the scientist and the scientific enterprise in the pursuit of truth is opened to question, and the public trust is eroded (Baur et al. 2015).

Questions of conscious and subconscious biases that influence scientists

Several questions emerge, given that scientists are people with human frailties. Each merits mention (Soskolne 2015, 197):

- What drives misconduct in science?
- What tempts scientists away from the pursuit of truth?

- How does misconduct derail scientific discourse?
- How does misconduct infiltrate the public policy process and hence global, regional and local environmental health?

Epidemiological research, as in any science, can be manipulated at the study design stage; for instance, experimental and control groups can be selected in ways that introduce bias and thus fail to provide valid point estimates of effect. It is recognized by the Council on Education for Public Health (CEPH), the accrediting body for schools and programmes in public health, that ethics training, strong mentorship and oversight are essential components for accreditation. It is through such training that the likelihood of poor science and practice are minimized.

Of the many biases that can arise in population health research, the ones invoked by powerful interests in support of the dominant paradigm can be found in Porta (2008) as follows:

- Suppression/Oppression Bias
- Repression Bias

These biases operate when a line of proposed research is denied research funds (the former) or not even proposed (the latter) for fear that, if addressed, the dominant paradigm's very existence could be threatened. Equivalently, at the end stage of a research project, suppression bias operates when a research report is denied publication rights for fear that its dissemination could upset the *status quo*.

Why ethics in the professions?

Ethics training is deemed essential not only to keep thoughtful people intent on doing good on track, or to keep our own house in order, but also for socializing students; we also need to equip students with the skills needed to speak truth to power based on valid science.

Ethics principles also provide a normative basis for rational behaviour policy, transparency of collective actions, and accountability for actions taken. Having ethics guidelines facilitates thoughtful consideration of options in moving forward.

Ethical decision-making is required at every step in both epidemiological research and in practice. In neither realm can we be naïve, needing at all times to remain aware of forces at play that may be introduced to influence both the scientific design of a study and its interpretation, as well as how it may be used to inform policy formulation. Great vigilance and personal integrity are required to counter the influence of financially interested parties and corrupt and morally bankrupt governments. Understanding ethical norms can help professionals in various circumstances to navigate their way to an ethical decision.

Core values and mission statements for the professions

In all disciplines, core values and mission statements are intended to provide the anchor not only for the work we do, but also for our collective motivation. The latter in the public health disciplines includes the need to maintain, enhance and promote health in communities worldwide, and to work to protect the public health interest above any other interest.

Our ethics and values determine in large part our behaviours. People have the moral duty, in the public interest, to call others on their exhibited poor conduct. In the professional context, this ought to be done in a collegial way rather than one of confrontation. Sometimes, however, peer pressure is not effective to correct poor decisions before harm can arise. Also, calling people on what are seen as poor decisions has its challenges, especially in the context of speaking truth to power.

The scientific ethic

The ethic of science defines the boundaries that must be respected by those who wish recognition as part of the scientific community. Ethics for professionals are expressed as normative statements of rules of conduct/behaviour recognized in respect to a profession's particular class of human actions. Most professions are expected to be self-regulating, ensuring adherence to the specified rules of conduct/behaviour by its members. According to Reece and Siegal (1986), under the ethical theory of Deontology (a duty-based theory in moral philosophy), scientists have a duty to:

- Use appropriate methods
- Be objective
- Be honest in reporting
- Publish results, whether positive, no effect or negative
- Prohibit distortion in, for example:
  - Falsification of data
  - Biases inherent to study design
  - Proper analytical procedures
  - Objective interpretation
- Do one's own work and avoid plagiarism
- Acknowledge sources
- Avoid exploitation of graduate students

In essence, good ethical conduct and good science are inextricably linked and mutually reinforcing.

Bioethics extended to eco-epidemiology

Medical ethics, as currently applied, is most commonly based on the four bioethical principles described by Beauchamp and Childress (2008) as:

- Respect for autonomy, requiring that the researcher respects the research participant's right to self-determination
- Beneficence, requiring the researcher to do good by way of the research participant

- Non-maleficence, requiring the researcher to do no harm to the research participant
- Justice, requiring of the researcher the fair and equitable allocation of risks and benefits to all research participants without discrimination

These four principles, considered for the purposes of this discussion as *first-order principles*, must be applied in the evaluation of any proposed medical research project. In terms of their practical application, there is no hierarchy among the four principles and, in every situation, there is a tension among each of them. The researcher must aim to maximize each of the four principles through every step of the research process. What these principles do is force the researcher to transparently defend the position being taken in proposing the series of actions required of each research participant in relation to each of the four principles. In so doing, a basis for accountability and subsequent review or evaluation is made possible.

Those engaged in public health research, and particularly those engaged in eco-epidemiology, must extend the four biomedical principles above to recognize their duty to:

- Protect the most vulnerable in society (e.g. unborn, children, Inuit, frail elderly). This principle is akin to that of justice in biomedical research.
- Involve communities in our research (i.e. verify the community relevance of the research being proposed). This principle is akin to that of respect for autonomy in biomedical research.
- Maintain integrity in public health (i.e. the researcher must serve the public health interest above any other interest). This principle is akin to that of both beneficence and non-maleficence in biomedical research.

For the purposes of this discussion, a first-order principle is a primary, overarching consideration, while a second-order principle is one that derives from, and elaborates on the first-order principle.

Second-order principles flow from the above three identified duties in public health as follows:

- Environmental justice
- The polluter pays
- Precautionary principle
- Solidarity
- Post-cautionary principle
- The seventh generation principle

The first of these – environmental justice – is related to 'justice' under the biomedical framework. We can ask while our research is being done:

- Who is taking the risks?
- Who is deriving the benefits?

The second of these – the polluter pays – also is related to 'justice' under the biomedical framework. From this we seek justice by incentivizing the internalization of costs related to any harms associated with the polluting source.

The third of these – the precautionary principle – is related both to 'non-maleficence' and 'respect for autonomy' under the biomedical framework. This is apparent when examining the risk from a certain agent, in which case the presence of uncertainty shall not be used as a reason for postponing cost-effective measures to prevent such exposure.

The fourth of these – the principle of solidarity – is related to all four of the first-order principles under the biomedical framework. This becomes apparent from The Golden Rule in which we are reminded to not do unto our neighbour that which we would not wish to have done to ourselves. We want for ourselves to be treated with respect in our right to self-determination, to do good, to do no harm, and to enjoy justice.

The fifth of these – the post-cautionary principle – is related to each of 'beneficence', 'non-maleficence' and 'justice' under the biomedical framework. This is so because we come to recognize that the precautionary action that had not been taken in a timely fashion leaves alternative options that will be less effective than had the precautionary options been applied in a timely way.

The sixth of these – the seventh generation principle – is related to all three of 'beneficence', 'non-maleficence' and 'justice' under the biomedical framework. This becomes apparent when an examination of the potential consequences of a decision taken today on the children to be born seven generations hence are considered, and it is approved only if no ill-effects are anticipated. This principle is closely related to that of 'inter-generational equity'.

It becomes quickly apparent in applying the above first- and second-order principles that the techniques used to skew results and generate junk science (see the following section) are unethical.

Classical techniques that skew results: from biased methods to junk science

Some scientists are engaged in the 'doubt science' industry (see Epstein 1978; Davis 2002, 2007, 2010; McCulloch and Tweedale 2008; Michaels 2008; Oreskes and Conway 2010; Hedges 2015). They constitute a formidable force, if only for the reason that moneyed interests are limitless relative to the efforts exercised by those who see the ill being done and work hard, usually in a volunteer capacity, to counter the influence of those tempted by lucrative consulting contracts.

Cranor (2011) has assembled generally well-known techniques used by such people as they contribute to 'junk science', the latter being produced usually through funding provided by powerful interests. The latter is used to infiltrate the literature such that, in court proceedings, doubt will work in favour of the defendant and make it unlikely that policy change will ensue. The standard techniques that these scientists use to foment uncertainty about cause and effect include:

- Statistically under-powered studies
- Inadequate follow-up methods
- Inadequate follow-up time
- Contaminated controls, and a broad range of degree and types of exposure among the presumed exposed group
- Ignoring known synergies among components of the mixture of chemicals to which people are exposed
- Inadequate laboratory practices that systematically under-estimate exposures
- Inappropriate analytical methods for calculations
- Unbalanced discussion
- Selective disclosure of competing interests
- Linear-reductionist quantitative methods without post-normal qualitative approaches to complement them

In addition, arguments used to delay action in support of maintaining the *status quo* include classical techniques used to skew research results such as:

- Making a biased or selective interpretation
- Ignoring mechanistic information for inferring effects
- Exaggerating differences between human and toxicology studies, the insistence being on separating effects seen in animals from effects in humans, or the converse as is convenient
- Ignoring the fact that molecular structures predict hazard potential

Finally, classical techniques employed that skew and delay policy, and also create an unhelpful division among scientists, include:

- The insistence on first demonstrating effects in local populations of exposed people despite demonstrated effects in humans elsewhere
- The failure to make explicit the implicit value judgements that go into deciding appropriate standards of evidence for drawing policy-relevant conclusions (viz. by the researcher suppressing dominant interests and values that may skew the results)

A fuller exposition of the above strategies/techniques can be found in Cranor (2011).

Governance amid ideological influences in a globalizing world

Powerful moneyed interests, typically with a neo-liberal bent, are contributing vast sums of money not only to buy the services of consultants for hire, but also for the establishment and ongoing operations of ideological think tanks (Brown 2008).

Specific egregious examples of the distortion of science have been seen from such entities, with tobacco being perhaps the best known. The amount of money contributed by wealthy, ideologically driven entities, contributing so heavily to the generation of much of the junk science that continues to infiltrate the scientific literature, is vast. This stands in stark contrast to the typically volunteer efforts of some scientists who work hard to counter the onslaught of efforts designed to undermine public interest science.

Prior to the exposé of ideological think tanks by Brown (2008), what was perhaps the most damaging publication for policy action on climate change came from Lomborg (2001). Close on its heels, among others, the Koch brothers (Koch Industries) out of Texas, USA, with vast oil wealth, contributed large sums of money to ideological think tanks like the Chicago-based Heartland Institute whose role, among other points of focus, has been to deny the scientific evidence demonstrating both the existence and cause of climate change. Government inaction on climate change in many countries is, in large part, attributable to the fomenting of doubt from the work sponsored by and related to the mission of and tactics employed by such entities.

Many such examples, from tobacco to asbestos and climate change, give one pause to reflect on the definition of the term 'sociopath': power-seeking, anti-social con artists with no social conscience. These examples also cause one to wonder about, given that the thrust of this chapter has been on professional ethics, the integrity and moral fibre of the individuals who are complicit in such practices (Baur et al. 2015). Not to say that this ought not to happen in the real world; after all, business does what business must do in its pursuit of endless global growth and profit. However, what are needed are counterforces that serve to protect the public interest.

Ethics complemented with virtuous traits of character

To complement considerations of principle-based ethical analysis, Weed and McKeown (1998) suggested that virtue ethics be considered. They note that to be a professional of integrity we must appreciate the traits of a virtuous character. Virtues, they note, do not replace ethical rules or duties (see 'The scientific ethic' above). Rather, an account of professional ethics is more complete if virtuous traits of character are identified, such as:

* Humility   – Respect the input & opinions of others / Self-effacement
* Fidelity   – Honour one's commitments / Promote trust
* Justice   – Act fairly
* Patience   – Take time to hear others' viewpoints
* Industry   – Do your level best / Excel
* Veracity   – Tell the truth / Be honest
* Compassion – Empathize
* Integrity   – Demonstrate good moral character

- Serve   – Protect the most vulnerable / Serve the public interest
- Prudence   – Err on the side of caution / Demonstrate good judgement

These virtues resonate with most in the public health field and are self-explanatory. Some professionals do attempt to be assertive when it comes to protecting the public interest. This assertiveness emanates from a consideration of both principles and virtues, and particularly when considering one's duties as a scientist.

Voluntary professional societies, like the International Society for Environmental Epidemiology (ISEE), developed a procedure for supporting beleaguered colleagues and/or potential whistle-blowers. This procedure provides a way of responding to an appeal by any environmental epidemiologist and health scientist who claims to be made to feel threatened for having identified a hazard and/or for proposing to study a suspected hazard (ISEE revised March 2009). Being a voluntary society, the only support that can, however, be provided is moral support; legal avenues are not practical, given the absence of financial resources, and infrastructure for enforcement does not exist.

The way forward

True democracy can be achieved only through a well-informed public underscored by an improved government science, technology and innovation strategy that should:

- Offer incentives to non-profit professional organizations in support of capacity-building to expose junk science, particularly where applied science works at the nexus of policy
- Introduce disincentives (i.e. regulatory penalties) for those engaging in producing junk science

By way of readily accessible documents on ethics, and different from the United Nations Universal Declaration of Human Rights (1948) with an almost exclusive rights-based focus, The Earth Charter (2002) is a duties-based soft law instrument designed essentially to save us from ourselves. The launch in 2002 of The Earth Charter underscored the need to consider that, with every right, there is an associated duty.

The four major categories of ethical principles in The Earth Charter refer to:

- Respect and care for the community of life
- Ecological integrity
- Social and economic justice
- Democracy, non-violence, and peace

The Earth Charter is accessible in about 63 different languages. It can be read in less than 20 minutes. It behoves all of us to become familiar with this global blueprint for a set of values and ethics that could guide us onto a sustainable path to protect both present and future generations.

For evidence-based policy that serves the public interest, the professional familiar with the pressures arising from competing interests and the contextual narrative will be best equipped to navigate the system within which she/he works in support of public interest science. Familiarity with both principle-based and virtue-based ethics contributes to keeping our collective house in order. While not all 'corporate' science is bad science, we need now to stand up to global moneyed influence to ensure greater balance in our mission to protect the public interest. Professional societies like the *International Joint Policy Committee of the Societies of Epidemiology* (IJPC-SE) perform a vigilant function (see www.ijpc-se.org).

References

Baur X., Budnik L. T., Ruff K., Egilman D. S., Lemen R. A. and Soskolne C. L. (2015) 'Ethics, morality, and conflicting interests: how questionable professional integrity in some scientists supports global corporate influence in public health', *Int J Occup Environ Health 21*, 172–75.

Beauchamp T. L. and Childress J. F. (2008) *Principles of Biomedical Ethics.* Oxford University Press, Oxford.

Brown D. A. (2008) 'The ominous rise of ideological think tanks in environmental policy-making', in Soskolne C. L. (ed), *Sustaining Life on Earth: Environmental and Human Health through Global Governance,*. Lexington Books, Lanham, 243–56.

Butler C. D., Dixon J. and Capon A. G. (eds) (2015). *Health of People, Places and Planet: Reflections Based on Tony McMichael's Four Decades of Contribution to Epidemiological Understanding.* Australian National University Press, Canberra. Downloadable free of charge at http://press.anu.edu.au?p=320071. Accessed 19 October 2015.

Council on Education for Public Health (CEPH). http://ceph.org/about/. Accessed 19 October 2015.

Cranor C. F. (2011) *Legally Poisoned: How the Law Puts Us at Risk from Toxicants.* Harvard University Press, Boston.

Daily G. C. (ed) (1997) *Nature's Services: Societal Dependence on Natural Ecosystems.* Island Press, Washington D.C.

Davis D. (2002) *When Smoke Ran Like Water: Tales of Environmental Deception and the Battle against Pollution.* Basic Books, New York.

Davis D. (2007) *The Secret History of the War on Cancer.* Basic Books, New York.

Davis D. (2010) *Disconnect: The Truth about Cell Phone Radiation, What the Industry Has Done to Hide It, and How to Protect Your Family.* Dutton Adult, New York.

The Earth Charter (2002) www.earthcharterinaction.org/invent/images/uploads/echarter_english.pdf. Accessed 19 October 2015.

Epstein, S. S. (1978) *The Politics of Cancer.* Sierra Club Books, San Francisco.

Funtowicz S. and Ravetz J. (1992) 'Three types of risk assessment and the emergence of post-normal science', in Krimsky S and Golding D (eds), *Social Theories of Risk.* Praeger, London, 251–74.

Hancock T., Spady D.W. and Soskolne C.L. (eds) (2015) *Global Change and Public Health: Addressing the Ecological Determinants of Health: The Report in Brief.* Canadian Public Health Association, Ottawa. www.cpha.ca/uploads/policy/edh-brief.pdf. Accessed 19 October 2015.

Hedges C. (2015) *Wages of Rebellion: The Moral Imperative of Revolt.* Knopf, Canada.

Hill A. B. (1965) 'The environment and disease: association or causation?' *Proceedings of the Royal Society of Medicine 58*, 295–300.

International Society for Environmental Epidemiology (ISEE). *Procedure for Dealing with Beleaguered Colleagues.* www.iseepi.org/About/Docs/iseeprocedurefordealingwithbeleaguered colleagues.pdf. Accessed 19 October 2015.

Kübler-Ross E. (1969) *On Death and Dying: What the Dying Have to Teach Doctors, Nurses, Clergy and Their Own Families.* Scribner, New York.

Lomborg B. (2001) *The Skeptical Environmentalist: Measuring the Real State of the World.* Cambridge University Press, UK.

McCulloch J. and Tweedale G. (2008) *Defending the Indefensible: The Global Asbestos Industry and Its Fight For Survival.* Oxford University Press, New York.

Michaels D. (2008) *Doubt Is Their Product: How Industry's Assault on Science Threatens Your Health.* Oxford University Press, New York.

Orsekes N and Conway E. M. (2010) *Merchants of Doubt: How a Handful of Scientists Obscured the Truth on Issues from Tobacco Smoke to Global Warming.* Bloomsbury Press, London.

Porta M. (ed) (2008) *A Dictionary of Epidemiology, Fifth Edition.* Oxford University Press, New York.

Reece R. D. and Siegal H. A. (1986) *Studying People: A Primer in the Ethics of Social Research.* Mercer, Macon, GA, 62–70.

Rotmans J. (1998) 'Methods for IA (Integrated Assessment): the challenges and opportunities ahead', *Environmental Modelling and Assessment 3*, 155–79.

Soskolne C. L. (2005) 'On the even greater need for precaution under global change' (Reprinted from *The European Journal of Oncology Library*, Vol 2, 2003), *Human and Ecological Risk Assessment 11*, 97–106.

Soskolne C. L. (2015) 'Public health and environmental health risk assessment: which paradigm and in whose best interests?' in Westra L, Gray J, Karageorgou V (eds), *Ecological Systems Integrity: Governance, Law and Human Rights.* Earthscan, London, Chapter 16, 191–200.

United Nations Universal Declaration of Human Rights (1948) http://watchlist.org/wordpress/wp-content/uploads/Universal-declaration-of-human-rights.pdf. Accessed 19 October 2015.

Weed D. L. and McKeown R. E. (1998) 'Epidemiology and virtue ethics', *International Journal of Epidemiology 27*, 343–49.

Whitmee S., Haines A., Beyrer C., Boltz F., Capon A. G., Ferreira de Souza Dias B., Ezeh A., Frumkin H., Gong P., Head P., Horton R., Mace G. M., Marten R., Myers S. S., Nishtar S., Osofsky S. A., Pattanayak S. K., Pongsiri M. J., Romanelli C., Soucat A., Vega J., Yach D. (2015) *Safeguarding Human Health in the Anthropocene Epoch: Report of The Rockefeller Foundation–Lancet Commission on Planetary Health.* Published online 16 July 2015, http://dx.doi.org/10.1016/ S0140-6736(15)60901-1. http://press.thelancet.com/PHCommission.pdf. Accessed 19 October 2015.

2 Environmental ethics and environmental policies

Marie Claire Cantone and Matteo Andreozzi

Introduction

In Western thought, the substantial identity between human beings and moral patients (recipients of actions judged from the ethical point of view) has historically prevented the expansion of moral concern beyond human communities. Nevertheless, several environmental problems are currently seriously undermining the traditional belief that the moral community should be restricted to human beings alone. New theories, especially in the fields of biology, ethology and ecology, together with recent scientific discoveries demonstrating how human activities are jeopardizing ecosystem services, urge for a paradigmatic change in our moral convictions (Millennium Ecosystem Assessment 2005a). Unfortunately, the more thoroughly we become aware of these problems, the more we realize that we have to rectify the errors of the past, if we still want to live on this planet. We must, in essence, correct the exploitation, abuse and damage to nature that were committed through superficiality or ignorance. We must strive to build a world vision, a culture and a society that do not yet exist. Even if we focus our energies on solving basic, practical problems such as climate change, deforestation and the loss of biodiversity, the solution lies in something which is much more deeply rooted in human cultures. An important step is to become aware of the global environmental crisis our earth is facing, but if we really want to take effective measures, we need first to change our cultural principles and our way of thinking (Andreozzi 2013).

We used to think of nature as an unlimited resource available for human use. Moreover, the continuous growth of our technological power has led to at least three major contemporary crises attributable to irresponsible human activity (Millennium Ecosystem Assessment 2005b). First, the *environmental crisis*, which involves landscapes and natural resources and affects the supply of cultural and vital services emerging from life–environment relationships. It addresses humans indirectly, through their desires, and consists of a rapid and exponential process of deterioration, whose consequences will reverberate for a long time to come. Second, the *ecological crisis*, which affects the ecosystem services that protect life on the planet. We are referring to irreversible damage of more than half of these services. It addresses both humans and other living beings indirectly, through their needs. Last, the *biological crisis*, which directly involves all of life. The speed and the rate of extinction of various life forms have increased dramatically, while biodiversity has declined. The *environmental crisis* is strictly related to human needs and rests on the human perception of the environment as a simple sum of services which are not linked to each other; the *ecological crisis* regards the hidden connections existing between all natural activities; the *biological crisis* concerns the survival of all life on planet Earth, which has now been put in jeopardy. Although alarming, these crises provide a pretext for efforts to be made to bring about change. In fact, this pretext is raised by many scholars in environmental ethics, who have taken up the challenge and opened an extremely urgent and inspiring call for academic research. This is not the call to apply traditional ethical paradigms to a new practical ethics field – the environment. This is the call for a *new ethical paradigm* – one that is able to extend moral values and moral status to non-human and non-paradigmatic entities, regarding them as moral patients (Rolston 2012).

How could concerns for the environment based on the need to respect ourselves, future generations, other cultures or religious beliefs change things in an effective way? For example, in this perspective, electric cars seem to represent a solution that respects the environment. Nevertheless, the electricity which makes them move is derived in large part from the use of fossil fuels, which in this case pollute far from us. Thus, with electric cars we respect predominantly ourselves and our urban life – not the environment. This is because this kind of concern preserves the instrumental values of nature that we have already recognized for a long time – creating the problems we have to handle nowadays. What we need is to accept the latter call – extending the status of moral patient beyond the ideal paradigmatic human being – and to do it with enthusiasm and with a strong personal commitment to issues of extreme relevance for the global agenda.

The originality and relevance of environmental ethics

Environmental ethics is extremely original and relevant in the broader contemporary debate on humans and nature. While its originality consists in the decentring of ethical reflection from an exclusively human scope, its relevance is based mainly on its questioning of the notions of moral value and moral status when applied to new categories of moral patients, thus leaving open the possibility to construct ethical systems able to *truly* respect them. Each ethical theory is an attempt to arrange our ethical judgements into a system, and so explain and guide our ethical decisions through a certain number of principles (Kernohan 2012, 6). There are different types of ethical theories. As Andrew Kernohan suggests (2012, 6–7), we can classify the most popular approaches, as well as better understand the special role of environmental ethics, if we look at the typical situation to which an ethical judgement applies (see Figure 2.1).

A typical situation involves a moral agent (typically, a person) performing an action which leads to consequences related to some beneficiary or victim, who is the moral patient. Focusing on different components of the ethical situation described above generates different ethical approaches. If we focus on the character of the moral agent, asking if they are virtuous or vicious, we are dealing with

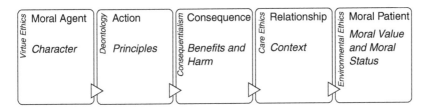

Figure 2.1 A typical ethical situation.

virtue ethics. Deontology focuses on the principles that guide the action, while consequentialism focuses on the benefits and harm produced by it. Care ethics places the attention on relationships by contextualizing the entire ethical situation. The big question of environmental ethics is: which entities have moral value and moral status, and should therefore be considered as moral patients? Hardly anyone has ever handled this question throughout the whole history of philosophy: the few authors who have addressed the problem did not consider the option to move it beyond the here-and-now relationship between humans (persons, corporations or governments). We are now required to extend the circle of moral concern. It does not mean denying the moral relevance of human beings, extending our same moral status to non-human entities, or refusing the validity of classic ethical approaches.

Even without abandoning the most accepted ethical theories, it is nonetheless possible to refuse the ethical and ontological supremacy of human beings and thus admit the need to respect different kinds of non-human and non-paradigmatic moral patients. Indeed, environmental ethics expands the status of moral patients beyond five dimensions (Andreozzi 2015). The first dimension is *space*: this means to extend moral concern beyond the geographical borders that keep closer persons separated from strangers. The second is *time*. We need to move the ethical community borders beyond the present and imminent future, and start thinking also generations into the distant future. The third is *humankind*. We humans are not the only living beings able to have a cognitive and sentient life, and thus to value our own life from a conscious perspective: indeed, non-human animals also care about their lives. The fourth dimension is *sentience*. This is because, in saying that a living being is interested in (wants, desires, hopes for, cares about, etc.) something, we are not ruling out situations in which something is in a living being's interest (will contribute to their good, well-being or welfare), even though they are not consciously interested in it (Regan 1976). The last dimension is *individuality*: our moral concerns should not be direct toward singular entities only, but species, ecosystems, ecological processes and climate too. As a result, the moral circle should be extended in order to include at least eight non-paradigmatic moral patients: distant people, future people, sentient beings, living beings, evolutionary processes, ecosystems and the Planet Earth (see Figure 2.2).

It is also necessary in this perspective to keep a clear distinction between the moral values and the moral status of these moral patients: even if it is imperative to admit the existence of bearers of non-instrumental values that are not (present

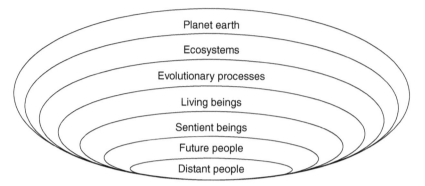

Figure 2.2 The extension of the moral circle.

and near) humans, this would not necessarily give them a moral status similar to ours. Moral value and moral standing express a variety of meanings and refer to different fields of study. This means that the two concepts pose different questions. Regarding the former notion – the value of nature – we should thoroughly answer at least three questions: What is value? What is the origin of value? What is of value? In reference to the latter – the moral status of nature – we should ask: Which entities should we consider? What should we consider about these entities? How much weight should we give to these considerations? Providing separate answers to the different questions behind the two concepts is a required step toward rethinking the way in which we should relate with nature, as well as the way we should handle matters of policy regulations concerning nature. Indeed, this is the only way to reserve the same respect to natural entities that we owe to moral patients. Such a theoretical proposal is not only in agreement with Western culture – as it can overcome anthropocentrism without going against humanism – but it is also able to both uphold the necessity to extend the moral community beyond humanity and guarantee the protection of the environment (Kernohan 2012, 8–10).

Approaches to the problem

Environmental ethics developed as a discipline in the early 1970s, under the increasing concerns and awareness of the 1960s, when scientists all over the world started to bring attention to the effects that population growth, industrial development and economic expansion were having on the natural world. The discipline deals with ethical issues surrounding the environment, aiming at finding ethical justifications and moral motivations for global environmental protection. Nevertheless, it cannot be reduced to the mere application of traditional ethical theories to the natural world. This implies a 'change of values' related to the environment and the need to find new 'centres of values'. Several philosophers have given quite different answers to this fundamental problem and different environmental ethics have emerged. Environmental ethics includes at least four major schools of thought with the aim of systematizing the values of the environment: enlightened or weak anthropocentrism, zoocentrism (which includes both animal liberation and animal rights theories), biocentrism and ecocentrism.

Classic ethical theories endorse a narrow anthropocentric paradigm: they assign moral standing only to here-and-now people. 'Anthropocentrism' literally means 'human-centred': only human beings are at the centre of moral values. Nevertheless, there is no contradiction in remaining anthropocentric while extending the status of moral patients to distant people and future people. These people have indeed the same characteristics as nearby and present people. Whatever has a moral value for narrow anthropocentric theories, has a value for distant and future people. Therefore, these people also have a moral standing from an anthropocentric perspective. But here is the twist that leads to enlightened or weak anthropocentrism: since we cannot directly interact with people at a physical or temporal distance from us, we are required to respect these people in what is instrumentally valuable for them. What, more than natural resources, is the fundamental basis for human well-being? Everyone in the world depends on nature and ecosystem services to provide the conditions for a decent, healthy and secure life (Millennium Ecosystem Assessment 2005a). It follows that we have moral duties toward the environment, even though these are indirect duties derived from the direct duties we recognize toward human beings alone. In short, we need to shift from the belief that human beings are the owners of nature and assume the more suitable role of administrators.

Despite the fact that a number of philosophers (Hargrove 1989, Hargrove 1992, Norton 1984, Norton 1995, Passmore 1974a, Passmore, 1974b) truly believe this is a more than adequate paradigm for handling the need for environmental protection, other philosophers claim it is time to abandon the human-centred approach for an animal-centred, life-centred, or ecological-centred approach. Authors such as Peter Singer and Tom Regan historically extended the status of moral patients to several non-human animals (mostly mammals) by arguing that if the capacity for pain and pleasure or mental awareness were enough to give a morally valuable standing to human beings, they should be enough to give moral status also to non-human animals (Regan 1983, Singer 1975). Indeed, this is the core of zoocentric approaches to environmental ethics, by analogy to zoology, the scientific study of animals. Biocentric ethics defends the moral value of life and thus involves ethical theories in which all living beings have moral status. Life-centred values have been defined since antiquity, as we can see for example in the biblical edict 'choose life', and in some Buddhist principles. The most influential argument for a biocentric ethic in Western philosophy was given by the philosopher Paul Taylor (1986). He argues as follows:

1 Some entities have an objective good of their own.
2 An entity has an objective good of its own if, and only if, it is a teleological centre of life.
3 All living things are teleological centres of life.
4 Therefore, each living thing has an objective good of its own.

5   We have good reason to adopt the biocentric outlook on nature according to which the objective good of any living thing is of no more inherent worth than that of any other.

6   All living things, including humans, have equal inherent worth.

7   Rational agents should give to all living things the same respect that they do to human beings. (Kernohan 2012, 168)

According to Taylor, we are not required to treat all living things in the same way; however, we must give them the same respect. There are important differences between humans and other living beings, and these differences must imply different moral statuses, despite there being no difference in the moral values behind these ethical standings. In Peter Singer's words:

> The differences that exist between men and women are equally undeniable, and the supporters of Women's Liberation are aware that these differences may give rise to different rights. Many feminists hold that women have the right to an abortion on request. It does not follow that since these same people are campaigning for equality between men and women, they must support the right of men to have abortions too. Since a man cannot have an abortion, it is meaningless to talk of his right to have one. Since a pig cannot vote, it is meaningless to talk of its right to vote. […] The extension of the basic principle of equality from one group to another does not imply that we must treat both groups in exactly the same way, or grant exactly the same rights to both groups. Whether we should do so will depend on the nature of the members of the two groups. The basic principle of equality, I shall argue, is equality of consideration; and equal consideration for different beings may lead to different treatment and different rights. (Singer 1976, 150)

Finally, theories of environmental ethics that extend moral values and moral status to evolutionary processes, ecosystems and the Planet Earth are called ecocentric. As biocentric ethics claims that we have the moral obligation to defend and promote the welfare of all living beings, and that we must do so for their own interest and not only for their instrumental values, ecocentric ethics extends these principles to the entire natural community. Aldo Leopold and John Baird Callicott's land ethic, Holmes Rolston III's Earth ethic, and Arne Næss' deep ecology are the most representative instances of such an ethical perspective (Callicott 1987, Callicott 1989, Callicott 1999, Leopold 1949, Næss 1989 [1974], Rolston 1986, Rolston 1988, Rolston 2012). According to the most common interpretation of their theories, since, when a criterion or principle extends to new cases it still applies to the cases where it applied before the extension, humans and other living beings keep their moral values and moral status, but they should be rooted in the same great flourishing of the natural environment.

The most important insight derived from all these different approaches to the problem is as simple to understand as it is difficult to admit: humans should no longer be considered as masters of the universe, but rather as simple parts of nature.

We cannot derive from this fact the duty to defend and promote the moral values of non-human natural entities at any cost. We are required to give the same moral consideration to the moral status that is specific to each moral patient. There are several cases of conflict of interests between humans and the natural environment, but a world is still conceivable in which respect for people can reasonably coexist with respect for the environment. In some cases a real resolution of these conflicts may require sacrificing some human values, and in other cases we cannot ask for such a sacrifice: it depends on the context and the circumstances. Without denying the instrumental values of the environment, we should resolve conflicts of interest by referring to moral values and moral status: these are the most appropriate categories to adjust our ethical behaviour in both general and specific situations. In the words of UNEP, 'ethics is an open-ended process with the potential to expose new challenges and generate new possibilities. It is a process of making choices that enable better ways of seeing and doing things' (Jickling et al. 2006, 23).

From environmental ethics to environmental policies

The relevance of environmental ethics in offering moral motivations for environmental protection should not be reduced to its philosophical level, but extended to a political–legal level. UNEP goals (n.d.), for example, include creating new environmentally friendly behavioural patterns and lifestyles, and fostering ethical responsibilities. All relevant environmental programs are set in force by political organs such as governments, parliaments and public administrations. Decision-making policies fostered by such entities in environmental protection cannot be separated from ethics and from the effect they will have on future generations (ENV-ETHICS Project n.d.). Policy regulations and environmental laws are important tools in the frame of economics and social life: their purpose is to reduce the impact of human activity on the natural environment. Environmental associations, political parties and other stakeholders give their important contribution in setting environmental goals, but at the same time the actual effect is in substance and in practice related to the politically accepted environmental goals, through standards and recommendations which are recognized at the political/legal level.

Caring for the environment is something on which we must reach a consensus. It is also something that might require considerable enforcement, and we can argue whether rules can govern virtuous intentions. As discussed in 2002 in the paper 'Enforcing environmental ethics: civic law and natural values' by Holmes Rolston III, and taken up again more recently, we might ask how much environmental ethics should be included in environmental policies (Rolston 2002, Rolston 2011). Furthermore, we can consider whether legal enforcement can contribute to changing habits and inducing new ethical behaviour, and whether such enforced ethics could be considered useful in the framework of environmental protection. Even if an enforced ethics is incomplete (i.e. if people are not polluting for fear of punishment, their ethics may be considered only as nominal ethical behaviour), environmental behaviour is perhaps the most important objective in environmental policy and in related educational activities.

The European Community Environmental Policy includes different measures on environmental protection and on sustainable development which consider the environmental, social and economic dimensions. As we can see from Article 3 of the Treaty on European Union (TEU) environmental protection is clearly expressed, but at the same time emphasis is placed on the economic aspects with importance placed on sustainable development:

> The Union shall establish an internal market. It shall work for the sustainable development of Europe based on balanced economic growth and price stability, a highly competitive social market economy, aiming at full employment and social progress, and a high level of protection and improvement of the quality of the environment. It shall promote scientific and technological advance. (European Union 1992)

The need to harmonize environmental knowledge with ethical values, as well as the need to achieve changes in behaviour and to internalize ethical values, is clearly present in some efforts and experiences which were recently promoted by the EU by setting a policy framework for almost all environmental regulations in the Member States. Since the 1970s, the EU has agreed on over 200 pieces of legislation concerning the environment, but we know that legislation needs to be properly applied and the challenge lies in its implementation. Environmental Action Programmes have been launched in Europe since 1973 (40 years ago) as a political declaration of intent, which take all the measures planned for a certain period. The 7th Environmental Action Programme, 'Living well within the limits of our planet', was adopted in November 2013 (EU 2013). This programme should support the implementation both within the Union and on an international level of the outcomes of, and the commitments undertaken to, the 2012 United Nations Conference on Sustainable Development (Rio + 20). Its aim is to transform the global economy into an inclusive and green economy in the context of sustainable development and the reduction of poverty.

Sustainable development is present in different parts of the programme and can be seen as an attempt to minimize the trade-off between the economy and environmental protection, in also considering not compromising the ability of future generations to meet their needs. At the same time, decisions on the environment cannot be separated from a relevant level of ethics: environmental management is indeed also a question of ethics. We can argue whether reference to environmental ethics and attention on the 'more-than-humans', the term suggested by UNEP for non-humans (Jickling et al. 2006), could be explicitly incorporated into action programmes, and whether greater emphasis on environmental protection could then be obtained. Turning to the term 'ecological sustainability' could give priority to environmental protection, and the introduction of specific attention on the more-than-humans could bring new emphasis. The concept of sustainable development can put aside the perception given by environmental protection, and the need to protect non-human species, which is already widely accepted, remains linked to an ethical approach perceived as something limited mainly to the area of individual choices.

Global needs concerning protection of the environment from ionizing radiation

The International Committee on Radiological Protection (ICRP) is a non-governmental charity organization which aims at providing recommendations and guidance on protection against the risks associated with exposure to ionizing radiation. Throughout its history, the Committee has promoted the protection of the environment by focusing its attention on the environment of mankind: the transfer of radionuclides through the environment and the related risk for human beings. ICRP Recommendations Publication 26 (1977) included assumption of the concept that 'if man is adequately protected then other living things are also likely to be sufficiently protected'. Within the same context, ICRP Recommendations Publication 60 (1991) considers that 'the standards of environmental control needed to protect man to the degree currently thought desirable will ensure that other species are not put at risk'.

The wider attention brought to environmental awareness by the UN Rio Declaration on Environment and Development (1992) increased the societal expectation that environmental protection should be assured and not simply assumed. Drawing on these cultural changes, the ICRP started developing a new kind of attention towards the environment. In 'A framework for assessing the impact of ionising radiation on non-human species' (ICRP 2003), the ICRP switched its focus and started developing a new framework aimed at assessing the relationship between exposure and dose, and between dose and effect for non-human species. The publication clearly expresses that this attention is not the result of any specific concern regarding environmental hazard, but more to pursue the societal goal of environmental protection on the basis of scientific and ethical principles, by which a policy for the protection of non-human species could be achieved.

ICRP started to develop policy guidance for environmental protection in which one of the most important challenges is complementing environmental protection with the protection of humans. ICRP (2008, 2009) fosters a parallel approach (see Figure 2.3) by developing a small set of landmark specimens (Reference Animals and Plants − RAP): a limited number of hypothetical entities representing different types of animals and plants used as a reference point for the procedure of estimating radiation dose. The RAP is a basis for judging the severity of likely effects of ionizing radiation on non-humans. The support for the decision-making regarding public health and environmental protection considers a 'reference male and female' and dose limits; constraints and reference levels for human radiation protection; 'reference animals and plants'; and derived consideration reference levels for environmental protection. The new ICRP recommendation (2007) effectively extended the system of protection in order to address protection of the environment, including flora and fauna, in a clearer and more explicit way. The main aim is 'to prevent or reduce the frequency of deleterious radiation effects to a level where they would have a negligible impact on the maintenance of biological diversity, conservation of species, or the health and status of natural habitats, communities and ecosystems'.

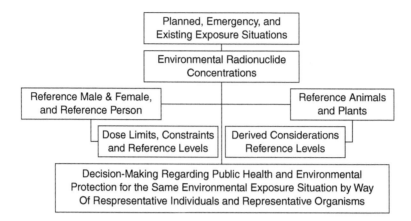

Figure 2.3 A common approach for the radiological protection of humans and
       non-human species.

Source: ICRP

   Together with the publication of the 7th EAP, the new Basic Safety Standards
Directive (BSS) of the European Commission has been approved. The EU BSS
refers to the Euratom Treaty (the Treaty establishing the European Atomic Energy
Community created in 1957 to coordinate the Member States' research programmes for the peaceful use of nuclear energy) and in particular to Art. 2, '*In
order to perform its tasks, the Community shall establish uniform standards to protect the
health of workers and of the general public to ensure that they are applied (…)*', and Art. 30,
'*Basic standards shall be laid down within the Community for the protection of the health
of workers and the general public against dangers arising from ionizing radiations (…)*'.
The first EU BSS Directive was adopted in 1959, and then amended up to the
eighth and last publication, published in 2014. The main objective of the EU BSS
Directives which have followed over time is the health protection of workers
and of the general public against the dangers arising from ionizing radiation. In
this framework, protection of the population includes protection of the environment as a pathway from the environmental sources to the exposure of humans
to radiation. The contamination of the environment may result in a source of
exposure to members of the public who are directly affected, and moreover the
state of the environment can have a long-term impact on human health. The
Member States are required to bring into force laws and administrative provisions
in order to comply with the Directive. Over time, the revision of the successive
EU BSSs, as in the case of the IAEA International BSS, aimed to be consistent
with ICRP Recommendations, and in particular with EU BSS Directive 59/2013
(EU 2014), as the last IAEA BSS (IAEA 2014) is in general consistent with the last
ICRP Recommendations (2007) and with new specific ICRP recommendations,
as in the case of new dose limits for workers to the lens of the eye (ICRP 2012).

As discussed above, despite ICRP not specifically indicating if it is endorsing an anthropocentric or non-anthropocentric approach in protecting the environment, it subscribes to the global need to maintain biological diversity, ensure conservation of species and protect the ecosystem – and specifically promotes a common approach to human and environmental protection by proposing a framework for assessing the impact on non-human species.

Conclusion

Despite the lively debate concerning environmental policies and the relevance that deeper questioning of this relationship would have for public debate and policy regulation on the natural world, the literature on this subject contains an irrefutable omission. There is a recognized and increasing need for protection of both human and non-human systems, and this need is also required to prove sustainability for generations to come. Today's knowledge and technology are already able to significantly reduce the human impact on nature and, at the same time, to meet the growing needs for food and other primary services. We already have the means to handle contemporary world crises. The involvement of stakeholders could be useful in stimulating reflection on this issue and to increase the level of knowledge and accountability. A dialogical approach is to be strongly considered, where science, ethical and social values, and political processes need to play a key role, but no comprehensive analysis and systematic study of the connection between ethics and environmental policies exists in literature, in the different fields of application.

In the context of protection from ionizing radiation, for example, we can notice that IAEA BSS, in line with ICRP publications, considers that protection of the environment includes the protection and conservation of both animals and plants, and their biodiversity, but the EU BSS did not take this opportunity to extend the scope of radiation protection in the same way. The preparation of the EU BSS document, through a number of drafts, started to consider complementing the protection of workers and the public with specific consideration of the biota (Janssen et al. 2013), based on the idea that ICRP guidance needed to be transferred into an enforceable legal requirement, but it does not appear in the final approved document.

Better protection of nature requires coordinated efforts across all sections of governments, businesses and international institutions; however, the greater need is to change our perception of life and nature (Millennium Ecosystem Assessment 2005a, 6). Such knowledge and technological changes are unlikely to be fully achieved unless we start to put nature at the centre of our ethical paradigm. It follows that first of all we need to consider the full value of nature through a better consideration of the non-human natural world. Environmental policies cannot solve all natural crises in one move. In fact, the main job that needs to be done concerns the way individuals live, and therefore the choices we make in our daily life. In other words, the first step that we need to take is to make an ethical personal effort.

28   *Cantone and Andreozzi*

References

Andreozzi M. (2013) 'Relationships over entities', *Relations. Beyond Anthropocentrism* *1*(1), 7–10.

Andreozzi M. (2015) *Le sfide dell'etica ambientale. Possibilità e validità delle teorie morali non-antropocentriche*. LED, Milano.

Callicott J. B. (1987) *Companion to a Sand County Almanac: Interpretive and Critical Essays*. The University of Wisconsin Press, Madison.

Callicott J. B. (1989) *In Defense of the Land Ethic: Essays in Environmental Philosophy State*. University of New York Press, Albany.

Callicott J. B. (1999). *Beyond the Land Ethic: More Essays in Environmental Philosophy*. University of New York Press, Albany.

ENV-ETHICS Project (n.d.) *Env-Ethics*. www.env-ethics.com/en/. Accessed 19 September 2015.

European Union (1992) 'Treaty on European Union', *Official Journal of the European Communities* C325/5-C325/181.

European Union (2013) 'Decision No. 1386/2013/EU of the European Parliament and of the Council on a General Union Environment Action Programme to 2020 "Living well, within the limits of our planet"', *Official Journal of the European Union* L 354, 20 December 2013, 171–200.

European Union (2014) 'Council Directive 2013/59/Euratom laying down basic safety standards for protection against the dangers arising from exposure to ionising radiation, and repealing Directives 89/618/Euratom, 90/641/Euratom, 96/29/Euratom, 97/43/Euratom and 2003/122/Euratom', *Official Journal of the European Union* L 13, 17 January 2014, 1–73.

Hargrove E. C. (1989) *Foundations of Environmental Ethics*. Prentice Hall, Englewood Cliffs.

Hargrove E. C. (1992) 'Weak anthropocentric intrinsic value' *The Monist 75*(2), 183–207.

IAEA BSS (2014) 'Radiation protection and safety of radiation sources: international basic safety standards', *IAEA Safety Standards Series*, GSR Part 3, Vienna.

ICRP (1977) 'Recommendations of the ICRP', ICRP Publication 26, *Ann. ICRP 1(3)*.

ICRP (1991) '1990 Recommendations of the International Commission on Radiological Protection' ICRP Publication 60, *Ann. ICRP 21(1–3)*.

ICRP (2003) 'A framework for assessing the impact of ionising radiation on non-human species', ICRP Publication 91, *Ann. ICRP 33(3)*.

ICRP (2007) 'The 2007 recommendations of the International Commission on Radiological Protection' ICRP Publication 103, *Ann. ICRP 37(2–4)*.

ICRP (2008) 'Environmental protection – the concept and use of reference animals and plants', ICRP Publication 108, *Ann. ICRP 38(4–6)*.

ICRP (2009) 'Environmental protection: transfer parameters for reference animals and plants', ICRP Publication 114, *Ann. ICRP 39(6)*.

ICRP (2012) 'ICRP statement on tissue reactions / early and late effects of radiation in normal tissues and organs – threshold doses for tissue reactions in a radiation protection context" ICRP Publication 118, *Ann. ICRP 41(1/2)*.

Janssens A., Necheva C., Tanner V. and Turai I. (2013) 'The new Basic Safety Standards Directive and its implications for environmental monitoring, *Journal of Environmental Radioactivity 125*, 99–104.

Jickling B., Lotz-Sisitka H., O'Donoghue R. and Ogbuigwe A. (2006) *Environmental Education, Ethics, and Action: A Workbook to Get Started*. UNEP, Nairobi.

Kernohan A. (2012) *Environmental Ethics: An Interactive Introduction*. Broadview Press, Peterborough, Ont.

Leopold A. (1949) *A Sand County Almanac, and Sketches Here and There*. Oxford University Press, New York.

Millennium Ecosystem Assessment (2005a) *Ecosystems and Human Well-Being*. Synthesis Island Press, Washington, DC.

Millennium Ecosystem Assessment (2005b) *Ecosystems and Human Well-Being: Statement from the Board*. Island Press, Washington, DC.

Næss A. (1989 [1974]) *Ecology, Community, and Lifestyle: Outline of an Ecosophy*. Cambridge University Press, New York.

Norton B. G. (1984) 'Environmental ethics and weak anthropocentrism', *Environmental Ethics* 6(2), 131–48.

Norton B. G. (1995) 'Why I am not a nonanthropocentrist. Callicott and the failure of monistic inherentism', *Environmental Ethics* 17(4), 341–58.

Passmore J. A. (1974a), 'Attitudes to nature' in Peters R. S. (ed), *Royal Institute of Philosophy Lectures, Vol. 8: Nature and Conduct*. MacMillan, London, 251–64.

Passmore J. A. (1974b) *Man's Responsibility for Nature: Ecological Problems and Western Traditions*. Charles Scribner's Sons, New York.

Regan T. (1976) 'Feinberg on what sort of beings can have rights?' *Southern Journal of Philosophy* 14(4), 485–98.

Regan T. (1983) *The Case for Animal Rights*. University of California Press, Berkeley and Los Angeles.

Rolston H. (1986) *Philosophy Gone Wild: Essays in Environmental Ethics*. Prometheus Press, Buffalo, NY.

Rolston H. (1988) *Environmental Ethics: Duties to and Values in the Natural World Temple*. University Press, Philadelphia.

Rolston H. (2002) 'Enforcing environmental ethics: civic law and natural value', *International Research in Geographical and Environmental Education* 11(1), 76–79.

Rolston H. (2011) 'Civic law and natural value: enforcing environmental ethics', *Environmental Law News: Special Yosemite Commemorative Issue*, 23–28.

Rolston H. (2012) *A New Environmental Ethics: The Next Millennium for Life on Earth*. Routledge, New York.

Singer P. (1975) *Animal Liberation: A New Ethics for Our Treatment of Animals*. Random House, New York.

Singer P. W. (1976) 'All animals are equal' in Regan T. and Singer P. (eds), *Animal Rights and Human Obligations*. Prentice Hall, Englewood Cliffs, 148–62.

Taylor P. (1986) *Respect for Nature: A Theory of Environmental Ethics*. Princeton University Press, Princeton.

UNEP (n.d.) *UNEP's Environmental Education and Training – EETU's Goals*. www.unep.org/training/about/. Accessed 19 September 2015.

United Nations (1992) *Report of the United Nations Conference on Environment and Development, held in Rio de Janeiro*. http://cil.nus.edu.sg/rp/il/pdf/1992%20Rio%20Declaration%20on%20Environment%20and%20Development-pdf.pdf. Accessed 19 September 2015.

3 Justice, environmental health laws and relations between people

Carl Cranor

Introduction

A major concern about the law is how it governs relations between citizens in a community. Frequently this is expressed as a concern about justice. As John Rawls put it, 'Justice is the first virtue of social institutions …' (Rawls 1999, 3). This chapter examines one part of the United States legal system and one part of that, namely a certain group of environmental health laws, that govern the vast majority of chemical creations proposed for commercialization and actually commercialized. What relations are presupposed between citizens who create chemical products and those who use or are exposed to the chemical product? Are these laws just in accordance with a major theory of justice, namely Rawls'? A test case for answering these questions is how well these laws would protect the most vulnerable and most susceptible of people in the community, namely developing children. Once they are born children are citizens as much as full adults. How well do current laws protect children as they develop from embryos through childhood and the teenage years to adulthood? I argue that one class of laws, postmarket laws, with a large portion of this attributable to the Toxic Substances Control Act (TSCA), do not protect children well at all. TSCA is quite important because it guides the entry of new substances into the market and it grandfathered as safe 62,000 when it was enacted. It and other postmarket laws leave chemical products in the market until there is scientific evidence that they pose risks or cause harms, long delaying protections for children and adults alike. I argue that these laws fail the test of justice and fail by three other measures for assessing relations between citizens in a community.

Environmental health laws provide different models for protecting citizens including children. I focus on a class of laws, postmarket laws, that do an especially poor job of preventing exposures, diseases and dysfunctions for children. These laws in the U.S. and many countries govern the vast majority of chemical creations, some of which will be toxic. Finally, children are citizens too and legally and morally deserving of protections from toxic substances.

Generic legal strategies to protect the public health

There are two generic strategies for addressing chemical creations. *Premarket* testing and scientific review laws seek to identify risks from products *before* they enter commerce and people are exposed (U.S. OTA 1987, 199–200). Pharmaceuticals and pesticides are the main chemical products subject to premarket laws and are a comparatively small portion of chemical creations. Proposed chemical products are required to undergo a battery of tests and scientific review by the Food and Drug Administration (FDA) for pharmaceuticals or the Environmental Protection Agency (EPA) for pesticides before they may enter commerce. The products remain in the market until the public health agency, which bears a legal and scientific burden to change the status quo, decides to reduce exposures or remove the products.

Postmarket laws by contrast permit proposed chemical creations to enter commerce without undergoing any routine battery of tests for toxicity and then they permit products to remain in commerce until a public health agency bears a scientific and legal burden of proof to reduce exposures or remove the products from commerce. When the Toxic Substances Control Act (TSCA) was enacted it grandfathered as safe 62,000 chemical creations and it did not require new chemicals to be routinely tested for their toxicity. Yet it governs the vast majority of new chemicals and can backstop the removal of others that might first be considered under other postmarket laws such as the Clean Air Act, the Clean Water Act, and the Safe Drinking Water Act to name a few (Schierow 2009).

Toxicology

In order to discuss the law and relations between people my initial focus is on children during their development. Humans are most susceptible to exposures to toxic substances and radiation or even other perturbations of their biology as they develop from pre-conception to embryos through birth and teenage years to adulthood, and into old age.

Why are children so susceptible to disease? The answer is in what is called 'the developmental origins of health and disease'. The developmental origins of disease (just half of the slogan) is based on the idea that '*In utero* nutrition and/or *in utero* or neonatal exposures to environmental toxicants alter susceptibility to disease later in life [by affecting] the programming of tissue function that occurs during development' (Heindel 2008, 78) The biological programing of tissues and organs 'to altered [structural] and/or functional character of the tissues, organs and systems' that can lead to diseases, dysfunctions or premature death (Heindel, 2008, 78).

A plausible mechanism for many of these effects is in the epigenetic function of genes. 'These toxicant-induced pathogenic responses are most likely the result of altered gene expression or altered protein regulation [not a change in the genetic sequence] resulting in altered cell production and cell differentiation …' (Heindel 2008, 78). In turn these can lead to adverse effects in tissues, organs and a person's or animal's whole biology. Disorders that might arise from exposures to toxicants or other biological perturbations include 'cardiovascular disease, obesity, type 2 diabetes and metabolic disturbances, osteoporosis, chronic obstructive lung disease, some forms of cancer and some mental illnesses' (The International Society for the Development of Disease 2015). In general, during development embryos, fetuses, newborns and young children 'tend to be more sensitive to adverse environmental influences … [with] tissues undergoing rapid cell division, and [having] much less capacity to metabolize [and detoxify] xenobiotics than [do adults]' (Miller et al. 2002, 412)

When we add the developmental basis of disease to the known contamination of people (farmworkers often not citizens) plus humans' permeability to toxicants, this suggests a problem needing a legal and scientific paradigm change to address adequately. We cannot prevent contamination, but we do need to create legal institutions to prevent toxic contamination. U.S. citizens are contaminated by more than 300 manmade substances, including PFCs (perfluorinated compounds), PBDEs (polybrominated diphenyl ether flame retardants), PCBs (ploychlorinated biphenyls), organochlorine pesticides, phenols, phthalates, PAHs (polycyclic aromatic hydrocarbons) and perchlorate. There will be more as the Centers for Disease Control develops a greater number of reliable protocols for detecting toxicants in human bodies. Many are known toxicants (CDC 2015). Every pregnant woman is contaminated with at least 43 substances (Woodruff et al. 2011; ACOG 2013), and women's contamination starts prior to conception and is shared with developing children *in utero* – the placenta is no significant barrier (ACOG 2013). Babies are born with many industrial chemicals in their bodies, some toxic (Fimrite 2009).

Women's chemical burden is shared with developing foetuses and newborns. At one time the womb was seen as something like an impermeable capsule, strongly resistant to circulating drugs or toxicants (Needleman and Bellinger 1994, ix). Despite this seeming conventional view it was beginning to be contradicted about the same time by the social catastrophes of methylmercury (1960s), thalidomide (1960s) and diethylstilbestrol (DES) in 1971.

In utero exposure to methylmercury as a result of pregnant women eating fish resulted in children being born with cerebral palsy and sometimes limb abnormalities along with other dysfunctions such as sensory disturbance, poor muscle control, mental retardation and constricted visual field (Honda et al. 2006, 171–76). A pregnant mother's exposure to the pharmaceutical Thalidomide, which had been poorly tested for toxic effects, caused a variety of birth defects: 'seal limbs', shortened arms or legs or misplaced appendages, deformed spines and missing ears or eyeballs (Dufour-Rainfray et al. 2011). Neurological problems, heart disease, kidney abnormalities and autism were also present in some children (Hilts 2003, 153; Schardein and Macina 2007, 131).

Women who took the synthetic estrogen, DES, another at best poorly tested pharmaceutical, gave birth to female offspring who contracted vaginal/cervical cancer about twenty years later. When some of these same daughters reached the age of about 40 they had 'approximately twice the risk of breast cancer as unexposed women of the same age and with similar risk factors' (U.S. NCI, 2011).

Finally, very recent research strongly suggests that in the late 1960s teenage women with DDT (Dichlorodiphenyltrichloroethane) exposures just before puberty contracted breast cancer about twenty years later at rates five times higher than adult women with comparable exposures (Cohn et al. 2007, 1408). In addition those 54-year-old exposures continue to have adverse effects. The daughters born to mothers who had *in utero* DDT exposures now have breast cancer rates about four times higher than women not exposed to DDT in utero (Cohn et al. 2015). Analogously, 'Radiation … [also] increases breast cancer risk most strongly when exposures occur early in life' (Miller et al. 2002, 412).

It is clear from these examples that toxicants in pregnant women are shared with their foetuses. As a major developmental biologist puts it, there is 'no placental barrier per se: the vast majority of chemicals given the pregnant animal (or woman) reach the fetus in significant concentrations soon after administration' (Schardein 2000, 5). The ability to cross the placenta also applies to new technologies such as plastic nanoparticles (Environmental Health News 2010).

Not only are children quite susceptible to toxic exposures during development, they can be exposed to *larger doses of toxicants relative to the body weight* than the mother, via cord blood and breast milk (Grandjean et al. 2008, 74) Mercury concentrations can be at least 5 times higher in foetal brain than in mother's blood (Honda et al. 2006, 176). Lipophilic substances, such as PCBs and the brominated flame-retardants, can have concentrations in cord blood and breast milk at much higher rates than in the mother's circulating blood (Heinzow 2009, 324–25). Developing foetuses have 'universal exposure' to BPA (bisphenol A), and free BPA (more harmful) has been found in higher concentrations in foetal livers than in maternal blood or urine (Nahar et al. 2013). Greater exposures continue after children are born because they have higher metabolism, breathing, absorption and circulation rates than adults. They take in more fluid and food per body weight (Miller et al. 2002, 412).

The toxicity problems for children mount up – they are more susceptible to adverse effects, they have greater exposures per body weight than adults, and they have lesser and fewer biological defences against toxicants compared with adults. The immune system is not developed *in utero*, and takes some time to develop after birth. The blood brain barrier that constitutes an obstacle to some toxicants from entering the brain is not fully developed until about the age of six months. A typical defence, namely, enzymes that can detoxify substances, are typically undeveloped or underdeveloped early in life (Cranor 2011, 98; Dietert and Pipenbrink 2006). However, there are some enzymes that turn less or non-toxic substances into more toxic substances, but since these too are less developed, infants and young children can avoid some toxicants that adults cannot.

The combination of greater susceptibility, greater exposures and lesser defences makes children particularly vulnerable to toxic exposures. Two organ systems in particular, the brain and the immune system, face particular problems. During development the brain must grow from a single cell into billions following 'precise pathways' in the 'correct sequence' to function normally. The brain undergoes great growth *in utero* and in the first six months of life, yet its development is not complete until a person reaches adulthood (Grandjean and Landrigan 2006). The immune system, like the brain, is comparably susceptible. Both seem to have 'one chance to get it right' (Dietert and Zelikoff 2010). Michael Skinner's research shows that toxicants can disrupt the reproductive system, leading to numerous problems in both male and female offspring in animal studies. While it may not be 'one chance to get it right', ill-timed exposures to toxicants can cause the reproductive system to 'get it wrong', and likely not have an opportunity to repair damage (more below).

In addition to the above – children are more susceptible, have greater exposures per body weight, have lesser defences to toxic substances – they also have longer lifespans during which diseases and dysfunctions can develop. For instance, some substances, such as some pesticides and ethylene oxide, can cause Parkinson's disease. If a person has sufficient exposures these can decrease cells in the brain that produce dopamine essential for voluntary muscular control. However, as long as a person is otherwise reasonably healthy, the brain can compensate for dopamine cells that under-produce. This can occur for a while. However, as healthy cells age, they can compensate less. Consequently, if a person is exposed as a child, they have a longer lifetime for the symptoms of Parkinson's to become manifest and likely at an earlier age than if the person had been exposed as an adult. Earlier exposure may well lead to earlier diseases and earlier disruptions of one's life as a consequence.

Beyond the generic susceptibility and vulnerability of children, they have considerable genetic variation, just as do adults. Consequently, some will be more vulnerable and some less vulnerable to toxic exposures. Scientists have identified genes that make some children more susceptible to polycyclic aromatic hydrocarbons (typical by-products of combustion) (Perera et al. 1999), some more vulnerable to the toxic effects of organophosphate pesticides (Huen et al. 2009) and still others are more susceptible to the toxic effects of methylmercury (Julvez et al. 2013) While all children typically would be more susceptible to these adverse effects than adults, those with the particular genes just indicated would be more susceptible than an average child.

Sometimes substances of similar chemical classes can 'add to' the effects of other substances from a related chemical class; this is true of dioxin-like substances (Kortenkamp, 2007, 98–99). This 'class' of substances attaches to the same receptor in a cell, so it does not matter whether one is exposed to a dioxin or a furan; both groups of substances attach to the same receptor. However, substances attaching to the same cellular receptor are not necessary to produce additive effects for exposures to toxicants. There can be independent additive effects from different chemical substances that can increase vulnerability, but not affect the same cellular receptors. Several substances that affect different 'upstream' pathways can jointly produce additive effects on circulating thyroid hormones: dioxin-like PCBs, non-dioxin-like PCBs, perchlorate and brominated fire retardants (PBDEs). Each of these chemicals each operating by different pathways can reduce thyroid concentrations in pregnant women, potentially creating neurological risks to foetuses. In addition, 'exposures to environmental contaminants have the potential to affect upstream immune indicators, including antibody synthesis, T-cell function, and other measures of immunocompetence, which can result in compromised downstream resistance to infection' (Woodruff et al. 2008, 1573).

In at least some instances it does not take large concentrations or large exposures to toxic substances to trigger diseases. Children in many cases seem exquisitely sensitive to low doses of chemical products. Even tiny doses can cause adverse effects. For instance, there seems to be no lowest concentration for several substances that can trigger disease: lead (causing neurological effects and heart problems) (Canfield et al. 2003; Lanphear 2005; Silbergeld and Weaver 2007, 141), mutagenic carcinogens (causing cancers) (Eastmond 2012), Thalidomide (single pill) (Claudio et al. 2000, 6), DES (causing obesity in mice) (Vom Saal 2014). A single dose of valproic acid (an anti-convulsive drug) in animals is sufficient to cause autism-like behaviour

(Dufour-Rainfray et al. 2011, 1256). For at least some adverse effects caused by endocrines extremely low doses may sometimes cause greater harm than larger doses (Vandenberg et al. 2012).

When researchers compare adverse effects caused by chemical exposures in mature adults and developing children they have found that for radiation and DDT, teenage exposures are much worse than adult exposures (human data) (Miller et al. 2002, 412; Cohn et al. 2007). The same is true for Thalidomide and DES. Thalidomide mothers had only minor effects from the drug, while some children were born with substantial morphological defects (human data). DES mothers were not initially affected by the drug, but later had increased rates of breast cancer, while some of their daughters had both cervical cancer and then later breast cancer.

The previous results suggest that children's exposure in the womb or in early childhood are especially problematic. While this is true, even a father's exposures, what one might call 'Bad Daddy' factors, can cause adverse effects to children in utero. For instance, toxic contamination of males with chemotherapeutic agents, lead, mercury, pesticides and solvents can lead to degradation of sperm quality, miscarriages, childhood leukaemia, birth defects and childhood cancer. Men contaminated with Paxil, anaesthetic gases and morphine can lead to sperm fragmentation, miscarriages, chronic late blooming, abnormal, underweight offspring and stillbirths (Anthes 2010).

Quite alarming and surprising is that animal data have shown that *some ill-timed exposures during development of reproductive organs can cause transgenerational harms.* Exposure of male rats during reproductive organ development to some pesticides and bisphenol A (individually) causes sperm damage, sterility, prostate disease, kidney disease, immune system abnormalities, testis abnormalities and tumour development (e.g. breast) (Anway et al. 2006; Anway et al. 2008). Analogous results were seen in female rats exposed in utero. Exposure *in utero* to one toxicant can cause polycystic ovarian disease (infrequent ovulation, multiple persistent ovarian cysts [seen in 6–18 per cent of women], and primary ovarian insufficiency [POI]). These conditions can persist through four generations, making them transgenerational (Nilsson et al. 2012).

A major take-home message from the above examples is that very often what we might think of as *transient* chemical exposures can become biologically *embedded* in individuals, in their children or grandchildren (multigenerational), and, with appropriate timing, in family lines in great grandchildren and beyond (transgenerational). That is, what may appear to be mere transient exposures in fact can become more permanent in our lives if they become embedded in the biology of an individual, transferred from a parent to a child and biologically embedded in a child, perhaps only to show up much later in life, or, in some extreme instances revealed in animal data, transferred *in utero* from mother to child when reproductive organs are developing and causing adverse effects in grandchildren, great grandchildren and beyond (in short becoming part of family lines).

While this research is in the early stages, the evidentiary picture – with parts of the picture filled with numerous data points, others partially filled and some blank – is solid and quite worrisome.

What should be done?

The U.S. legal system and probably many others regulate the vast majority (80–90 per cent) of chemical substances with *postmarket* laws as noted above. The main law for created chemicals in the U.S. is the Toxic Substances Control Act (TSCA). If a company proposes a new chemical, it must include only minimal information about it. The company must provide 'all available data on chemical identity, production volume, by-products, use, environmental release, disposal practices, and human exposures ... and all existing health and environmental data in the possession of the submitter, parent company, or affiliates, and a description of any other relevant health or environmental data known to or reasonably ascertainable by the submitter' (Society of Chemical Manufacturers n.d.). A company need not include data about toxic properties. The U.S. Environmental Protection Agency (EPA) has 90 days to review the product for toxic effects. If it finds none, it may be manufactured. If there is evidence of toxic effects, the EPA may request further data. However, to request more toxicity data requires a sufficiently elaborate rule-making process that takes considerable agency effort. This tends to discourage such requests so over time the EPA has developed 'voluntary' provisions by which they negotiate with companies on the needed data. Subsequently, most extra data is acquired, if at all, by this process (Schierow 2009). TSCA also grandfathered 62,000 substances in a chemical inventory in 1979 as safe. Both new compounds and the grandfathered substances remain in commerce until a public health agency bears a scientific burden of proof and a legal burden under the appropriate law sufficiently strong to change the status quo to reduce exposures or remove them.

The TSCA legal structure for new chemicals differs from U.S. laws governing pharmaceuticals and pesticides, both of which require at a minimum premarket toxicity testing of the products, impartial scientific review of those tests and agency approval before the product can enter commerce. Both the Federal Food, Drug and Cosmetic Act and the Federal Insecticide, Fungicide and Rodenticide Act require the company to show that their products do not pose toxic risks to the public. They also require that the products are appropriately efficacious for their tasks.

While the TSCA is the main law that addresses new chemicals at the point of manufacture, I regard it as a postmarket law simply because it does not have premarket toxicity testing provisions as do the laws for pharmaceuticals and pesticides. Many other laws, such as the Clean Water Act, the Clean Air Act and the Safe Drinking Water Act largely address contaminants/pollutants in different media while the issue of 'new' chemicals does not arise. In my view they should be required to list major pollutants that might enter the water, soil or air and test them for toxicity. However, that is not likely to occur anytime soon.

Postmarket laws pose a number of problems for a society. They encourage wilful toxic ignorance on the part of companies, and this becomes propagated to environmental health agencies and the larger public. For 80 to 90 per cent of new industrial chemicals there is no or little knowledge about whether they are toxic or not. At present companies may choose to test their creations for toxicity or not. However, the TSCA creates powerful incentives not to test. If a company tests its product and finds adverse effects and submits these to the EPA, the agency then has scientific reasons to request more tests or related tests. Thus, the company would be creating problems for itself: why test? If company A tests its products and company B does not, A's cost structure is higher than B's so A is at something of a competitive disadvantage to B. Again, why test? Thus, little premarket toxicity testing is done under the TSCA.

Postmarket laws create barriers to better health protections. Reducing toxic risks is so difficult that improved health protections become glacially mired in procrastination, obfuscation and endless disputes about science and other issues. For the EPA merely to produce risk numbers for products – this means finding the potency of a substance and what exposures plus potency would generate risks to citizens – can take considerable time. In 2008 the General Accountability Office found that the EPA's office for determining risks data, the Integrated Risk Information System, was bogged down with a number of substances.

Trichloroethylene (TCE), a widely used solvent and metal degreaser, is a common environmental contaminant in air, soil, surface water and groundwater. 'TCE has been linked to cancer, including childhood cancer, and other significant health hazards, such as birth defects' (U.S. GAO 2008, 39–40). TCE also likely causes Parkinson's disease (Goldman et al. 2012). This substance has been in the risk hopper for more than twenty years as of 2008; by now that time has become 27 years. Dioxin is a bioaccumulating, human carcinogen, likely transgenerational toxicant and endocrine disruptor (Manikkam et al. 2012) that in 2008 had been in risk procedures for more than seventeen years (U.S. GAO 2008, 41). By now it has been in process for 25 years. Perchloroethylene (perc), used in dry cleaning, metal degreasing, and in making some consumer products, is a probable carcinogen and a common groundwater contaminant that has been under review for more than twenty years (U.S. GAO, 2008, 41). Developing risk numbers for formaldehyde has been a messy process. It is a known human carcinogen that also damages the respiratory system. There were early efforts to establish risk numbers in 1989 and 1990, but there have been various stops and restarts since then. One effort to provide a risk assessment had to be restarted because new data became available. One could say that efforts to establish risk data have been in process for 26 years. Naphthalene, 'used in jet fuel and in the production of widely used commercial products such as moth balls, dyes, insecticides, and plasticizers', is a probable human carcinogen. It has been under review for more than sixteen years (U.S. GAO 2008, 35).

Because so little is known about most chemical creations and it can often take so long to remove or reduce risks that may cause, this makes haphazard guinea pigs of adults and children alike, increasing their risks. Premarket testing and approval laws (e.g. for drugs and pesticides) are not free from critique but much better: some developmental effects of pharmaceuticals and pesticides have been missed. These will also need improvement.

Justice

The above consequences of postmarket laws pose problems of justice for a community. Postmarket laws do not prevent and cannot prevent a number of children and adults from diseases if they are exposed to toxicants. Moreover, these injustices result from the actions of fellow citizens who create chemical products, but do not conduct appropriate research into their toxic properties. These are diseases that do not 'just happen to us' as do naturally occurring diseases, such as measles, mumps, polio or the plague.

There are several ways in which diseases caused by exposures created by fellow citizens are unjust. For this assessment I rely on a standard theory of justice by John Rawls. As I argue elsewhere, people can be treated unjustly by being invaded by chemical creations of unknown toxicity and then having to await what might occur – the chemicals may or may not be toxic and people may be harmed, or may have to deal with such serious diseases or dysfunctions that one's opportunity range in the society is truncated (Cranor 2017).

Such invasions by themselves constitute legal battery (and we might think of an equivalent 'moral' battery, as Mary Lyndon and I have independently argued (Cranor 2011, 182; Lyndon 2012, 487–99). Battery consists of an agent knowingly causing another person, 'directly or indirectly, to come in contact with a foreign substance in a manner which the other will reasonably regard as offensive' (Mink v. University of Chicago 1978, 715). One person need not actually harm another, a 'technical invasion of the integrity of the plaintiff's person by even an entirely harmless, but offensive, contact entitles him to vindication of his legal right by an award of nominal damages, and the establishment of the tort cause of action entitles him also to compensation for the mental disturbance inflicted upon him' (Mink v. University of Chicago 1978, 715). As Lyndon puts it, 'If it is tortious to seriously insult or startle someone, it would seem an even greater transgression of social boundaries to inflict a silent, invisible bodily contact with a possible toxicant, leaving those "touched" to await whatever may come' (Lyndon 2011, 496).

Moreover, a battery satisfies Rawls' idea of the freedom of the person, namely, the right to be 'free from psychological oppression and physical assault and dismemberment (integrity of the person)'. Providing such protections are part of the security and safety for citizens that are ordinarily prerequisites for carrying out life plans and conceptions of the good life. Consequently, even if one is not harmed, the legal concept of battery provides grounds for the claim that one suffers battery and injustice if one has merely been invaded by a product untested for its toxicity. This constitutes a violation of one's social boundaries for which we should be protected.

'Battery [a foundational legal cause of action] protects bodily integrity and individual autonomy, creating the essential status and space for social interactions. Indeed, proscribing harmful or offensive physical contacts is a structural prerequisite for a functional society' [provides a legal outlet to reduce violence] (Lyndon 2011, 487).

If a product actually causes a disease or dysfunction in a person, this too would be a violation of Rawls' freedom of the person principle. If the harm is sufficiently serious that a person's normal opportunities in the community are truncated or frustrated, this would be a more serious injustice. It would be a violation of what Rawls calls his fair equality of opportunity principle. Elsewhere I have extended his idea to legal failures hat damage citizens' health (Cranor 2011, 220–22). The idea is that some injuries can seriously undermine the range of opportunities citizens will have in a community over a lifetime. If they do, while this is a harm, it is sufficiently intrusive in a person's life, that it should receive recognition as an opportunity-interfering harm. Serious diseases and dysfunctions undermine a person's opportunities to carry out life plans and even to change them. If a person contracts a serious form of leukaemia, but continues to survive it, he may still find even normal life to be substantially truncated. Here is how a rare form of leukaemia affected one person involved in a tort suit in the U.S. Brian K. Milward contracted acute promyelocytic leukaemia (a rare form of myelogenous leukaemia) at age 47.

Nearly a decade of chemotherapy, along with diabetes and a rare bowel disorder, have left him battling what he calls 'absolutely ridiculous' fatigue. Retired and on disability, he remembers returning to work twice. First, he resorted to napping to endure an eight-hour shift. When his boss assigned him to office duty, pushing paper and making calls, he still fell asleep at his desk.

'I can't really do anything', said Milward, 57 – at least, not what he loves: repairing race cars, working in his yard, playing with his grandchildren. 'It just sucks when you get a cancer like this' (Lombardi, 2014).

Finally, diseases caused by exposures to chemical creations or radiation can also exacerbate unjust distributions of income and wealth, especially if they adversely affect those who are worse off in a community. If this occurs such effects would also be injustices under another aspect of Rawls' principle of justice, but I do not develop this further here.

Justice typically concerns the relations between people in a community and my focus here is on distributive justice. What I have suggested is that exposure to chemical products or radiation released by one group of people in a society can adversely affect others citizens and be unjust. The argument is that conceptions of justice can give us insights into relations between citizens in a community. There are other perspectives that can add to this.

A second way we can characterize between citizens is to contrast how citizens must be treated if they are subjected to a medical experiment concerning a new pharmaceutical, such as in a drug trial, compared to how they are treated under postmarket laws when exposed to a chemical creation that has been approved under the TSCA. To make this point I juxtapose the ethical protections for persons who participate in medical experiments with the legal protections for citizens who are exposed to general chemical creations.

There are a number of requirements on medical experiments that typically must be satisfied. Typically participants in medical experiments must (a) *consent* to participate in the research. However, in order for them to do this, their consent must be based on their informed and mentally competent understanding of the risks. In order to have this understanding, researchers conducting the experiment must (b) have done sufficient prior research on risks that participants might face so that they can give them reasonable assurances of safety. The participants must also understand the risks so they can give proper consent. (c) There must be appropriate oversight from impartial and independent scientific and ethical committees. Finally, there typically are special concerns to protect children and concern for the safety of participants is central to conducting medical experiments.

Now imagine that experimental participants have the opportunity to participate if pharmaceutical trials – exposure to a new drug, a new chemical. The above conditions must be satisfied. Most importantly for the comparison to which I draw attention, the researcher must do appropriate prior research on the chemical to determine whether it poses any risks and so that reasonable assurances of safety can be provided for participants.

In contrast, for citizens in the U.S. subject to chemicals approved under the TSCA we cannot be sure any of these conditions are satisfied. There are no prior preparations and reasonable assurances of safety for those who are exposed. There are not necessarily careful assessments of safe exposures. There is no independent scientific and ethical oversight for each substance that enters commerce, in contrast to the protections under the pharmaceutical laws. There is no special concern to protect children from the chemical creations and postmarket laws do not show concern for people who might be contaminated.

When we juxtapose these two different sets of 'protections', we should experience cognitive dissonance. In each case citizens are involved. However, there are exquisite protections for medical experiments but for the release of analogous chemical creations under postmarket laws there are not explicit and necessary protections. This should not only cause cognitive dissonance, but also give us considerable pause about how we are treating citizens under postmarket laws. People exposed to tiny, invisible, undetectable substances that may or may not pose risks are treated quite differently.

In each case participants on the one hand and citizens on the other are not necessarily exposed to risks; it is merely possible that there may be risks. In one circumstance researchers test for them in order to ensure proper protections for others, but in the other they are not required to do so and do not ensure the safety of fellow citizens. This does lead to the conclusions that citizens subject to untested chemical creations are treated as haphazard guinea pigs. How they are treated is not a proper experiment, but they are subjected to substances that may have possible risks, without any protections, awaiting, as Lyndon puts it, to 'see what happens' (Lyndon 2011, 496).

Finally, there is a fourth way to compare relations between how citizens are treated in a community, that is, by reviewing some of the major differences between three areas of the law. Consider some requirements on the criminal law, premarket laws for chemical creations, and postmarket laws for chemical creations.

Typical criminal laws in general but obviously not in every instance protect citizens from violations of their rights that are the result of largish, perceptible physical objects, that is, humans who violate others in the community. I have in mind here such things as violent crimes – murder, nonnegligent manslaughter, rape, robbery and aggravated assault. All these involve physical interactions with others. In addition, some property crimes – burglary, larceny-theft, and motor vehicle theft – in many instances may also involve interactions between offenders and victims.

Interactions between offender and victims assist self-protection, broader social protection and evidence gathering. Together these add to the protections the law provides, and, I suggest, because there are circumstances that assist the law in functioning, it has an easier task than protecting people from tiny, invisible, undetectable molecules.

In part because people are largish physical objects that can be easily perceived, as molecules cannot, this can perhaps assist a person in avoiding criminal interactions in the first place. One can avoid dangerous situations to the extent one can perceive or is aware of them. For certain property offenses, such as burglary, a person might institute other kinds of self-protections – burglar alarms to protect property, safes to protect valuables and so on. These instances of self-protection in conjunction with the law help one to avoid harm and violations.

Many kinds of harm the criminal law seeks to prevent also have properties that assist in catching criminals. To the extent that some crimes occur in public spaces, others may see them and provide evidence. If there is an interaction between perpetrator and victim, the victim can help identify the offender and perhaps provide other evidence that assists in finding and catching him or her.

The nature of many crimes also assists evidence gathering (from residual traces of the crime). For example, bombings, murders, thefts, rapes and burglaries often leave traces behind that can lead to the perpetrator or other information that ultimately can assist detectives.

The criminal law also prevents a potential perpetrator from being wilfully ignorant about what he or she contemplates doing. Responsibility and excusing conditions in the criminal law ensure that in order to be found guilty of a crime one must have been aware (in one of several senses) that one's actions made harming others the *object* of action, *practically certain* to inflict harm, or *aware* of a risk of causing harm to others. To be found properly guilty of a crime one of these conditions must be satisfied and any one of them ensures that one could not be wilfully ignorant of what one contemplates doing. Finally once an offender is arrested, the crime and harm associated with it typically ceases.

Now compare the criminal law with *premarket testing and review laws* typical of pharmaceuticals. Testing creates practical discouragement of wilful ignorance about new products a company might wish to commercialize. Testing *per force creates information* about any risks associated with the products, provided that testing protocols are well designed. Scientific review may catch risks that company testing did not reveal. This provision of the law serves much the same purpose as responsibility conditions in the criminal law.

In contrast to the criminal law, the bearers of harm in pharmaceuticals are molecules – tiny, invisible, silent entities that are unavailable to our senses. Thus, a person taking a drug can do little to ensure against risks as one can do something to protect oneself from many criminal risks. While these features undermine self-protection and preclude others from identifying toxic attacks because they are inaccessible to our senses, the institutions governing pharmaceuticals provide other protections. Physicians, informed by knowledge of a patient's medical record including other drugs she might be taking, can provide guidance in choice of drugs to avoid risks. Pharmacists can also assist.

However, if pharmaceuticals cause harm as some can, the risks and harm continue with the product in the market until it is withdrawn or removed legally. Pharmaceuticals typically do not leave traces behind that assist in their detection, as do crime scenes. Scientists must utilize subtle scientific studies statistically to detect that products cause harm, or use animal, mechanistic and other data to piece together evidence of harm.

In addition, if scientific studies show a pharmaceutical poses greater risks than were initially identified, physicians and pharmacists offer one line of protection for patients. Finally, drugs that turn out to be too risky for patients to take (many drugs have some kinds of risks) may not be easy to remove from the market. In this respect they are like pesticides and general industrial chemicals. However, even here for patients taking such drugs, pharmacists, physicians and adverse publicity may well be able to guide patients in a safer direction. Pharmaceutical companies likely do not welcome adverse publicity about their products, even while they fight their removal from the market, and this may assist quicker removal.

Postmarket laws for industrial chemicals are quite different from both the criminal law and premarket testing and scientific review laws. This casts doubt on the ethics of postmarket laws for protecting the public.

In the U.S. under the Toxic Substances Control Act, there is no routine toxicity testing of products before they enter commerce and citizens are exposed and 62,000 substances were grandfathered as 'safe'. Both new and existing substances remain in commerce until there is sufficient evidence that they are not safe and the EPA or another public health agency can issue a rule reducing risks or removing the products from commerce.

Thus, unlike both the criminal law and pharmaceutical laws, companies easily can know nothing about their products' risks. Even though under the TSCA a company must submit its industrial chemical for review, the agency has very little time to review it (90 days, with a possible 90 day extension) and it typically has almost no data with which to make a risk judgement. Consequently, the TSCA invites companies to have wilful ignorance about their products.

After chemical creations are in products or released more generally in the environment from disposal or deterioration of the original products, any risks that might accompany them are dispersed widely. Researchers have found PCBs in animal and human bodies in the arctic where none were produced and very few were used. These substances have migrated northward via evaporation-deposition processes along with the winds and enter the bodies of fish and sea mammals. Inuits eat the fish and some of the mammals, thus contaminating their bodies (Cone, 2005). In the southern hemisphere Tasmanian Devils are substantially contaminated with flame retardants (Hansford, 2015) And, of course humans are substantially contaminated with more than 300 chemical creations (above).

Thus, chemical creations are widely dispersed and if they pose risks, as many do, the risks will be similarly distributed. However, chemicals cannot not be as easily corralled or captured as many (but not all) criminals can be. They are also unlike pharmaceuticals that are distributed by means of prescriptions written by physicians and issued by pharmacists; there is not a record of them – who is exposed and how much they are exposed. Consequently, any risks will continue until there are no exposures sufficient to cause harm. However, this can be especially long for persistent chemicals.

Citizens can do little and sometimes nothing to protect themselves from toxic substances. They cannot see, smell, feel or detect them in any way as they can to some extent detect when they are at risk from others' criminal conduct. Other people cannot warn them when they might be at risk. Others cannot identify chemical culprits as they can sometimes identify criminal culprits. Chemicals do not leave physical traces behind at the site of harm as criminals often leave traces at crime scenes. No one typically can identify sources of harm or clues to what caused a disease or other malady without substantial scientific investigation.

A person cannot choose a different chemical exposure as patients might be prescribed different pharmaceuticals. Also, there are no 'physicians' or 'pharmacists' for industrial chemicals who can guide consumers away from them. General industrial chemicals resemble serial criminals that continue to cause harm, only they are so much more difficult to 'catch' than those committing crimes. Harms caused by industrial chemicals are hardly 'one-off' events as many typical crimes are.

Our brief contrasts between postmarket laws for chemical creations on the one hand, with the criminal law and pharmaceutical laws on the other, emphasizes the substantial ethical and legal shortcomings of such laws for protecting the public. Because citizens can do almost nothing to protect themselves from chemical creations (as they can for many crimes) and others cannot assist in the enforcement of the law or the catching of offenders, the law and its structure must compensate for these shortcomings. The obvious way to provide that compensation is to institute premarket testing and scientific review laws for general industrial chemicals somewhat analogous to those for pharmaceuticals and pesticides.

Pharmaceuticals are designed to be biologically active – to modify a person's biology in beneficial ways. They are also created to enter our bodies in a controlled and specified manner. Consequently, pharmaceuticals must be tested to ensure that they have beneficial effects and any toxic side effects are minimal or non-existent.

Pesticides are also created to be biologically active and disrupt the functioning of insects, fungi and rodents, *inter alia*. However, they are not designed to enter humans' bodies. Nonetheless, we know that they will invade by means of ingestion, inhalation and absorption through the skin, depending upon the product in question (U.S. EPA 2001). Pesticides are not designed to be biologically active in and disrupt humans' biology, but they can do so (depending upon the dose in question). Neither are pesticides designed to enter our bodies in a controlled fashion as are pharmaceuticals. Yet they do so haphazardly. Nonetheless, the U.S. Congress chose to require toxicity testing of pesticides before they enter commerce and citizens are exposed, so that they do not pose unreasonable risks to people (with special concerns to protect children) when they do adventitiously enter our bodies.

Similarly, general industrial chemicals should be subject to premarket testing and scientific review as are pesticides. These substances are neither designed to be biologically active in human bodies nor in the bodies of other living things, nor are they designed to enter our bodies as pharmaceuticals, but they enter just as surely as do pesticides and some have serious adverse effects. People have been contaminated by lead, perfluorinated compounds, polychlorinated biphenyls, brominated flame retardants, mercury compounds, dioxins, bisphenol A, bisphenol S and other phenols, the phthalates, various classes of pesticides, heavy metals and numerous other compounds. And, in some cases they have been harmed by the invasions, especially children. For many of these compounds researchers do not yet understand the full range of adverse effects.

Conclusion

In the U.S. and probably many countries, postmarket environmental laws govern the vast majority of general chemical creations. They do not protect children and the rest of us from exposures and poorly protect us from risks and harms. The relations between citizens that these laws create are unjust in various ways (based on a widely accepted theory of justice). They compare very unfavourably with other areas of the U.S. legal system (and I suspect with others as well) in their protections of citizens from risks and harms.

Yet there is a way forward, namely, instituting premarket toxicity testing and scientific review that might resemble in some ways the regime for pesticides (not pharmaceuticals). This would help to compensate for the profound shortcomings of postmarket laws compared with the criminal and pharmaceutical laws. Thus, we can do better, but it will take legislation to do so.

Molecular contamination from pesticides or general industrial chemicals is inevitable and unavoidable. We do not know when they invade and there is no place to hide or to avoid them. Some of them will be toxic. Current laws permit toxic contamination, wilful ignorance of toxicity, slothful reduction of risks and little prevention of environmentally induced diseases.

References

American College of Obstetricians and Gynecologists (ACOG), Committee on Health Care for Underserved Women (2013) 'Committee opinion: exposure to toxic environmental agents', Committee Opinion, Number 575.

Anthes E. (2010) 'The bad daddy factor drinking, smoking, taking prescription meds or failing to eat a balanced diet can influence the health of men's future children', *Pacific Standard*. www.psmag.com/books-and-culture/the-bad-daddy-factor-25764 [Accessed June 2015].

Anway M. D., Leathers C. and Skinner M. (2006) 'Endocrine disruptor vinclozolin induced epigenetic transgenerational adult-onset disease', *Endocrinology 55*, 5515–23.

Anway M. D., Rekow S. S. and Skinner M. K. (2008) 'Transgenerational epigenetic programming of the embryonic testis transcriptome', *Genomics 91*, 30–40.

Bellinger B. and Needleman, H. L. (2003) 'Intellectual impairment and blood lead levels', *New England Journal of Medicine 349*, 500–502.

Canfield R. L., et al. (2003) 'Low-level lead exposure and executive functioning in young children', *Child Neuropsychology 9*, 35–53.

Centers for Disease Control and Prevention (CDC) (2015) *Fourth National Report on Human Exposure to Environmental Chemicals*. www.cdc.gov/biomonitoring/pdf/FourthReport_UpdatedTables_Feb2015.pdf [Accessed 2 July 2015].

Claudio L., Kwa W. C., Russell A. L., et al. (2000) 'Testing methods for developmental neurotoxicity of environmental chemicals', *Toxicology and Applied Pharmacology 164*, 1–14.

Cohn B.A., La Merrill M., Krigbaum N.Y., et al. (2015) 'DDT exposure in utero and breast cancer', *Journal of Endocrinology and Metabolism 100*, 2865–72.

Cohn B. A., Wolff M. S., Cirillo P. M. and Sholtz R. I. (2007) 'DDT and breast cancer in young women: new data on the significance of age at exposure', *Environmental Health Perspectives 115(10)*, 1406–14.

Cone M. (2005) *Silent Snow: The Slow Poisoning of the Arctic*. Grove Press, New York.

Cranor C. F. (2011) *Legally Poisoned: How the Law Puts Us at Risk from Toxicants*. Harvard University Press, Cambridge, MA.

Cranor C. F. (2017) *Tragic Failures: How and Why We Are Harmed by Toxic Substances*. Oxford University Press, New York and Oxford.

Dietert R. R. and Piepenbrink M. S. (2006) 'Perinatal immunotoxicity: why adult exposure assessment fails to predict risk', *Environmental Health Perspectives 114*, 477–83.

Dietert R. R. and Zelikoff J.T. (2010) 'Identifying patterns of immune-related disease: use in disease prevention and management', *World J Pediatr 6*, 111–18.

Dufour-Rainfray D.,Vourc' P.,Tourleta S., et al. (2011) 'Fetal exposure to teratogens: evidence of genes involved in autism', *Neuroscience and Biobehavioral Reviews 35*, 1254–65.

Eastmond D. A. (2012) Environmental Toxicology, University of California, Riverside, personal communication.

Environmental Health News (2010) 'Plastic nanoparticles can move from mom to baby through placenta', www.environmentalhealthnews.org/ehs/newscience/plastic-nanoparticles-can-cross-placenta/ [Accessed 29 March 2010].

Fimrite P. (2009) 'Study: chemicals, pollutants found in newborns', *SFGate*, December 3, 2009. www.sfgate.com/health/article/Study-Chemicals-pollutants-found-in-newborns-3207709.php [Accessed 12 May 2015].

Goldman S. M., Quinlan P. J., Ross G. W., et al. (2012) 'Solvent exposures and Parkinson disease risk in twins, *Ann. Neurol. 71*, 776–84.

Grandjean P. and Landrigan P. (2006) 'Developmental neurotoxicity of industrial chemicals', *Lancet 368*, 2167–78.

Grandjean P. et al. (2008) 'The Faroes statement: human health effects of developmental exposure to chemicals in our environment', *Basic and Clinical Pharmacology and Toxicology 102*, 73–75.

Hansford D. (2015) 'Flame retardants found in rare Tasmanian Devils', *National Geographic News*. http://news.nationalgeographic.com/news/2008/01/080128-devils-cancer.html [Accessed 28 June 2015].

Heindel J. J. (2008) 'Animal models for probing the developmental basis of disease and dysfunction paradigm', *Basic and Clinical Pharmacology and Toxicology 102*, 76–81.

Heinzow B. G.J. (2009) 'Endocrine disruptors in human breast milk and the health-related issues of breastfeeding', in *Endocrine-Disrupting Chemicals in Food*, I. Shaw (ed).Woodhead Publishing, Cambridge, 322–55.

Hilts P. J. (2003) *Protecting America's Health: The FDA, Business, and One Hundred Years of Regulation*.Alfred A. Knopf, New York.

Honda S., Hylander L. and Sakamoto M. (2006) 'Recent advances in evaluation of health effects on mercury with special reference to methylmercury—a minireview', *Environmental Health and Preventive Medicine 11*, 171–76.

Huen K., Harley K., Brooks J., et al. (2009) 'Developmental changes in PON1 enzyme activity in young children and effects of PON1 polymorphisms', *Environmental Health Perspectives 117*, 1632–38.

International Society for the Developmental Origins of Disease (2015) www.mrc-leu.soton. ac.uk/dohad/index.asp [Accessed 15 June 2015].

Julvez J., Smith G. D., Goldin J., et al. (2013) 'Prenatal methylmercury exposure and genetic predisposition to cognitive deficit at age 8 years', *Epidemiology 24*, 643–50.

Kortenkamp A. (2007) 'Ten years of mixing cocktails: a review of combination effects of endocrine-disrupting chemicals', *Environmental Health Perspectives 115*, 98–105.

Lanphear B. P. (2005) 'Origins and evolution of children's environmental health', in 'Essays on the future of environmental health research: a tribute to Kenneth Olden', special issue, *Environmental Health Perspectives*.

Lombardi K. (2014) 'Benzene and worker cancers: "an American tragedy"', *Center for Public Integrity*. www.publicintegrity.org/2014/12/04/16320/benzene-and-worker-cancers-american-tragedy [Accessed 12 January 2015].

Lyndon M. L. (2012) 'The toxicity of low-dose chemical exposures: a status report and a proposal: review of *Legally Poisoned: How the Law Puts Us at Risk from Toxicants*', *Jurimetrics 52*, 457–500.

Manikkam M., Guerrero-Bosagna C., Tracey R., Skinner M. K. (2012) 'Dioxin (TCDD) induces epigenetic transgenerational inheritance of adult onset disease and sperm epimutations, *PLOS ONE*, 7 e46249, www.plosone.org; GAO, 2008, 42.

Miller M. D., et al. (2002) 'Differences between children and adults: implications for risk assessment at California EPA', *International Journal of Toxicology 21*, 403–18.

Mink v. *University of Chicago*, 460 F. Supp. 713–23 (1978).

Nahar M. S., Chunyang L., Kannan K., et al. (2013) 'Fetal liver bisphenol A concentrations and biotransformation gene expression reveal variable exposure and altered capacity for metabolism in humans', *J Biochem Mol Toxicol 27*, 116–23.

Needleman H. L. and Bellinger D. (eds) (1994) *Prenatal Exposure to Toxicants*. Johns Hopkins University Press, Baltimore.

Nilsson E., Larsen G., Manikkam M., et al. (2012) 'Environmentally induced epigenetic transgenerational inheritance of ovarian disease', *PLoS One 7*(5), e36129.

Perera F. P., Jedrychowski W., Rauh V. and Whyatt R. M. (1999) 'Molecular epidemiologic research on the effects of environmental pollutants on the fetus', *Environmental Health Perspectives 107*, 451–60.

Rawls J. (1999) *A Theory of Justice (Revised ed.)*. Harvard University Press, Cambridge, MA.

Schardein J. L. (2000) *Chemically Induced Birth Defects*, 3rd ed., Marcel Dekker, New York.

Schardein J. L. and Macina O. T. (2007) *Human Developmental Toxicants: Aspects of Toxicology and Chemistry*. Taylor and Francis, Boca Raton, FL.

Schierow L. J. (2009) 'The toxic substances control act (TSCA): implementation and new challenges', *Congressional Research Service Report #7-5700*, 1–39.

Silbergeld E. K. and Weaver V. M. (2007) 'Exposures to metals: are we protecting the workers? *Occupational and Environmental Medicine 64*, 141–42.

Society of Chemical Manufacturers and Affiliates. 'EPA's new chemicals program under TSCA: the basics', www.chemalliance.org/topics/?subsec=27&id=689 [Accessed 1 June 2015].

U.S. Congress, Office of Technology Assessment (U.S. OTA) (1987) *Identifying and Regulating Carcinogens*. Washington Governmental Printing Office, Washington, DC.

U.S. Environmental Protection Agency (U.S. EPA), Office of Pesticide Programs (2001) 'General principles for performing aggregate exposure and risk assessments, www.epa. gov/pesticides/trac/science/aggregate.pdf [Accessed 21 June 2015].

U.S. Government Accountability Office (U.S. GAO) (2008) 'Chemical assessments: low productivity and new interagency review process limit the usefulness and credibility of EPA's integrated risk information system', GAO-08-440, 1–89.

U.S. National Institutes of Health, National Cancer Institute (U.S. NCI) (2011) 'Diethylstilbestrol (DES) and cancer', www.cancer.gov/about-cancer/causes-prevention/risk/hormones/des-fact-sheet [Accessed December 2012].

Vandenberg L. N., Colborn T., Hayes T. B., et al. (2012) 'Hormones and endocrine-disrupting chemicals: Low-dose effects and nonmonotonic dose responses', *Endocr Rev.* *33*, 378–455.

Vom Saal F. (2014) University of Missouri, personal communication.

Woodruff T. J., Zota A. R. and Schwartz J. M. (2011) 'Environmental chemicals in pregnant women in the United States: NHANES 2003–2004', *Environ Health Perspect 119*, 878–85.

Woodruff T. J., Zeise L., Axelrad D. A., et al. (2008) 'Meeting report: moving upstream-evaluating adverse upstream end points for improved risk assessment and decision-making', *Environmental Health Perspectives 16*, 1568–75.

Part II

Principles

4 A common morality approach to environmental health ethics

Friedo Zölzer

A global ethical basis for environmental health

A global perspective of ethics

According to the definition proposed by the World Health Organisation, 'Environmental health addresses all the physical, chemical, and biological factors external to a person, and all the related factors impacting behaviours. It encompasses the assessment and control of those environmental factors that can potentially affect health. It is targeted towards preventing disease and creating health-supportive environments'. Environmental health is therefore a global issue. Some aspects may pertain to a locality or a region, but others are not thus restricted.

Radioactivity, for instance, is an environmental factor that potentially affects health, and it sometimes does so at a particular workplace or in the area around a particular facility. But the global fallout from the nuclear weapons tests of the 1950s and the Chernobyl disaster in 1986 have made it clear that once released into the atmosphere, radioactivity is not to be contained within boundaries. Accidents in chemical plants such as Seveso in 1976 and Bhopal in 1984 may have left many people with the impression that they were due to bad management that would not occur in more advanced countries. But apart from that being a pious hope, the subtle and gradual pollution of water and soil with toxic compounds of all kinds, which are impossible to keep out of food products (even those advertised as 'organic'), has certainly become a global phenomenon. And to give just one more example, the rise in the atmospheric carbon dioxide concentration is not only of concern because of climate change and its direct consequences, but also because of the expected indirect impact on the health of vast populations around the world.

Attempts to address the ethical questions arising in the context of environmental health have not – as far as I can see – taken account of this global nature of the enterprise. They have been based on concepts familiar to people brought up in a 'Western' cultural context. The classical schools of utilitarian and deontological ethics have featured prominently in the discussion of ethics of radiation protection, for instance. That is precisely the approach which I would like to challenge here, and have tried to challenge elsewhere (Zölzer 2013). After all, less than 30 per cent of the world's population are living in Europe and the Americas, but over 50 per cent in Asia and another 20 per cent in Africa and the Middle East. Can we really expect the majority of mankind to adopt ethical arguments stemming from a context largely alien to them?

Global approaches to questions of values and norms in general are becoming more and more common. A milestone in this development was the 'Universal Declaration of Human Rights' (United Nations General Assembly 1948). In the second half of the twentieth century and especially around the turn to the twenty-first, a number of other international statements on human rights followed, such as the 'Declaration of the Rights of the Child' (United Nations General Assembly 1959), the 'Declaration on Human Environment' (United Nations Conference on Human Environment 1972), the 'Declaration on Environment and Development' (United Nations Conference on Environment and Development 1992), the 'Universal Declaration on the Human Genome and Human Rights' (UNESCO 1997) and the 'Universal Declaration on Bioethics and Human Rights' (UNESCO 2005).

The idea of human rights, i.e. inalienable rights that belong to every human being, of course goes further back in the history of philosophy. Usually, the Stoic school of philosophy (third to sixth century B.C.) is considered the first to have developed the thought. De las Casas (early sixteenth century) was nevertheless still ahead of his time when he advocated the universality of human rights, stating that 'all peoples of the world are humans. ... The entire human race is one' (Carozza 2003). The idea gained prominence in the era of enlightenment, mainly with Locke (1689) arguing that 'by nature' human beings have a right to 'life, liberty, and property'. Kant (1795) emphasized the interconnectedness of human rights and human dignity and their fundamental importance for the international context, as 'the community of nations of the earth has now gone so far that a violation of right on one place of the earth is felt in all'.

With the rise of globalization over the past few decades, philosophers have addressed the need for, and possibility of, global ethics from various points of departure. A few examples may suffice here. Habermas (1998) speaks of a 'post-national constellation' in which we find ourselves, and claims that 'world citizenship ... is already taking shape today in worldwide political communications'. Interested in human flourishing and its global dimension, Sen (2009) has written extensively about the 'idea of justice', which he shows to be central to various cultures around the world, past and present. One of his close associates, Nussbaum (2004), has identified a number of 'core capabilities' which all individuals in all societies should be entitled to, thus constituting the base of her account of 'global justice'. Appiah (2006) explores the reasonability of cosmopolitanism, which he defines as 'universality plus difference'. While emphasizing 'respect for diversity of culture', he suggests there is 'universal truth, too, though we are less certain that we have it all already'. Bok (1995) suggests that 'certain basic values [are] necessary to collective survival' and therefore constitute a 'minimalist set of such values [which] can be recognised across societal and other boundaries'. That does not preclude the existence of 'maximalist' values, usually more culture-specific, nor the possibility that they can 'enrich' the debate, but there is a 'need to pursue the enquiry about which basic values can be shared across cultural boundaries'.

An area in which cross-culturally shared ethical principles, values and norms are actively discussed is interfaith dialogue. One outcome of such activities was the 'Declaration towards a Global Ethic' signed at the Parliament of the World's Religions 1993 in Chicago by the representatives of more than 40 different religious traditions. It proceeded from the assumption that 'There already exist ancient guidelines for human behaviour which are found in the teachings of the religions of the world and which are the condition for a sustainable world order' (Küng and Kuschel 1993). Interfaith declarations on more specific topics such as business ethics and environmental ethics have followed (Webley 1996; Orth 2002).

Biomedical ethics as a model

The most widely applied framework of biomedical ethics is probably the one developed by Beauchamp and Childress (1979). Although not originally conceived as a cross-cultural kind of ethics, it turns out to be compatible with such an approach. It does not proceed from the assumption of one comprehensive moral standard (such as utility in the case of utilitarianism, or universalizability in the case of deontology), but is based on four less general principles (respect for autonomy, non-maleficence, beneficence and justice). In the more recent editions of their book, the authors assume that these principles are rooted in 'common morality', which is 'not relative to cultures or individuals, because it transcends both' (Beauchamp and Childress 2013).

Beauchamp and Childress are not really interested in the question of where and how the 'common morality' can be found. When they introduced the term, they just claimed that 'all morally serious persons' (Beauchamp and Childress 1994) or in a later edition 'all persons committed to morality' (Beauchamp and Childress 2013) would agree with their four principles. I do not find this convincing, because there is no way of ascertaining what 'all' such persons think or feel, to say nothing of the difficulties of defining 'morally serious' or 'committed to morality'. More effort is needed to show that these principles have cross-cultural validity – or to find others that are more widely acceptable.

We could, of course, use empirical research to test the assumption that we have got the underlying principles right, but I am not convinced that anthropological or cultural studies alone would be meaningful. A universal 'opinion poll' which would find out what people around the globe are thinking about the pertinent questions would just reflect current dispositions and would be very much subject to fluctuations. We have to look for something with greater long-term validity.

Orientation has been provided throughout the ages by the religious and philosophical traditions of the different cultures. Although our 'Western' society is largely secularizsed, and fundamentalism, fanaticism and extremism have brought religion into discredit, we cannot ignore the fact that these traditions continue to be of great influence for people not versed in 'Western' secular philosophy. And even in the 'West', the importance of Christianity is probably still much greater than the number of people attending Sunday church service would suggest. The views of Europeans and Americans have been shaped at least as much by Christian values passed on from generation to generation for centuries, as by the philosophical traditions of the enlightenment era. An analysis of 'common morality' can therefore not pretend that religion has no role to play in the twenty-first century.

My suggestion then is that the most important documents for establishing a 'common morality' are the sacred scriptures of the world's great religions, such as the Vedas and the Bhagavadgita for the Hindus, the Sermons of Buddha for the Buddhists, the Torah for the Jews, the Gospels for the Christians, the Quran for the Muslims, the Writings of Bahá'u'lláh for the Bahá'ís, and so on. They provide a framework of orientation for the believers (even though there may be some disagreement regarding their exact meaning), because they are considered to be divinely inspired. A non-believer will of course have some difficulty with this notion, but may at least appreciate that these scriptures reflect values deeply rooted in the various cultures. Another category of useful documents for our purpose are those produced by way of intra- and inter-religious dialogue, because they already reflect cross-cultural agreement.

There are also relevant cultural expressions outside the context of (organized) religion. Thus, we should not ignore oral traditions in the form of proverbs, stories, legends and myths, especially those of indigenous peoples who have no written records. We should also take into consideration secular texts of various kinds which have had a formative influence over the centuries. The Hippocratic Oath comes to mind, or the works of certain philosophers of ancient Greece and China (even if Confucius' writings are perhaps more appropriately classified as sacred scripture). In addition to these time-honoured traditions, some modern documents like the above mentioned 'Universal Declaration of Human Rights' or the 'Universal Declaration on Bioethics and Human Rights' have been suggested to already constitute the 'common heritage of humankind' (ten Have and Gordijn 2013).

I have elsewhere (Zölzer 2013) attempted to show that indeed the four principles of biomedical ethics are rooted in the written and oral traditions of mankind. Some of that discussion I will repeat below. I have also argued that the cross-cultural approach allows us to identify additional principles relevant for disciplines related to, but distinct from biomedicine. At the time, I was writing about radiation protection, but the same applies, I think, for environmental health, or for public health in general. Other authors have – without explicit reference to 'common morality' – made their own proposals for principles that would either substitute or supplement those of Beauchamp and Childress. In the following I will have a closer look at some of these, so as to not miss out on important aspects when proposing a set of cross-cultural values for environmental health ethics.

In a popular textbook on environmental health, a chapter by Jameton (2010) addresses questions of ethics. A number of 'general principles of ethics' are listed that have a bearing on environmental health. The author refers to them without further discussing their origin or background, and without any reference to their possibly being part of a 'common morality'. His seven suggestions are:

- Sustainability: *Conduct environmental health work in such a way that it meets the needs of both the present and future generations.* This is an example of a principle which is not of primary concern for biomedicine where the focus is on the individual patient. When it comes to environmental health, however, or public health in general, sustainability is highly important, and it will be discussed in greater detail below.

- Healthfulness: *The health of humans and the environment need to be restored, balanced and harmonized.* At first glance, healthfulness might seem to be an empty concept. After all, when we are concerned with 'environmental factors that can potentially affect health', it is self-evident that our aim is good health. But we could see here two of Beauchamp and Childress' principles in disguise, namely beneficence and non-maleficence, to be addressed shortly.
- Interconnectedness: *Environmental health actions have far-reaching consequences.* To say that all life on earth is closely interconnected is hardly controversial, but it is a statement of facts, not of norms and values, so I do not see it as helpful in our context.
- Respect for all life: *Environmental health work should be conducted with respect for both human and nonhuman life.* This to me, as much as I sympathize with it, seems more like a principle for environmental ethics in general. For the discussion of the ethical aspects of environmental health, i.e. the study of environmental factors affecting human health, I do not consider the status of nonhuman life to be of direct relevance.
- Global equity: *Everyone is entitled to just and equal access to the basic resources needed for an adequate and healthy life.* Here we have Beauchamp and Childress' principle of justice, and as should be clear from the foregoing, I very much support keeping in view the global applicability of this principle.
- Respectful participation: *Respect the considered and responsible choices of stakeholders, whether individuals or organizations.* As will be seen below, inclusiveness is one of the procedural principles which in my view follow from the more basic ones, and stakeholder involvement can be considered one of its practical applications.
- Realism: *Environmental health ethics should be founded on a realistic understanding of the health sciences and the risks and benefits of proposed activities and investments.* Here again it seems to me that we would be stating the obvious, as environmental health is supposed to be a scientific endeavour from the outset, and I do not think we would gain anything for our discussion of norms and values by (re-)stating the need for a realistic approach.

Altogether it seems to me that Jameton's choice of principles is informed by environmental sciences rather than biomedicine, and although I agree that environmental health has aspects of both I think it is better to maintain the well-established system of Beauchamp and Childress as a basis. Environmental health is a human-centred endeavour, and its ethics would lack substance if it neglected the work done in the medical field.

Two other proposals to be taken into consideration here are not specifically aimed at environmental health ethics, but at the broader area of public health ethics. Under the title, 'How many principles for public health ethics', Coughlin (2008) discusses what would be needed if Beauchamp and Childress' approach was to be applied beyond biomedicine, and comes up with two new proposals. Schröder-Bäck et al. (2014) reflect on a possible basis for a curriculum of public health ethics in a paper entitled 'Teaching seven principles for public health ethics'. Similar to Coughlin they do not doubt the usefulness of Beauchamp and Childress' principles, but suggest adding three more. I can therefore restrict the following short review to five additional principles:

- Precaution: *Precautionary measures should be taken even if some cause and effect relationships are not fully established scientifically.* When he discusses this principle, Coughlin writes mainly about sustainability. While the implications for future generations are an important aspect of precaution, its greatest concern is with acting under uncertainty, and it should therefore be invoked as an independent principle, as discussed below.
- Solidarity: *Solidarity or social cohesion … relates to how united, connected, and cooperative a society is.* Although it seems to me that Coughlin relates this principle too closely with a specific school of ethics, communitarianism, I agree with his idea that the interests of society as a whole, the common good, sometimes need to be considered in addition to and separately from those of the individuals immediately affected.
- Health maximization: *The primary end sought is the health of the broader constituency of the public.* This sounds similar to the above-mentioned healthfulness, which I have tried to argue is beneficence and non-maleficence in disguise. Schröder-Bäck et al., however, claim that these two, because they focus on the individual, cannot serve to maximize health in a population. The concern, which in itself I do not dispute, seems to be addressed by giving importance to solidarity, or the common good as just explained.
- Efficiency: *There is a moral duty to use scarce health resources efficiently.* Schröder-Bäck et al. discuss the problems of adequately defining efficiency, especially if we do not want to limit ourselves to economic terms only, but quite apart from these considerations it seems to me that there is nothing new in this principle if we have already widened our view from beneficence and non-maleficence for the individual to solidarity and the common good.
- Proportionality: *In weighing and balancing individual freedom against wider social goods, considerations will be made in a proportionate way.* This is, as pointed out by Schröder-Bäck et al. themselves, a methodological principle, not really on the same level as the others. We will discuss below how one of the challenges of the Beauchamp and Childress approach is to balance the different principles, which all have *prima facie* validity, in case they conflict with each other. This is not an easy matter, but to me it does not seem to be made easier by throwing in another ill-defined concept such as proportionality.

My understanding of the principles important for environmental health has also been shaped by discussions that I had the privilege of taking part in as a member of Task Group 94 (Ethics of Radiation Protection) of the International Commission on Radiological Protection. As I am writing this, their report has not yet been finalized, but drafts have been shared at symposia and conferences, and it is clear that the principles suggested to be essential for radiation protection are as follows: beneficence/non-maleficence, prudence, justice and dignity. Of these, prudence and dignity could be looked at as possible additions to the set of Beauchamp and Childress. Prudence is closely related to precaution, and will here be discussed in that context, although it may include further considerations. Dignity is often considered a corollary of respect for autonomy, but I treat it as an independent principle below. In this and in several other aspects, my approach is somewhat different from that of Task Group 94.

The four core principles

Respect for autonomy

When it comes to cross-cultural validity, the first of the four principles of Beauchamp and Childress is probably the most problematic. It has been criticized as being 'more or less ethno-ethics of American society' (Fox 1990; Matsuoka 2007), but of little relevance elsewhere in the world. In particular, some authors claim that people of Asian background would generally not agree with it, or at least define it differently from Beauchamp and Childress (Fan 1997; Fagan 2004; Kimura 2014). In 'Principles of biomedical ethics' the role of this principle is to ensure that the patient is the main decision maker in his or her own case. An important corollary therefore is the concept of 'informed consent', which means that neither therapy nor research can be carried out without the agreement of a competent patient. This understanding of autonomy is certainly common in what we call the 'West', but not so much in other parts of the world. There is at least anecdotal evidence that in Latin America, in Muslim Countries, in Africa, in China, and in South East Asia, decision making is not primarily a privilege of the individual patient, but very much a matter of the patient's family (Justo and Villarreal 2003). And it does not appear as if this was to be considered just a current phenomenon, whereas the written and oral traditions actually would have placed emphasis on autonomy as it is now understood in the 'West'. Nevertheless, there are quite a few Christian (Clarfield et al. 2003; Reilly 2006), Muslim (Aksoy and Elmali 2002; Rathor et al. 2013) and Confucian (Nie, quoted in Justo and Villarreal 2003; Tsai 2005) authors who assert that the principle is fully compatible with their world view. Others disagree, although they usually do not go as far as suggesting that respect for autonomy has no validity. They are just concerned about its relative importance vis-à-vis other principles. We will come back to this question of balancing different moral claims later.

Beneficence and non-maleficence

'To abstain from doing harm' is one of the central features of the Hippocratic Oath (Edelstein 1943), which was later adopted by Jewish, Christian and Muslim physicians (Pelligrino 2008). The principle is also mentioned, albeit indirectly, in similar texts from ancient China (Tsai, 1999). Of course it has always been understood that sometimes pain has to be inflicted to achieve healing and thus non-maleficence has to be weighed against beneficence. To work 'for the good of the patient' is part of the Hippocratic Oath as well, and it features quite prominently in the mentioned Chinese medical texts.

More generally, i.e. outside the context of medicine, both beneficence and non-maleficence can be seen as core principles in any system of religious ethics. A central concept of both Hinduism and Buddhism is ahimsa which means kindness and non-violence to all living beings. The Bhagavad Gita praises the 'gift which is made to one from whom no return is expected', whereas the Dhammapada states, 'A man is not great because he is a warrior or kills other men, but because he hurts not any living being'. Both the Torah and the Gospel express the same thought in a different way by exhorting everybody to 'love your neighbour as yourself'. More concretely, the Talmud observes that to 'to save one life is tantamount to saving a whole world', while the apostle Paul suggests that 'whenever we have the opportunity, let's practice doing good to everyone'. The Quran asserts that 'Whoever rallies to a good cause shall have a share in its blessings; and whoever rallies to an evil cause shall be answerable for his part in it'. Nevertheless Islamic jurisprudence has the guideline that 'if a less substantial instance of harm and an outweighing benefit are in conflict, the harm is forgiven for the sake of the benefit' (references in Zölzer 2013).

Justice

The 'Golden Rule' is one of the most common ethical guidelines around the world. It is found in every single tradition one may choose to look at, and even its wording is strikingly uniform. A few examples must suffice: 'One should never do that to another which one regards as injurious to one's own self' (Hindu). 'Hurt not others in ways that you yourself would find hurtful' (Buddhist). 'Never impose on others what you would not choose for yourself' (Confucian). 'That which is hateful to you, do not do to your fellow. That is the whole Torah; the rest is the explanation; go and learn' (Jewish). 'Therefore whatever you want people to do for you, do the same for them, because this summarises the Law and the Prophets' (Christian). 'None of you [truly] believes until he wishes for his brother what he wishes for himself' (Muslim). 'If thine eyes be turned towards justice, choose thou for thy neighbour that which thou choosest for thyself' (Bahá'í). Because of its general acceptance, this rule is also foundational to the above-mentioned 'Declaration toward a Global Ethic' of the Parliament of the World's Religions 1993. It is obvious at least from some of the versions quoted here that the Golden Rule can also serve as support for the principles of non-maleficence and beneficence. But it seems to me that its greatest importance is for the idea of justice. It asks everyone to consider the interests of the other as if they were his or her own, and thus demands reciprocity (references in Zölzer 2013).

Justice as such is verifiably an element of 'common morality' as well. The Bhagavad Gita contains the promise that 'He who is equal-minded among friends, companions and foes … among saints and sinners, he excels'. In the Sermons of

Buddha the following statement is found:'He, whose intentions are righteousness and justice, will meet with no failure'. The Psalms observe that, 'He loves righteousness and justice; the world is filled with the gracious love of the Lord', whereas in the introduction to the Proverbs the reader is assured that here he will acquire 'the discipline that produces wise behaviour, righteousness, justice, and upright living'. Muhammad advises his followers to be 'ever steadfast in upholding equity…, even though it be against your own selves or your parents and kinsfolk'. And Bahá'u'lláh writes that 'No light can compare with the light of justice. The establishment of order in the world and the tranquillity of the nations depend upon it' (references in Zölzer 2013).

A look at secular philosophy will be instructive here, as justice has not only been of prime importance since Antiquity, but has also been systematically studied early on (Johnston 2011). Aristotle, for instance, distinguished between different forms of justice, and his analysis has exerted decisive influence on later thought. The form that is implied by the sacred scriptures quoted above is 'distributive justice'. It concerns the allocation of goods and burdens, of rights and duties in a society. But even this one form can be viewed from different perspectives. Which allocation of goods and burdens is just? An egalitarian one, one that considers merits, one that considers needs, or one that respects historical developments? All this is not clear at the outset, and needs to be made the subject not only of philosophical debate, but also of cross-cultural discourse.

The four additional principles

In my earlier paper on 'A cross-cultural approach to radiation ethics' (2013), I discussed human dignity as a corollary to respect for autonomy, and suggested precaution, concern for the underprivileged and intergenerational equity as additional relevant principles which can be traced in the written and oral traditions of mankind. I still think the choice was also a good one for the ethics of environmental health, but inspired by the above review of proposals made by other authors, I will now use slightly different terms, replacing concern for the underprivileged with solidarity, and intergenerational equity with sustainability. It seems to me that what I had in mind were just aspects of these broader concepts.

Human dignity

Human dignity is no doubt closely related to Beauchamp and Childress' respect for autonomy. Some authors have even discussed whether the former should not actually replace the latter, but others have criticized this by saying we would replace a relatively well-defined concept by a very vague one. I do agree with those who understand dignity as the more fundamental principle and respect for autonomy rather as the derived one which concretizes it for certain situation. On the other hand, as the Beauchamp and Childress system is well established, I think it is better to leave the four core principles as they are and consider human dignity as an additional, correlated one.

It is probably true to say that very few people would deny its applicability to just about any area of human activity. It is expressed in different ways around the world, but the basic idea is virtually ubiquitous – that of a dignity pertaining equally to all humans. In the Bhagavad Gita, Krishna says, 'I am the same to all beings.... In a Brahma ... and an outcast, the wise see the same thing'. Similar statements are reported of Buddha and Confucius. In the Bible, the prophet Malachi asks, 'Do we not have one father? Has not one God created us?' The concept is also clearly expressed in the Quranic verse, 'We have conferred dignity on the children of Adam ... and favoured them far above most of Our creation'. And in Bahá'u'lláh's writings we find this: 'Know ye not why We created you all from the same dust? That no one should exalt himself over the other' (references in Zölzer 2013).

These are just short glimpses from different religious sources, but the broad agreement on the notion that all human beings share the same dignity is also reflected in the 'Declaration toward a Global Ethic' of the Parliament of World's Religions in 1993. It says that 'every human being without distinction of age, sex, race, skin colour, physical or mental ability, language, religion, political view, or national or social origin possesses an inalienable and untouchable dignity, and everyone, the individual as well as the state, is therefore obliged to honour this dignity and protect it' (Küng and Kuschel 1993).

Moreover, human dignity has for centuries been invoked by secular philosophers. This strand of thought begins with Stoicism, continues through the Renaissance, and leads up to Enlightenment (Kretzmer and Klein 2002). In our time, together with the above-mentioned religious traditions, it has played a very prominent role in the drawing up of the 'Universal Declaration of Human Rights' of 1948 and the 'Universal Declaration of Bioethics and Human Rights' of 2005.

Precaution

Whereas non-maleficence focuses on the immediate and obvious harm caused by medical procedures, we may encounter problems when dealing with environmental factors at relatively small doses, where effects can only be inferred from observations in an entirely different dose range. Such is the case with radiation, where the best available data for cancer induction come from the study of atomic bomb survivors in Hiroshima and Nagasaki with an average dose of 200 mSv, but when we speak about occupational radiation exposure or exposure from accidental releases of radioactivity in the areas around Chernobyl and Fukushima, we need to gauge effects at doses smaller by one or more orders of magnitude. In a situation like this, we are compelled to make reasonable estimates of the harms caused, but at the same time we have to be aware of the uncertainties with which we do the assessment.

In recent decades, there has been a lot of talk about the 'Precautionary Principle', especially in the context of environmental issues. For instance, the United Nations Conference on Environment and Development in Rio de Janeiro 1992, also called the Earth Summit, proposed the following: 'Where there are threats of serious or irreversible damage, lack of full scientific certainty shall not be used as a reason for postponing cost-effective measures to prevent environmental degradation' (United

Nations Conference on Environment and Development 1992). Another important version is the one drawn up by a group of scientists from different disciplines gathered at the Wingspread Conference 1998: 'When an activity raises threats of harm to human health or the environment, precautionary measures should be taken even if some cause and effect relationships are not fully established scientifically' (Wingspread Conference 1998).

Of course, the principle in its modern form cannot be expected to appear in the written and oral traditions of different cultures. Exhortations to prudence, however, are ubiquitous, and they are generally interpreted, by people referring to those traditions for orientation, as suggesting a precautionary approach. Thus, in the Mahabharata, Krishna advises to 'act like a person in fear before the cause of fear actually presents itself', whereas Shotoku Taishi, the first Buddhist regent of Japan, puts it this way: 'When big things are at stake, the danger of the error is great. Therefore, many should discuss and clarify the matter together, so the correct way may be found'. Confucius simply says that 'The cautious seldom err'. In the Proverbs, we find the following statement: 'Those who are prudent see danger and take refuge, but the naïve continue on and suffer the consequences'. Muhammad reportedly counselled one of his followers who complained that God had let his camel escape: 'Tie up your camel first, then put your trust in God'. For an explicit reference to the Precautionary Principle I will give just one example, the statement of a representative of the Australian Aboriginals and Torres Strait Islanders: 'Over the past 60,000 years we, the indigenous people of the world, have successfully managed our natural environment to provide for our cultural and physical needs. We have no need to study the non-indigenous concepts of the Precautionary Principle [and others]. For us, they are already incorporated within our traditions' (references in Zölzer 2013).

Solidarity

Beneficence is mainly concerned with the well-being of one particular person – in the medical context the patient. Beyond that, however, the interest of others affected, or even the general public, is certainly also a factor that none of our traditions would disregard. This is what is implied by the principle of solidarity. It has also been referred to as social coherence, or we could say, consideration of the common good.

A particular concern in this context is a situation in which profits and burden are distributed unequally, i.e. the good is provided preferentially to one group of individuals and the harm to another. In this case, I think the cross-cultural approach has indeed something to contribute. Many if not all philosophical and religious traditions agree that special attention must be given to the underprivileged. We find a similar way of thinking in Rawls' *A Theory of Justice* (1971), where he states that 'social and economic inequalities are to be arranged so that they are to be of the greatest benefit to the least-advantaged members of society'. Rawls is generally considered a deontological philosopher, but in this particular instance I do think his theory very much reflects 'common morality'.

So, let us again have a look at the primary sources. The Rig Veda recommends, 'Let the rich satisfy the poor implorer, and bend his eye upon a longer pathway. Riches come now to one, now to another'. The Buddha promises, "He who pursues wealth in a lawful way, and having done so gives freely of his wealth thus lawfully obtained – by so giving … he begets much merit'. Confucius' counsel is: 'Exemplary people help the needy and do not add to the wealth of the rich'. In the Psalms it is stated that 'Blessed is the one who is considerate of the destitute; the Lord will deliver him when the times are evil'. Of Jesus Christ we read, 'Since you didn't do it for one of the least important of these, you didn't do it for me'. And Muhammad says about the 'doers of good' that they '[would assign] in all that they possessed a due share unto such as might ask [for help] and such as might suffer privation' (references in Zölzer 2013).

Sustainability

As mentioned above, precaution is often seen as addressing mainly the problems caused for future generations. While it is true that uncertainties about health effects are usually greater and sometimes of a completely different nature for the future than for the present, the point of the Precautionary Principle is how to behave under uncertainty in general. The consideration of the well-being of future generations, on the other hand, seems to be captured best by the principle of sustainability. More specifically, many authors speak about intergenerational equity. Equity does not mean the same as equality, so we do not necessarily have to treat future generations the same as our own, but we have to treat them fairly. Sustainability can therefore be considered a corollary to the core principle of justice.

The idea that coming generations have to be taken care of when we make decisions (be it about environmental factors affecting health, or other issues) can claim cross-cultural agreement. Both Hinduism and Buddhism are very much concerned with the idea of *karma*, which sees each thought or action as part of an ever-continuing cycle of cause and effect. In line with this, a Hindu delegation to the World's Parliament of Religion stated, for instance, that 'we must do all that is humanly possible to protect the Earth and her resources for the present as well as future generations', and the Dalai Lama made a similar pronouncement: 'Now that we are aware of the dangerous factors, it is very important that we examine our responsibilities and our commitment to values, and think of the kind of world we are to bequeath to future generations'. The responsibility for those who come after us is expressed somewhat differently in the Torah, where God speaks to Abraham, 'I'm establishing my covenant between me and you, and with your descendants who come after you, generation after generation, as an eternal covenant', and this concept of eternal covenant is equally important for Christians and Muslims. Bahá'u'lláh adds still another component to this by saying, 'All men have been created to carry forward an ever-advancing civilization', which according to a statement of the Bahá'í International Community 'offers hope to a dispirited humanity and the promise that it is truly possible both to meet the needs of present and future generations'. Here we can also mention African customary law, which is aptly summarized by a Nigerian chief as follows: 'I conceive that land belongs to a vast family of whom many are dead, a few are living, and countless hosts are still unborn'. And as an example of recent international documents, we can look at a passage from the report of the United Nations World Commission on Environment and Development of 1987 ('Brundtland Commission'), which maintains that development must meet 'the needs of the present without compromising the ability of future generations to meet their own needs' (references in Zölzer 2013).

The four procedural principles

The principles discussed so far, both the core principles proposed by Beauchamp and Childress and the additional ones which can be understood as corollaries or extensions of those core principles, can also be applied to questions of risk communication or other issues coming up with the implementation of environmental health regulations. My suggestion here is to see inclusiveness as an application of human dignity and respect for autonomy, accountability as most closely related to non-maleficence and precaution, empathy as a practical manifestation of beneficence and solidarity, and transparency as associated with justice and sustainability.

Inclusiveness

If we ask for the main procedural value behind the much discussed concept of stakeholder involvement, inclusiveness would seem to be the first choice. Respecting people's autonomy is incompatible with making decisions for them. That would be disregarding their human dignity. Instead, everybody concerned should be somehow included in the decision making – which is the central idea of stakeholder involvement.

It must be admitted that participatory approaches to decision making have historically played a minor role. However, it is possible to point to traditions which consider it highly desirable to solve questions of general interest by way of consultation. Thus it is from one of the oldest sacred scriptures, the Rigveda – 'Meet together, speak together, let your minds be of one accord.... May your counsel be common, your assembly common, common the mind, and the thoughts of these united' – to one of the newest, the Tablets of Bahá'u'lláh: 'Take ye counsel together in all matters, inasmuch as consultation is the lamp of guidance which leadeth the way, and is the bestower of understanding'. It is well known that the primitive Christian and Muslim communities provided space for open consultation, an ideal which was soon lost from both religions' mainstream, and has only been revived, to some extent, more recently. A relevant statement of Shotoku Taishi, the first Buddhist ruler of Japan, has already been quoted above: 'When big things are at stake … many should discuss and clarify the matter together, so the correct way may be found'. Sen, in his *Identity and Violence* (2006), presents evidence that the democratic ideas of classical Greece for centuries found no echo anywhere in Europe, while the form of government in some Asian city-states at the same time can be described as democratic. All this must be considered anecdotal evidence, but it shows that it may be worthwhile looking for participatory approaches in different traditions. At least it demonstrates that the value of inclusiveness is not an invention of modern times and is well compatible with traditions (references in Zölzer 2016).

Accountability

Researchers, regulators and communicators in environmental health all carry responsibility towards the stakeholders, even if these are to some degree involved in decision making. Especially when it comes to the negative effects on human health, we will want to hold accountable those who have not done their investigations carefully, who have failed to react properly to the available data, or who have not been forthcoming with information. Anything else would be contrary to non-maleficence and prudence.

Given the emphasis placed by all religions and philosophies of the world on proper behaviour, it would be hard to find any source not referring to the actor's responsibility for what he or she did or did not do. Of Mahatma Gandhi, to quote a modern representative of Hinduism, we have the statement that 'it is wrong and immoral to seek to escape the consequences of one's acts', and Buddha says, 'Don't look at others' wrongs, done or undone. See what you, yourself, have done or not'. Confucius expresses it in much the same way: 'The noble person places demands upon himself, the petty person blames others'. The prophet Jeremiah warns that God will 'give every man according to his ways, according to the fruit of his deeds'. Similarly the Apostle Paul emphasizes responsibility to a higher authority: 'So then each of us will give an account of himself to God'. And an oral tradition of Muhammad contains this statement: 'Each of you is a guardian and is responsible for those whom he is in charge of' (references in Zölzer 2016).

Empathy

I have not seen this principle being suggested in the context of environmental health, but I do think it is of great importance for the practical implementation of theoretical insights. Showing beneficence to an individual, or solidarity with the underprivileged, is not primarily a matter of rational insight, but rather of identifying and understanding other people's views and emotions, even though one's own situation might be quite different. Empathy has recently been described as essential for human-centred design processes (Kolko 2014).

The term 'empathy' goes back to the nineteenth century and as such cannot be expected to be found in much older written and oral traditions. Compassion, loving kindness, and a caring attitude however are mentioned everywhere. In the Bhagavad Gita, Krishna says: 'Who is incapable of hatred toward any being, who is kind and compassionate, free of selfishness … such a devotee of Mine is My beloved'. Buddha praises 'loving kindness and compassion' as two of the most important attitudes that the believer should cultivate. 'Care for all others' is central to Confucius' teachings. The Talmud contains this statement: 'Loving kindness is greater than laws; and the charities of life are more than all ceremonies'. And in one of the epistles ascribed to the apostle Peter we find this exhortation: 'Be of one mind, sympathetic, loving toward one another, compassionate, humble'. An Islamic oral tradition relates that Muhammad said to his followers: 'You won't be true believers unless you have compassion, and I am not referring to the mercy that one of you would have towards his companion or close friend but I am referring to mercy or compassion to all'. And an American Indian Proverb recommends, 'Never criticize a man until you've walked a mile in his moccasins' (references in Zölzer 2016).

Transparency

Transparency in decision making and implementation is closely related to stakeholder involvement as briefly discussed above, but more deeply, I think, it is related to justice, namely procedural justice. We would not consider it fair process, if things were done secretively, if truth was hidden, and if trust was misused. This also applies in relation to the coming generations who – if we want to treat them equitable – will have to be provided with correct and complete information about what we have left for them.

Honesty, sincerity, truthfulness and trustworthiness are unquestionably virtues that have their place in any religious and philosophical tradition. In the Mahabharata we find that 'it is always proper to speak the truth', and Buddha describes his true follower as a 'straightforward person … open and honest'. Confucius states: 'Every day I examine myself. … In intercourse with my friends, have I always been true to my word?' Similarly, in the Book of Job, the main character declares: 'My lips will not speak falsehood, and my tongue will not utter deceit'. The Gospel of Matthew contains the following exhortation: 'But let your communication be, Yea, yea; Nay, nay: for whatsoever is more than these cometh of evil'. The same terseness is found in the Qurán: 'Have fear of God, and be among the truthful'. And finally the Bahá'í Writings contain this observation: 'Truthfulness is the foundation of all human virtues. Without truthfulness, progress and success are impossible for any soul' (references in Zölzer 2016).

The importance of balancing

A summary of my proposal for core, additional and procedural principles is given in the following table. I have to admit, of course, that the strict one-to-one associations suggested by this form of presentation are untenable. As indicated, sustainability has to do with beneficence as well, not only with justice, and is also closely related to precaution. Solidarity is a matter as much of beneficence as of justice, and it should not only be practiced in correlation with beneficence, but also with non-maleficence. Inclusiveness could be discussed as being based on justice instead of human dignity, and vice versa transparency would seem to follow from human dignity almost as much as from justice. The table is thus to be taken with a pinch of salt, just showing some essential relationships, as well as (hopefully) lending some structure to the ideas put forward in this paper.

Core principles	Additional principles	Procedural principles
Respect for autonomy	Human dignity	Inclusiveness
Non-maleficence	Precaution	Accountability
Beneficence	Solidarity	Empathy
Justice	Sustainability	Transparency

From the foregoing, it seems clear that not only the four principles proposed by Beauchamp and Childress, but a number of additional principles, be they corollaries or extensions of the original four, or applications in terms of procedural ethics, are indeed based on values which are shared across cultures. They can be traced back to the religious and philosophical traditions that have provided moral guidance for people around the world over the centuries. That is not to say that secular ethics is wrong and useless, but just that a degree of worldwide consensus already exists and is reflected in those traditions. Whether environmental health in practice has always and everywhere reflected these values is a different question, but there is a growing awareness of their importance.

One aspect needs to be emphasized in conclusion, I feel. The values discussed above, similar to the principles of biomedical ethics, have only *prima facie* validity, which means they apply as long as there is no conflict between them. If there is, they need 'balancing', i.e. their relative importance must be weighed. I think it is here where cultural specificity can come in. Beneficence and human dignity, to give just one example, are held in high esteem everywhere around the world, but not in every situation is it possible to implement both of them to the same extent. There is sometimes a conflict between wanting to do good by for instance forbidding and penalizing a certain unhealthy behaviour on the one hand, and respecting people's autonomous right to decision making on the other. And if such a conflict arises, not everybody everywhere may give the same answer to the question which of the two is to prevail. Some degree of plurality is certainly acceptable, or even desirable, but we need be aware of the differences and discuss whether we want to retain them, or rather develop a common approach. Making the principles of environmental health ethics and the related procedural principles explicit, and assessing their cross-cultural validity, will help us in this endeavour.

References

Aksoy I. and Elmali A. (2002) '"Four Principles of Bioethics" as found in Islamic Tradition', *Medicine Law J. 21*, 211–24.
Appiah K.A. (2006) *Cosmopolitanism: Ethics in a World of Strangers.* W.W. Norton, New York, USA.
Beauchamp T. L. and Childress J. F. (1979[1], 1994[4], 2013[7]) *Principles of Biomedical Ethics.* Oxford University Press, Oxford, UK.
Bok, S. (1995) *Common Values.* University of Missouri Press, Columbia, MO, USA.

Carozza P.G. (2003) 'From conquest to constitutions: retrieving a Latin American tradition of the idea of human rights', *Human Rights Quart. 25*, 281–313.

Clarfield A. M., Gordon M., Markwell H. and Alibhai S. M. H. (2003) 'Ethical issues in end-of-life geriatric care: the approach of three monotheistic religions – Judaism, Catholicism, and Islam', *J. Am. Geriatr. Soc. 51*, 1149–54.

Coughlin S.S. (2008) 'How many principles for public health ethics', *Open Public Health J. 1*, 8–16.

Edelstein L. (1943) *The Hippocratic Oath: Text, Translation, and Interpretation*. Johns Hopkins University Press, Baltimore, MD, USA.

Fagan A. (2004) 'Challenging the bioethical application of the autonomy principle with multicultural societies', *J. Appl. Philos. 21*, 15–31.

Fan R. (1997) 'Self-determination vs. family-determination: two incommensurable principles of autonomy', *Bioethics 11*, 309–22.

Fox R. (1990) 'The evolution of American bioethics: a sociological perspective' in Weisz G. (ed), *Social Science Perspective on Medical Ethics*. University of Pennsylvania Press, Philadelphia, PA, 201–20.

Habermas J. (1998) *The Postnational Constellation*. MIT Press, Cambridge, MA, USA.

Jameton A. (2010) 'Environmental health ethics', in Frumkin H. (ed), *Environmental Health. From Global to Local*. John Wiley and Sons, San Francisco CA, USA, 195–226.

Johnston D. (2011) *A Brief History of Justice*. Wiley-Blackwell, Chichester, UK.

Justo L. and Villarreal J. (2003) 'Autonomy as a universal expectation: a review and a research proposal', *EUBIOS J. Asian Int. Bioethics 13*, 53–57.

Kant I. (1795) *Zum Ewigen Frieden. Ein philosophischer Entwurf* (transl. 2003, *Perpetual Peace: A Philosophical Sketch*). Hackett Publishing Company, Cambridge MA, USA.

Kimura R. (2014) 'Japan, bioethics', in Jennings B. (ed), *Bioethics*, Vol. 4., 4th ed. Macmillan Reference, Farmington Hills, MI, USA, 1757–66.

Kolko J. (2014) *Well-Designed: How to Use Empathy to Create Products People Love*. Harvard Business Review Press, Cambridge, MA, USA.

Kretzmer D. and Klein E. (eds) (2002) *The Concept of Human Dignity in Human Rights Discourse*. Kluwer Law International, The Hague, Netherlands.

Küng H. and Kuschel K. J. (eds) (1993) *A Global Ethic: The Declaration of the Parliament of the World's Religions*. SCM Press, London, UK.

Locke J. (1689) *Two Treatises of Government*. A. Churchill, London, UK.

Matsuoka E. (2007) 'The issue of particulars and universals in bioethics: some ideas from cultural anthropology', *J. Philos. Ethics Health Care Med. 2*, 44–65.

Nussbaum M. (2004) 'Beyond the social contract: capabilities and global justice', *Oxford Development Studies 32*, 3–16.

Orth G. (ed) (2002) *Die Erde – lebensfreundlicher Ort für alle. Göttinger Religions-gespräch 2002 zur Umwelt- und Klimapolitik*. LIT Verlag, Münster, Germany.

Pelligrino E. D. (2008) 'Some personal reflections on the "appearance" of bioethics today', *Studia Bioetica 1*, 52–57.

Rathor M.Y., Rani M. F.A., Shah A. S. B. M., Leman W. I. B., Akter S. F. U., Omar A. M. B. (2013) 'The principle of autonomy as related to personal decision making concerning health and research form an "Islamic viewpoint"', *J. Islam. Med. Ass. North Amer. 43*, 27–34.

Rawls J. (1971) *A Theory of Justice*. Harvard University Press, Cambridge, MA, USA.

Reilly D. (2006) 'A plea for relevance to daily practice', *FOCUS Fall 2006*, 18–20.

Schröder-Bäck P., Duncan P., Sherlaw W., Brall C., Czabanowska K. (2014) 'Teaching seven principles for public health ethics: towards a curriculum for a short course on ethics in public health programmes', *BMC Medical Ethics 15*, 73–82.

Sen A. (2006) *Identity and Violence: The Illusion of Destiny*. W.W. Norton, New York, USA.

Sen A. (2009) *The Idea of Justice*. Harvard University Press, Cambridge, MA, USA.

ten Have H. and Gordijn B. (2013) 'Global bioethics' in ten Have H. and Gordijn B. (eds), *Compendium and Atlas of Global Bioethics*. Springer, Dordrecht, 1–16.

Tsai D. F. C. (1999) 'Ancient Chinese medical ethics and the four principles of biomedical ethics', *J. Med. Ethics 25*, 315–21.

Tsai D. F. C. (2005) 'The biomedical principles and Confucius' moral philosophy', *J. Med. Ethics 31*, 159–63.

UNESCO (1997) *Universal Declaration on the Human Genome and Human Rights.* http://unesdoc.unesco.org/images/0010/001096/109687eb.pdf [Accessed 16 September 2015].

UNESCO (2005) *Universal Declaration on Bioethics and Human Rights.* http://unesdoc.unesco.org/images/0014/001461/146180e.pdf [Accessed 16 September 2015]

United Nations Conference on Environment and Development (1992) *Declaration on Environment and Development.* www.unep.org/Documents.Multilingual/Default.asp?documentid=78&articleid=1163 [Accessed 16 September 2015].

United Nations Conference on the Human Environment (1972) *Declaration on Human Environment.* www.unep.org/Documents.Multilingual/Default.asp?documentid=97&articleid=1503 [Accessed 16 September 2015].

United Nations General Assembly (1948) *Universal Declaration of Human Rights.* www.un.org/en/documents/udhr/index.shtml [Accessed 16 September 2015].

United Nations General Assembly (1959) *Declaration of the Rights of the Child.* www.unicef.org/malaysia/1959-Declaration-of-the-Rights-of-the-Child.pdf [Accessed 16 September 2015].

Webley S. (1996) 'The interfaith declaration: constructing a code of ethics for international business', *Business Ethics: A European Review 5*, 52–54.

Wingspread Conference (1998) *Wingspread Statement on the Precautionary Principle.* www.psrast.org/precaut.htm [Accessed 16 September 2015].

World Commission on Environment and Development (1987) *Our Common Future.* www.un-documents.net/our-common-future.pdf [Accessed 16 September 2015].

Zölzer F. (2013) 'A cross-cultural approach to radiation ethics' in Oughton D. and Hansson S.O. (eds), *Social and Ethical Aspects of Radiation Risk Management.* Elsevier Science, Oxford, UK, 53–70.

Zölzer F. (2016) 'Are the core values of the radiological protection system shared across cultures? *Annals of the ICRP 45S*, 358–72.

5 Bioethics, the Precautionary Principle and future generations

Robin Attfield

Introduction

The topic of this chapter is the Precautionary Principle, a principle which (despite international recognition) is not as widely known as it should be, and I will shortly be introducing it and explaining its relevance to environmental health and to bioethics in general. But since it is sometimes confused with the Principle of Maximin, I will also attempt to explain how these principles differ. I will then turn to some of the applications of the Precautionary Principle, and to the difference that heeding it (once it is interpreted in such as way as to be applicable to future quality of life) can make to the prospects of future generations.

In general terms, the Precautionary Principle declares that where there is reason to regard a substance or process as seriously or irreversibly damaging (usually but not invariably in environmental contexts), preventive action or regulation should be undertaken despite the absence of scientific certainty. While this is not a basic principle, like (for example) principles of distributive justice or of respecting persons, it nevertheless gives valuable guidance and valuably supplements other ethical principles when decisions have to be taken against a background of partial uncertainty.

This principle can take stronger or weaker forms. An example of a stronger form is the London Declaration on the Protection of the North Sea (1987). This Declaration authorizes the regulation of substances 'when there is reason to assume that certain damage or harmful effects on the living resources of the sea are likely to be caused by such substances, even where there is no scientific evidence to prove a causal link between emissions and effects' (Parker 1998, 634). If such a strong principle were widely adopted, a very great deal of regulation of potentially dangerous substances and processes would be authorized. An example of a weaker form is found in the Rio Declaration (1992), which states that 'where there are threats of serious or irreversible damage, lack of full scientific certainty shall not be used as a reason for postponing cost-effective measures to prevent environmental degradation' (Parker 1998, United Nations 1992).[1] This is weaker because a smaller range of potential damage is recognized and because other reasons than the lack of scientific certainty might be found against regulatory action. Yet even in this weak form, the Principle has great importance, because it was adopted into international law by all the countries represented at Rio, including yours and mine, and including those to which all the large pharmaceutical companies are subject.

The example of thalidomide

This being so, it is worth investigating whether the Principle applies to bioethics. A single relevant example may suffice to convey that the answer to this question is an affirmative one. Thus the drug thalidomide, which was primarily marketed in Europe and Australia, despite apparently having some beneficial uses (such as averting nausea), turns out to have had impacts that were frequently both serious and irreversible when prescribed to pregnant women.

So if anyone in a position of authority in Europe or Australia had become aware (at the time when this drug was being prescribed to pregnant women, in the late 1950s and the early 1960s) that these impacts were significantly possible, then the Precautionary Principle (if it had been recognized then) could have been invoked to prevent this being done, even in the absence of scientific consensus, and this would have resulted in people with missing limbs not being born, and people lacking such disabilities being born instead. Unfortunately this Principle was not widely recognized until 1992; but if it had been recognized earlier, considerable harm could have been circumvented or forestalled in these countries.

Even in the absence of this Principle, US regulators of the Food and Drug Administration refused permission for this drug to be marketed there, on a basis that effectively embodied a precautionary approach. This decision probably prevented the birth of thousands of babies who would have suffered from malformation, across a period of time including that in which thalidomide was actually marketed in Europe and Australia, right up to the stage at which the adverse impacts of thalidomide became apparent (Science Museum n.d.). This shows that a precautionary approach can sometimes be effective in the absence of acknowledgement of the Precautionary Principle. However, the devising and promulgation of an explicit principle, with clear specifications of the circumstances to which it applies, has made it possible in more recent decades to apply such an approach in a consistent manner to the introduction of new technologies and processes, and to the continuation of existing ones, including some that posed previously uninvestigated or unconfirmed risks to health, or in some cases to survival.

Application of the principle to bioethics and biomedicines

So we should now consider whether this Principle could be relevant to biomedicines in general, in the sense that it should be taken into account before they are put into circulation, and that they should be put into circulation only if there are no significant reasons to suppose that these drugs would have serious or irreversible impacts. Now many medicines have been derived from the biodiversity of areas such as rainforests, and indeed this supplies one of the central reasons for preserving such areas. Drugs such as vinblastine, which has revolutionized the treatment of Hodgkin's lymphoma, and vincristine, which has done the same for acute childhood leukaemia (Larrea 2013, 55) confer great benefits on humanity. Yet there are also risks affecting biomedicines, which in some cases may turn out to be comparable to those relevant to thalidomide. Thus plantations of crops for bio-medicinal uses could in principle harbour the same kinds of dangers as plantations of palm-olives for agricultural food production have had, plantations which have unintentionally led to increases in malaria, and on a large scale at that (Kaewwaen and Bhumiratana 2015). As it is, opium plantations, originally intended to produce morphine for medicinal purposes, are generating such serious social harms that in many places these crops are being destroyed (Obetzanov 2003). There again, the release into the environment of genetically modified varieties of species grown to produce improved medicines could in principle prove dangerous to native flora and fauna, with possible problems of cross-breeding and of the introduced varieties out-competing native ones.

It does not follow that biomedicine should be abandoned, or that most of its products should be banned. But it does follow that biotechnologists in general should be aware of the risks posed by the introduction of their own biological products, and that the same applies to practitioners of biomedicine in particular. Disregarding such dangers could involve culpable negligence, and involve respon-sibility, however indirect, for forms of serious or irreversible harm that could, with foresight, have been avoided. The Precautionary Principle applies, of course, to many other human practices, such as the release of carbon dioxide and other green-house gases into the atmosphere, with probable detriment to distant peoples, future generations and countless nonhuman species; taking it seriously at all levels of soci-ety, and intervening accordingly, could make a very large difference with regard to the irreversibility of our carbon footprint. Indeed this is an issue of enormous importance in the context of environmental health (Attfield 2014, 2015). Here, however, the potential applicability of the Precautionary Principle to bioethics in general and to biomedicine in particular is in focus, and, as we have seen, appears to be incontrovertible.

The Precautionary Principle and the Principle of Maximin

However, the very fact that the implications of the Precautionary Principle are both large and wide in their scope has led some scientists and philosophers to question its acceptability, despite its widespread acceptance and recognition in international law. The Precautionary Principle, it is said, amounts to the Principle of Maximin, according to which agents should select the course of action among their options of which the worst outcome would be the least bad (Rawls 1999).[2] This Principle bids us review the conceivable outcomes of our various options, and avoid all but the least risky of them; and the suggestion is that the Precautionary Principle says just the same. And since doing nothing is usually one of the options, and tends to leave the world in the state that it currently was in beforehand, quite often the least risky option would be precisely the option of doing nothing. Following the Principle of Maximin (and related policies) would therefore, the same critics claim, stultify adventurousness, enterprise and initiative, discourage experimentation (even in science, for which experimentation is pivotal), and make being cautious at all times a moral requirement.

However, the Precautionary Principle does not advocate such a Maximin principle or policy, for it does not focus on preventing the worst outcome that could conceivably happen (as the Principle of Maximin does), but, rather, on preventing outcomes that there is reason to consider as significant threats or dangers, outcomes, that is, that, as well as being of a serious or irreversible nature, are also significantly possible. While extreme risk aversion, in line with the Principle of Maximin, counsels not venturing out-of-doors in case of being run over by a bus or being struck by lightning, the Precautionary Principle actually advocates bold action to prevent, for example, tidal surges and forest fires, phenomena which most people recognize (on the strength of recent trends) as likely to increase in both magnitude and frequency because of anthropogenic climate change. So the Precautionary Principle is capable of upholding activism and interventionism. Far from eradicating initiative, it can empower fearless campaigning (like that of Greenpeace) for the sake of a sustainable future, as well as assisting in discerning which policies can rationally be risked, and which cannot. It can recognize that it is often inaction that would generate serious or irreversible harm, as when coastal erosion is left unchecked, or flooding is treated as beyond prevention, and that bold initiatives and reflective activism (whether in campaigning or in social policies) are the ways to avoid a drift to disaster.

So the Precautionary Principle should not be rejected on these grounds, nor misrepresented as advocacy of extreme caution. Indeed it should be applied to anti-technology campaigns as well as to technology, particularly when such a campaign could avoidably facilitate famine. Thus if a genetically modified strain of wheat or rice could rescue millions of people from starvation, without countervailing side effects, then the Precautionary Principle tells us that inaction is what we should avoid, rather than the smaller risks attending this innovation. Yet it applies also to technological innovations as well as to campaigns of protest, and we should not be distracted from adhering to it through caricatures such as its misrepresentation as a policy of Maximin-style cautiousness and extreme risk aversion (Attfield 2014, 2015).

Application of the Precautionary Principle to future quality of life

Besides, its scope may well be greater than at first appears. Some philosophers have pointed out that it is not possible to damage or harm most future people or creatures of other kinds, because harm is only possible where there is an alternative. But (they go on to say) many future individuals would only exist in one possible world or future scenario, and the adoption of different policies in the present would generate different future populations, rather than the same people but without damage or harm. So if the Principle concerns damage or harm, it applies only to individuals already alive or conceived, since their successors cannot strictly speaking be harmed or damaged at all (Schwartz 1978, 1979).

However, the philosopher who has reflected on these matters most penetratingly, Derek Parfit (1984), also holds that our responsibilities are not restricted to avoidance of harm to existing individuals. For through actions such as the policies we adopt we can often enhance the quality of life of whoever is alive in the future, meaning by this whichever population happens to occupy our continent or our planet in future times. Thus we could put in place policies and practices to prevent them suffering the impacts of high increases in average temperatures, and we could similarly make provision for them to inherit remedies for serious diseases; and where we can enhance the quality of future lives, we have the same responsibility to act accordingly as we have for avoiding harm to identifiable people in the present, even though we cannot know which future people will stand to benefit from present action. Parfit supports these claims through a series of thought experiments, and shows thereby that most of us actually presuppose that present actions that foreseeably deprive future people of resources or significant opportunities are just as unacceptable as harming people in the present.

It is true that our ability to know the impacts of present action on future people is sometimes a problem, as is our ability to know what is in their best interests. But we hardly doubt that future people will need a healthy and life-supporting natural and social environment, or that we can affect in the present whether these future needs will be satisfied, and this already shows that the problems of grasping future needs and the difference we can make to them can sometimes be overcome.

Parfit's claim amounts to acceptance that the Precautionary Principle applies to future impacts as well as present ones. Avoidance of serious or irreversible harm should be treated as including avoidance of serious or irreversible reductions in quality of life, both for future human and future nonhuman generations. Many people assume that it includes all this in any case, but it is wise to spell this out, in view of significant scepticism in some quarters on the part of people who seriously suggest that we have no responsibilities with regard to individuals who cannot yet be identified. For those who do not assume this, and for those who recognize that it is a mistaken view, the implications of the Precautionary Principle turn out to be even ampler than they are often taken to be, but no less credible nonetheless.

It is thus highly important that bioethicists, and biotechnologists too, including practitioners of biomedicine, study the Precautionary Principle and its implications for their various fields of practice. I was appalled to discover that genetics students of my own university had never heard of it, even though they were being trained to introduce into the world genetic innovations, whether for the sake of medicine or of practices such as agriculture, and I attempted to ensure that my teaching of ethics would put this right. The same applies to many other forms of biotechnology and to their practitioners, such as those working on biofuels, and indeed to students of biotechnology in general. College and university syllabuses should be modified so that all such students learn of and reflect on the Precautionary Principle. This probably applies also to students of bioethics, since many of the processes and practices considered by bioethicists are ones about which it makes sense to reflect on whether there are reasons to suppose that their impacts would be either serious or irreversible, or both (Attfield 2012).

Conclusion

To repeat, this is not said with a view to an overall curtailment of the applications of biomedicine or of biotechnology. As we have seen, some of these applications are benign, while the introduction of some is probably a positive obligation. There are, however, other applications, and other processes and practices of the kind considered by bioethical committees, that fall foul of the Precautionary Principle, which (at least in its stronger forms) authorizes preventive action, and (even in its weaker forms) declares that absence of a scientific consensus is no reason in itself against such action, even if, on occasion, there are other reasons. But one of these weaker forms is a version of the Precautionary Principle to which all the world's governments (except those of states that have begun to exist since 1992) are already committed, and which they have undertaken treaty obligations to observe.

Governments of signatory states should accordingly take action to embody study of the Precautionary Principle into the syllabuses of all their students of science and technology, as well as of bioethics, for in the absence of such measures, avoidable serious or irreversible harm and avoidable serious or irreversible loss of quality of future life are all too likely to occur. Everyone concerned with present and/or with future quality of life should do what they can to achieve this change of educational policy both in their own country and internationally.

Notes

1   Parker ascribes the identification of these examples to Barnabas Dickson.
2   This is how Rawls expresses the Maximin Principle (at pp. 152–3): 'The maximin rule tells us to rank alternatives by their worst possible outcomes: we are to adopt the alternative the worst outcome of which is superior to the worst outcomes of the others'. At p. 152, Rawls refers to an accessible and ampler discussion of this and other rules of choice under uncertainty in Baumol (1965), Chapter 24, and also to Luce and Raiffa (1957), Chapter XIII.
3   This book is a textbook on ethics, incorporating the history of ethics, value-theory, normative ethics, applied ethics (six fields), meta-ethics, and issues surrounding responsibility, determinism and free will.
4   A second edition of this work was published in 2014 at Newcastle-upon-Tyne, UK by Cambridge Scholars Publishing.

References

Attfield R. (2012) *Ethics: An Overview*. Continuum/Bloomsbury, London and New York.[3]
Attfield R. (2014) *Environmental Ethics*, 2nd ed. Polity, Cambridge and Malden, MA.
Attfield R. (2015) *The Ethics of the Global Environment*, 2nd ed. Edinburgh University Press, Edinburgh.
Baumol W.J. (1965) *Economic Theory and Operations Analysis*, 2nd ed., Prentice-Hall, Englewood Cliffs, NJ.
Kaewwaen W. and Bhumiratana A. (2015) 'Landscape ecology and epidemiology of malaria associated with rubber plantations in Thailand: integrated approaches to malaria ecotoping', *Interdisciplinary Perspectives on Infectious Diseases Volume 2015*, http://dx.doi.org/10.1155/2015/909106 [Accessed 20 November 2015].

Larrea C. (2013) 'Ecuador's Yasuni-ITT initiative: a critical assessment', in Lucas A. Andrianos (ed), *Sustainable Alternatives for Poverty Reduction and Eco-Justice vol. I* Chania, Greece: Institute of Theology and Ecology, Orthodox Academy of Crete, 41–63.[4]

Luce R. D. and Raiffa H. (1957) *Games and Decisions.* John Wiley and Sons Inc., New York.

Obetzanov I., Rutherford C.M. and Sommer S. (2003) 'Opium for heroin in Laos and Myanmar', *TED Case Studies* 125. http://www1.american.edu/TED/opium-burma.htm [Accessed 21 November 2015].

Parfit D. (1984) *Reasons and Persons.* Clarendon Press, Oxford.

Parker J. (1998) 'Precautionary Principle' in Ruth Chadwick (ed), *Encyclopedia of Applied Ethics vol. 3.* Academic Press, San Diego, 633–41.

Rawls J. (1999) *A Theory of Justice.* Oxford University Press, London and New York, 152–7.

Schwartz T. (1978) 'Obligations to posterity', in R. I. Sikora and B. Barry (eds), *Obligations to Future Generations.* Temple University Press, Philadelphia, 3–13.

Schwartz T. (1979) 'Welfare judgments and future generations', *Theory and Decision 11,* 181–94.

Science Museum (n.d) 'Thalidomide', *Science Museum Brought to Life: Exploring the History of Medicine.* www.sciencemuseum.org.uk/broughttolife/themes/controversies/thalidomide.aspx [Accessed 20 November 2015].

United Nations (1992) 'Report of the United Nations Conference on Environment and Development', Rio de Janeiro 3–14 June 1992, Annex 1 – Rio Declaration on Environment and Development. www.un.org/documents/ga/conf151/aconf15126-1annex1.htm, www.unep.org/Documents.multilingual/Default.asp?DocumentID=78& ArticleID=1163 [Accessed 20 November 2015].

6 Recent reflections on the ethical basis of the system of radiological protection

Christopher Clement and Jacques Lochard

Recent reflections on the ethical basis of the system of radiological protection

The system of radiological protection is a guide to human conduct, individual and societal, in this particular domain. The focus is on actions to be taken, or not, under different circumstances, to achieve the aim of protection of people and the environment without unduly limiting desirable human actions. Ethics is the branch of philosophy that deals with virtue and vice, good and evil, and with right and wrong human actions. As such, those who wish to understand radiological protection deeply must turn not only to the natural sciences of physics, chemistry and biology, but also to the humanities, philosophy and particularly the field of ethics.

Background

The system of radiological protection developed by the International Commission on Radiological Protection (ICRP) governs the regulation and practice of radiological protection worldwide. The first recommendations of ICRP's predecessor organization, the International X-Ray and Radium Protection Committee (IXRPC), were developed in 1928 (ICRP 1929). Right from the beginning, the emphasis was on scientific and practical aspects of protection. Nonetheless, the very act of making recommendations is, at its heart, ethical. Ethics deals with questions of human conduct, and the recommendations of ICRP deal with human conduct in the field of radiological protection.

It is difficult to say with certainty what discussions on ethics may have been held within ICRP in the early days, but nearly thirty years after these first recommendations, at the Ninth Annual Conference on Electrical Techniques in Medicine and Biology in 1956, Lauriston Taylor, then ICRP Chairman, declared: 'Radiation protection is not only a matter for science. It is a problem of philosophy, and morality, and the utmost wisdom' (Taylor 1957). Here is a clear indication that ICRP understood the importance of the ethical considerations that underlie the system of radiological protection.

Even so, it was not until the 1990s that the subject of ethics in radiological protection began to be dealt with directly in the literature. Important examples include that of Giovanni Silini, who reviewed the ethical foundation of the system in his Sievert Lecture delivered in 1992 (Silini 1992). He concluded by emphasizing that the system has been developed rationally, and at the same time with the desire to act reasonably. Articles published subsequently questioning the underpinning ethical theories (Oughton 1996; Schrader-Frechette and Persson 1997) led to recognizing that the system of radiological protection is rooted in the aspects of three major theories of ethics by combining the respect of individual rights (deontological ethics), the furthering of collective interest (utilitarian ethics) and the promotion of discernment and wisdom (virtue ethics) (Hansson 2007). Inspired by these reflections eminent professionals of radiological protection have continued to make progress in this direction (Gonzalez 2011; Valentin 2013).

In 2009, some informal discussions on elucidating the ethical basis of the system of radiological protection began to occur within ICRP. It had long been recognized that the system stood on three pillars: science, (ethical) values and experience. Great efforts had been made to understand and explain the scientific basis of the system in the publications of the ICRP, but very little had been done explicitly addressing the ethical basis.

In 2010, ICRP Committee 4 began a review of the literature on the subject. Progress was slowed for a time with attention focused on the Fukushima Daiichi nuclear power plant accident in March 2011, but in 2013 ICRP formed Task Group 94 on The Ethics of Radiological Protection. In relation to this, the Commission also initiated a series of regional workshops organized in collaboration with the International Radiation Protection Association (IRPA) in order to involve ethicists, philosophers, social scientists and radiation protection professionals from different regions of the world in its reflection on this important issue.

Objectives of the current effort

The objectives of Task Group 94 are to develop an ICRP publication presenting the ethical foundations of the system of radiological protection. The purpose of this publication is to consolidate the basis of the recommendations, to improve the understanding of the system, and to provide support for communication on radiation risk and its perception. It is also hoped that the discussions leading to the publication and after its release, along with continuing advances in science and experience, will help support the evolution of the system in the future. However, it is important to recognize that there are broader questions of ethics in radiological protection. One can consider at least three domains: the ethics in development of the system, the ethics in implementation of the system, and the ethics inherent in the system itself.

ICRP approved a code of ethics in 2014 to guide the behaviour of its members in developing the system of radiological protection. It focuses on commitment to public benefit, independence, impartiality, transparency and accountability. With respect to implementation of radiological protection, IRPA adopted a code of ethics for practitioners in 2004. The current ICRP effort undertaken by Task Group 94 does not attempt to delve into these areas; it focuses squarely on the ethics inherent in the system. To understand this, it is important to first understand a few key features of the system of radiological protection.

Fundamentals of the system of radiological protection

'The primary aim of the Commission's Recommendations is to contribute to an appropriate level of protection for people and the environment against the detrimental effects of radiation exposure without unduly limiting the desirable human actions that may be associated with such exposure' (ICRP 2007).

With respect to human health, this is 'to manage and control exposures to ionising radiation so that deterministic effects are prevented, and the risks of stochastic effects are reduced to the extent reasonably achievable' (ICRP 2007). In other words, to prevent negative health effects that can, at least in principle, be prevented, and to manage risks to health that may not be entirely preventable. With respect to the environment, the objective is to prevent or reduce the frequency of negative radiation effects to have a negligible impact on the maintenance of biological diversity; the conservation of species; and the health and status of natural habitats, communities and ecosystems. These two general protection objectives are achieved by following the fundamental principles of justification, optimization of protection, and individual dose limitation.

The principle of justification asserts 'that any decision that alters the radiation exposure situation should do more good than harm' (ICRP 2007). 'The consequences to be considered are not confined to those associated with the radiation – they include other risks and the costs and benefits of the activity. Sometimes, the radiation detriment will be a small part of the total' (ICRP 2007).

The principle of optimization of protection asserts that 'the likelihood of incurring exposures, the number of people exposed, and the magnitude of their individual doses should all be kept as low as reasonably achievable, taking into account economic and societal factors' (ICRP 2007). 'This means that the level of protection should be the best under the prevailing circumstances, maximising the margin of benefit over harm' (ICRP 2007).

The principle of application of dose limits asserts that 'The total dose to any individual from regulated sources in planned exposure situations other than medical exposure of patients should not exceed the appropriate limits recommended by the Commission' (ICRP 2007).

Very briefly, these three principles can be summarized as follows: do more good than harm, provide the best protection based on the prevailing circumstances, and do not expose any individual to an unfair share of risk. Not surprisingly, the primary aim, the protection objectives, and the fundamental principles all have strong scientific and ethical components.

Recent progress

The work of ICRP Task Group 94 on The Ethics of Radiological Protection has been strongly guided by the regional workshops held from 2013 to 2015. These included six organized in collaboration with ICRP, two in each of Asia, Europe and North America, as well as several other workshops and sessions in which ICRP members participated. The six 'main' workshops were:

- *The First Asian Workshop on the Ethical Dimensions of the Radiological Protection System*, organized by the Korean Association for Radiation Protection (an IRPA Associate Society) and hosted by the Korean Institute for Nuclear Safety, in Daejeon, Korea, August 27–28, 2013
- *The First European Workshop on the Ethical Dimensions of the Radiological Protection System*, organized by the Italian Association for Radiological Protection and the French Society for Radiological Protection (both IRPA Associate Societies), in Milan, Italy, December 16–18, 2013
- *The First North American Workshop on the Ethical Dimensions of Radiological Protection*, organized by the US Health Physics Society (an IRPA Associate Society), in Baltimore, Maryland, USA, July 17–18, 2014
- *The Second European Workshop on the Ethical Dimensions of the Radiological Protection System*, organized by the Spanish Society for Radiological Protection, the Italian Association for Radiological Protection and the French Society for Radiological Protection (all IRPA Associate Societies), in Madrid, Spain, February 4–6, 2015
- *The Second North American Workshop on the Ethical Dimensions of the System of Radiological Protection*, hosted by the Belfer Centre for Science and International Affairs, Harvard University, Cambridge, Massachusetts, USA, March 10–12, 2015
- *The Second Asian Workshop on the Ethical Dimensions of the Radiological Protection System*, hosted by Fukushima Medical University, Fukushima City, Japan, June 2–3, 2015

This chapter is based primarily on reflections of the authors on the *2nd International Symposium on the Ethics of Environmental Health* held in České Budějovice, Czech Republic, June 15–19, 2014. As such, it focuses on progress up to then, although some thoughts on progress since that time are also included. Nonetheless, the basic direction of the effort on ethics in radiological protection emerged during this symposium and the workshops that preceded it.

Well-being

Noting that protection of people is central to the system of radiological protection, the question of what this really means was raised at the First Asian Workshop. A partial answer was found in the World Health Organization (WHO) definition of health, which had been established in the WHO constitution of 1946 (WHO 1946): 'Health is a state of complete physical, mental and social well-being and not merely the absence of disease or infirmity'.

In contrast, the human health aim in the system of radiological protection focuses on physical effects: preventing deterministic effects and reducing risks of stochastic effects. Nonetheless, an element of social well-being is captured in the fundamental principle of optimization of protection, which states that exposures should be kept as low as reasonably achievable, taking into account economic and societal factors. In essence, the system aims to protect people from physical effects of radiation, but recognizes that in doing so one must take into account other potential harmful effects and also guard against 'overprotection' from radiation, which might result in other harms.

However, the system has not been designed to protect from harm to 'mental and social well-being' due to radiation. Previously, it was generally difficult to see how exposure to radiation could cause these types of effects, but the Fukushima experience has revealed that the presence of radiation from a nuclear accident in the public domain can cause serious concern and social disruption regardless of direct effects on physical health. It is not enough to ensure people are 'safe' from potential physical effects of exposure to radiation; attention must be paid to their overall well-being. The WHO definition of health encompasses both.

The Chernobyl accident, 25 years earlier, also caused similar problems, but these were overshadowed by the acute radiation sickness of more than one hundred workers (28 of whom died within the first three months after the accident), the dramatic increase in thyroid cancer incidence among those exposed at a young age, and some indication of an increased leukaemia and cataract incidence among the workers (UNSCEAR 2008). These effects have not been seen in Fukushima, and are not expected in the future (UNSCEAR 2014).

Whether, to what extent, and even how these types of indirect effects might be captured in the system of radiological protection is unclear. This will very likely be a topic for serious discussion in the years leading up to the next set of fundamental recommendations from ICRP.

Schools of ethical thought and common values

As noted earlier, there has been a surge in interest in the ethical, or more broadly philosophical, basis of the system of radiological protection since the early 1990s. These were generally individual efforts, and focused mainly on an examination of how the system was formed on the principles of the three major ethical schools of thought (deontological ethics, utilitarian ethics and virtue ethics). These efforts have been of considerable value, and have laid the foundation for the current effort. However, there have long been difficulties in reconciling how parts of each of these ethical theories could be assembled into a sensible and self-consistent whole.

The fundamental basis of each of these ethical theories is profoundly different. Virtue ethics defines actions as right if they come from a virtuous character. Utilitarian ethics defines actions as right if they result in a good outcome. Deontological ethics says actions are inherently right or wrong, regardless of the intent of the actor or the outcome of the action. These admittedly highly simplified but fundamental differences make 'mixing' elements of these theories a treacherous undertaking.

Some modern ethicists have rejected the ideal versions of the earlier theories. W.D. Ross, for example, examined the already well-understood flaws in deontological and utilitarian ethics, and emphasized the complexity of ethical decisions

(Ross 1930). In a kind of modern deontology, relying on ethical intuitionism, he stated that various obligations must be balanced depending on each circumstance, and that no single obligation can be absolute. So, in a sense, the right action is one that is taken after considering the relevant obligations as they relate to the specific circumstance.

Similarly, through the series of workshops, the Task Group focus has been on identifying ethical values[1] that must be balanced for each set of circumstances. It was generally agreed that these values could not have an *a priori* ranking or weighting; which values were most important would depend on the circumstances at hand.

Thus, the question was reshaped from 'How does one combine the various ethical theories to describe the ethical foundation of the system?' to 'What is the set of ethical values that underlies the system?'

Towards a fundamental set of values

The main focus of this current effort is to elucidate the ethical foundations of the system of radiological protection as it stands today. This is an exercise in analysis and clarification, to discern the ethical aspects which are imbedded in the system. As noted earlier, the system is fundamentally a guide to human conduct in the domain of radiological protection, and therefore, intentionally or not, explicitly or implicitly, must have an ethical basis. Although not the main focus of the current effort, this elucidation will also help guide the implementation and evolution of the system of radiological protection in the future.

Given this, it is natural to look first at the system itself, to find the key words, phrases and ideas that reveal its ethical foundation. However, it is also sensible to look outside the system for well-understood ethical underpinnings in related fields, to find the vocabulary needed to speak clearly about what is found, and to understand what may not be well addressed.

This is what has been done through the series of workshops. Participants sought a set of values: relevant to the system of radiological protection, shared as widely as possible, and that should be able to stand the test of being applied to current and foreseeable problems, with sensible results. It was generally agreed that a small set of values is better than a large one; as long as the set is complete it need not be redundant. The interim result is a set of four or five core ethical values:

Beneficence and non-maleficence (counted together or separately)
To do good, and to avoid doing harm
Prudence
To recognize and follow the most sensible course of action, especially in the face of uncertainty, avoiding unwarranted risk
Justice
The fair sharing of benefits and risks
Dignity
Treating individuals with unconditional respect, and preserving their capacity to deliberate, decide and act without constraint

Some have argued for a larger set of values, perhaps to include procedural values. In addition, addressing the concepts of reasonableness and tolerability, explicit in the system of radiological protection, as values has also been discussed. Nonetheless, the present chapter restricts itself to examining the four or five generally agreed core ethical values listed above.

These extremely brief descriptions of each value reflect the work yet to be done to better define them within the context of radiological protection. In the later workshops within the series referred to earlier this was sometimes a central point of discussion. Some attempts have already been made in the literature (Lochard 2016). Further discussion is needed, with input from many quarters.

This set of core ethical values was built through extensive discussions between professionals in radiological protection and philosophy. Many sources were considered; four are introduced here, each only briefly.

From the system of radiological protection

In a sense, this is perhaps the most important source of all, and there is no shortage of references within the system of radiological protection that reveal its ethical underpinnings.

Beneficence and non-maleficence are found at the very roots of the system. Recall that 'The primary aim of the Commission's recommendations is to contribute to an appropriate level of protection of people and the environment against the detrimental effects of ionising radiation exposure without unduly limiting the desirable human actions that may be associated with such exposure' and the principle of justification goes further to say 'that any decision that alters the radiation exposure situation should do more good than harm' (ICRP 2007).

Non-maleficence (avoidance of harm) is seen in the desire to protect people and the environment from detrimental effects. The call to avoid 'unduly limiting the desirable human actions' and to 'do more good' reflect beneficence.

Prudence is also essential to the system. The word 'prudence' appears many times in the publications of ICRP, e.g. 'The LNT [linear no-threshold] model is not universally accepted as biological truth, but rather, because we do not actually know what level of risk is associated with very-low-dose exposure, it is considered to be a prudent judgement for public policy aimed at avoiding unnecessary risk from exposure' (ICRP 2007). Here is an explicit recognition of the uncertainties of risks associated with very-low-dose exposures. Despite the absence of direct evidence of risk to humans at these very low levels, in the face of this uncertainty it has been judged 'prudent' to assume that the risk may not be zero.

Justice is reflected most obviously in the 'fundamental principle' of individual dose limitation. Optimization of protection could be implemented seeking only the greater good, with little regard for the welfare of individuals. This has long been a criticism of the utilitarian ethic from which this fundamental principle arises. However, individual dose limitation puts boundaries on optimization to ensure that no individual shares an undue share of risk. The use of constraints and reference levels in optimization serves a similar purpose.

Dignity is perhaps the least explicit of the core values in the writings of ICRP. Nonetheless, the system does refer to 'participation of relevant stakeholders' and frequently refers to the need for individuals to be 'informed' not only in the context of medial patients but more broadly (ICRP 2007).

From biomedical ethics

Other than natural background, by far the largest source of exposure of people to ionizing radiation is in medical diagnosis and treatment. For this reason, and the long and rich tradition of ethics in medicine, the work of Beauchamp and Childress (USDHEW 1978; Beauchamp and Childress 2001) was an important input. Furthermore, both medicine and radiological protection share the goal of protecting people (although the system of radiological protection also aims to protect the environment). So, it is no coincidence that the core ethical values align closely with the principles of biomedical ethics:

* Respect for autonomy
* Non-maleficence
* Beneficence
* Justice

Beneficence, non-maleficence and justice are explicitly shared principles/values.

The core ethical value of dignity has been discussed as being broader than, and encompassing, the principle of respect for autonomy. Autonomy speaks directly to an individual's capacity to deliberate, decide and act without constraint. Dignity also does this, but goes further by expressing a moral obligation to treat others with respect.

The relationship between the ethics of radiological protection and of biomedical ethics are further developed in several recent works (Malone and Zölzer 2016; Malone 2013).

From Confucius

What follows relies heavily on the presentation of this topic by Lui Senlin and Cho Kunwoo, both members of ICRP Committee 4 who participated in the series of workshops.

The value system of Confucianism consists of three cardinal guides, and five constant virtues. Of interest here are the latter, the five constant virtues of ren, yi, li, zhi and xin. Direct translations into English of the five constant virtues is an impossible and controversial task. Nonetheless, at least in a very superficial way, clear direct links can be drawn between the constant virtues and the ethical values.

> Ren (仁) is like benevolence and non-maleficence, and is at the base of the other four constant virtues.
> Li (禮) is like courtesy, related to the core ethical values of justice and dignity.

Yi (義) is like justice, a means to reaching harmony.

Zhi (智) is like wisdom, related to the core ethical value of prudence.

Xin (信) is like trust and honesty, closely related to the core value of dignity.

Although the relationships between the Confucian constant virtues and the core ethical values of the system of radiological protection are much more complex than hinted at here, even at a glance the parallels are obvious.

From cross-cultural ethics

The system of radiological protection, developed and promoted by the International Commission on Radiological Protection, is meant for the entire world. As such, the ethical basis of the system cannot rely only on 'western ethics' or any other 'regional' source of morality. It needs to reflect a common morality, accepted by the vast majority regardless of cultural, religious, political and other backgrounds.

The field of cross-cultural ethics seeks a 'common morality', not relative to cultures or individuals because it transcends both. The work of Beauchamp and Childress, referred to earlier, is a step in this direction. It sought mid-level principles with which they said all persons committed to morality would agree.

Cross-cultural ethics takes a different approach, seeking common elements in the written and oral traditions of different cultures through the ages. Just such an analysis shows that the Beauchamp and Childress principles of biomedical ethics are endorsed by the work of the great philosophers, scriptures of all the great religions, as well as the oral traditions of indigenous peoples (Zölzer 2013). At least indirectly, this also endorses much of the set of core ethical values of the system of radiological protection.

Zölzer also argues that human dignity is as widely accepted as the principles of biomedical ethics, and goes further to suggest that three derivative values should also be made explicit: precaution, sustainability and solidarity. He also suggests an additional four values important for communication and procedural ethics: honesty, accountability, empathy and participation. How to deal with these proposals remains to be discussed.

Conclusion

It is hardly fitting to use the word 'conclusion' as the effort described here is still very much underway. Even when ICRP publishes a report on the ethical basis of the system of radiological protection, the story will not be over. It will take some time to test and refine the set of core values, and it will certainly be necessary to examine how they are applied in various circumstances.

What is already clear is that focusing on a small set of core ethical values is a sensible and practical way to describe the ethical foundation of the system of radiological protection. This must be done avoiding jargon (of both ethics and radiological protection) to the extent possible, so that it is accessible to practitioners in both fields, and also to a broader audience.

Note

1   During the workshops, several discussions were had on what to call the concepts to be balanced when coming to a decision. The term '(ethical) value' was settled on. Although many thought that '(ethical) principles' was more in keeping with philosophical literature, it was agreed that this might cause undue confusion with the 'fundamental principles' of justification, optimization and individual dose limitation in the system of radiological protection.

References

Beauchamp T. and Childress J. (2001) *Principles of Biomedical Ethics*. Oxford University Press, New York.

Gonzalez A. J. (2011) 'The Argentine approach to radiation safety: its ethical basis', *Sci Technol Nucl Installations*, 1–15. http://dx.doi.org/10.1155/2011/910718 [Accessed 22 September 2015].

Hansson S. (2007) 'Ethics and radiation protection', *J. Radiol. Prot. 27*, 147–56. http://dx.doi.org/10.1088/0952-4746/27/2/002.

International Commission on Radiological Protection (2007) 'The 2007 recommendations of the International Commission on Radiological Protection', ICRP Publication 103, *Ann ICRP 37(2–4)*.

Lochard J. (2016) 'First Thomas S. Tenforde topical lecture: the ethics of radiological protection', *Health Phys 110(2)*, 201–10.

Malone J. (2013) 'Ethical issues in clinical radiology' in Oughton D. and Hansson S. O. (eds), *Social and Ethical Aspects of Radiation Risk Management*. Elsevier Science, New York, 107–29.

Malone J. and Zölzer F. (2016) 'Pragmatic ethical basis for radiation protection in diagnostic radiology', *British Journal of Radiology*, http://dx.doi.org/10.1259/bjr.20150713.

Oughton D. H. (1996) 'Ethical values in radiological protection', *Radiation Protection Dosimetry, 68*, 203-8.

Ross W.D. (1930) *The Right and the Good*. Oxford University Press, Oxford.

Schrader-Frechette K. and Persson L. (1997) 'Ethical issues in radiation protection', *Health Physics, 73(2)*.

Silini G. (1992) 'Sievert lecture – ethical issues in radiation protection' *Health Phys 63*, 139–48.

Taylor L. (1957) 'The philosophy underlying radiation protection', *AJR. Am. J. Roent. 77*, 914–19.

United Nations Scientific Committee on the Effects of Atomic Radiation (UNSCEAR) (2008) 'Sources and effects of ionizing radiation', *UNSCEAR 2008 Report to the General Assembly Scientific Annex D: Health Effects due to Radiation from the Chernobyl Accident*. United Nations Publications, New York.

United Nations Scientific Committee on the Effects of Atomic Radiation (UNSCEAR) (2014) 'Sources, effects and risk of ionizing radiation', *UNSCEAR 2013 Report to the General Assembly Scientific Annex A: Levels and Effects of Radiation Exposure due to the Nuclear Accident after the 2011 Great East-Japan Earthquake and Tsunami*.

U.S. Department of Health, Education and Welfare (1978) 'National Commission for the Protection of Human Subjects of Biomedical and Behavioral Research', *The Belmont Report DHEW* pub. no. (OS) 78-0012. U.S. Government Printing Office, Washington, DC. http://videocast.nih.gov/pdf/ohrp_belmont_report.pdf [Accessed 24 September 2015].

Valentin J. (2013) 'Radiation risk and the ICRP' in Oughton D. and Hansson S.O. (eds), *Social and Ethical Aspects of Radiation Risk Management*. Elsevier Science, New York, 17–32.

World Health Organization (1946) Preamble to the Constitution of the World Health Organization as adopted by the International Health Conference, New York, 19–22 June, 1946; signed on 22 July 1946 by the representatives of 61 States (Official Records of the World Health Organization, no. 2, p. 100) and entered into force on 7 April 1948.

Zölzer F. (2013) 'A cross-cultural approach to radiation ethics' in Oughton D. and Hansson S. O. (eds), *Social and Ethical Aspects of Radiation Risk Management*, Elsevier Science, New York, 53–70.

Part III

Decision making on environmental health problems

7 The phenomenology of environmental health risk

Vulnerability to modern technological risk, risk alienation and risk politics

Mark Coeckelbergh

Introduction

On 11 March 2011 an earthquake occurred near Honshu Island, the main island of Japan. This triggered a 15-metre tsunami, which caused damage to coolant systems of nuclear reactors in Fukushima and eventually led to nuclear meltdowns and release of radioactive material. Although more people died from the earthquake and the tsunami (more than 15,000 deaths as of February 2014), there was some radiation in the area and children from the contaminated areas had increased risk of getting thyroid cancer. Radioactive material found its way into drinking water and food supply. In Tokyo it was announced that safety limits for infants were exceeded. Radioactivity also entered the Pacific Ocean. Pollution on the coast and near the plant might persist. Many people living in the area near the power plant – hundreds of thousands – were evacuated. Many emergency workers were exposed to high levels of radiation; they risked their present and future health. Later an investigation found that direct causes of the accident were foreseeable and the power company admitted that it failed to take better measures to present disasters. A power plant closer to the epicentre of the earthquake withstood the disaster. Japanese authorities admitted poor oversight. An investigation committee concluded that there was poor crisis management. Following the disaster there was more public discussion about nuclear energy, inside and outside Japan. Some called for phasing out nuclear power. Germany accelerated plans to close and phase out its reactors (Strickland 2011; for an overview see also the Wikipedia entry on the Fukushima Daiichi Nuclear Disaster).

Accidents and disasters such as Fukushima raise interesting questions for the ethics and philosophy of environmental health risk. For instance, were these risks and this disaster 'natural' or not? Is there an 'objective' way of measuring this kind of risk? How should we respond to such risks? What is good risk management? What is left out in the narrative about causes, management and measures? What is the place of personal experience and cultural wisdom in narratives like this and, more generally, in responses to risk?

I discuss a case from the nuclear industry here, but similar questions could be asked about the chemical industry, about modern health care, about modern agriculture and so on. These are questions that are relevant to all environmental health risks and hence to those human activities that create these risks.

This chapter focuses on the subjective, social and cultural aspects of (our responses to) risk. The first part of the chapter focuses on the nature of risk and on the ways humans respond to risk and the corresponding vulnerability, in particular on the phenomenology of being-vulnerable to environmental risk. Drawing on my book *Human Being @ Risk* (Coeckelbergh 2013), I emphasize and briefly analyse the existential and cultural dimension of risk and vulnerability, and explore its implications for our thinking about environmental health risk. Then I argue that in modern technological culture there is a gap between the production of risk and the experience of risk, which has political consequences with regard to the power of persons and communities. I compare this modern situation with traditional risk cultures and raise the question if and how we can re-appropriate risk and re-empower people. I end with conclusions for coping with environmental health risk and call for a different risk politics.

Vulnerability to environmental health risk

Environmental health risk: Subjective and social-cultural aspects

Environmental health risk is never about science and technology alone. It is also about psychology, society, trust and identity. It is also about politics. It is about how we should live. It is about human existence.

To reveal these dimensions of risk, we may turn to well-known work in empirical psychology about risk perception (e.g. Slovic 2000), which seeks to quantify and analyse people's responses to risk, for instance fear of nuclear risk. But there are also cultural theories of risk (see for instance the work of Mary Douglas, e.g. Douglas 1992) and interesting ethnographical work on responses to risk, which goes beyond psychological explanations. For instance, there has been ethnographical research on responses to the Fukushima disaster. Figueroa (2013) has argued that as a consequence of the government's poor risk communication and in particular its inability to deal with public fears, citizens felt uncertain and distrusted the government, the regulators and the nuclear industry. He recommends a more participative approach to discussions about energy production.

However, the responses of citizens were not limited to passive fear and distrust; there were also much more active responses. Morita et al. also point to mistrust in official institutions and show 'civic efforts to make radiation data publicly accessible and easier to understand', in particular the making of a 'civic radiation monitoring map' by amateur citizens (Morita et al. 2012, 78). In the wake of the Fukushima disaster there were also social-political movements. Using ethnographical research, Ogawa documents anti-nuclear rallies and actions and shows that the activists were not only concerned with energy issues but also wanted a fairer society and proposed alternative ways of life (Ogawa 2013). Similarly, Niggemeier has shown that the protests opened up novel political opportunities and that the protests were even characterized as a New Social Movement (Niggemeier 2015).

It is also interesting to note how some people characterized the events in Fukushima as a natural disaster, whereas others pointed to 'Japanese culture'. For instance, Kinsella has mapped the responses in the U.S. nuclear community and found that on the one hand, nuclear producers stressed the earthquake and tsunami, thereby shifting responsibility to the natural world and minimizing the social and economic impact. On the other hand, the chairman of the Japanese commission that examined the failures also pointed to Japanese culture, which was then used as a rhetorical resource by people in the U.S. who argued that such an event could never happen in the U.S. (Kinsella 2013). Interestingly, Kinsella also notes that in the first case the 'natural' and the 'social' are separated: phenomena such as earthquakes and tsunamis are either seen as 'subject to precise scientific representation and technological control' or 'are fatalistically portrayed as inevitable and unforeseeable rather than as challenges to the prevailing system' (Kinsella 2013). [Note that Kinsella contrasts this approach to that of Actor-Network theory (see for instance the work of Callon, Latour and others – see for instance Latour 2005), which views both humans and non-humans in one political and negotiation process.]

The responses were also linked to identity and gender issues. For instance, Marioka has argued that there were gender differences in the health risk perception of radiation: mothers in general expressed more concern, whereas fathers saw radiation risk as a threat to economic stability and masculine identity. As a result, mothers' health concerns were dismissed (Marioka 2014). Sternsdorff Cistema has also shown that food safety was linked to culture: he has argued that in Japanese culture there are two ways of framing safe food:

> In Japanese, safe food is often described as having both anzen (安全) and anshin (安心). Anzen refers to the world of science and precision; it is a measurable and quantifiable form of safety that has thresholds and can be measured in units like 'below 100 bq/kg'. Anshin, on the other hand, speaks to questions of the heart, as many informants have pointed out to me. It is a subjective and emotional relationship to food. It is personal, and describes the degree of confidence one feels about the safety of food supplies. Both terms are often used in conjunction to describe foods as anzen anshin na shokuhin (safe and trustworthy food).
>
> (Sternsdorff Cistema 2013)

Thus, there are two relationships to food, an objective-scientific one and a subjective-emotional one, and in this approach safety requires *both*: 'food safety is not a question of science alone' but rather 'the scientific and the subjective co-exist in the production of safe food' (Sternsdorff Cistema 2013). Whether or not most Japanese people actually make or put so much importance on this particular distinction, this very way of thinking in terms of different but co-existing ways of relating to risk is very interesting.

Thus, one could ask whether risk is objective or subjective. The objective approach stands for risk assessment and risk management, and is based on scientific knowledge and measurement. The subjective approach has to do with our personal and cultural responses – which in turn are often objectified by the psychological and sociological sciences (see again for instance the work by Slovic on the psychology of risk perception or work on the social construction of risk, see for instance Nelkin 1989). Yet ethnographical research suggests not only that the latter, 'subjective' approach is also important to take into account in risk management and other 'objective' approaches, but *also* that we might be able move *beyond* a dualist understanding of risk altogether, beyond the binary 'subjective' 'perception' versus 'objective' risk.

There are various ways of doing this. One could for instance use Latour's work (e.g. Latour 1993) to question the nature-social distinction or look at how Japanese people deal with environmental health risk. In the following section, I will refer to both, but will mainly use my previous work in *Human Being @ Risk* (Coeckelbergh 2013) to propose a less dualistic approach to risk, including environmental health risk. In this way I take the Fukushima discussion to a more general level.

Risk and vulnerability cultures

The concept I propose to deal with the problem whether risk is objective or subjective is 'being-at-risk' and 'being-vulnerable'. The idea is that, phenomenologically speaking, 'risk is neither a feature of the world (an objective, external state of affairs) nor (…) a subjective construction by the mind, an internal matter, but is constituted in the subject-object relation. The same can be said of vulnerability' (Coeckelbergh 2013, 43). Whereas the concept of risk tends to mainly highlight the 'objective' side the phenomenon – we experience that something external puts us at risk – the concept of vulnerability highlights the 'subjective' side of it: the personal and social experience we have of being-vulnerable, the experience that something might happen to me and to us. But whatever side we highlight, risk and vulnerability can never be reduced to one side; on the whole risk and vulnerability are deeply relational and environmental in an existential sense: they emerge within the subject-object relation and concern the way we are attuned to, and respond to, our social-natural environment.

This way of thinking about risk enables us to go beyond the limitations of 'objective' risk science and risk management. It opens up different perspectives and reveals modern risk management as only one way of understanding and coping with risk. It means that there is, and that we must allow for, personal variation in coping with risk, which is not necessarily 'wrong'. It means that so-called 'cultural ways of understanding risk and vulnerability are not entirely different approaches which only belong to *other* cultures, but that the modern way of understanding risk – including environmental health risk – is as much 'cultural' as, say, so-called 'cultural' responses by whoever we construct as 'others' ('the Japanese', for instance). There are various risk and vulnerability cultures, and each of them has different ways of understanding risk and vulnerability and different ways of coping with risk and vulnerability.

For instance, there is something like a Dutch 'water technology culture', a specific Dutch way of understanding and dealing with a so-called 'natural' disaster, which is neither merely 'objective' nor merely 'subjective' but both (or neither). It is both technological and cultural, material and human. Let me explain.

For the Dutch, flood control is a matter of life or death. If the Dutch did not have flood control, a significant part of the country would be flooded since it is situated below sea level. Already in medieval times farmers made dwelling mounds in order to stay dry. Later they were connected: there were dikes. After the floods of 1953 the Dutch built many dikes and waters systems, the so-called Delta works which included the Eastern Scheldt storm surge barrier. The cultural narrative entangled with this technology is that of a heroic fight against nature. Later this changed to working with the water, rather than fighting it, and more room was given to rivers. Some areas of agricultural land were now allowed to be flooded.

To show how difficult it is to disentangle 'objective' and 'subjective' aspects of these risks and risk cultures (and indeed risk politics), consider how hard it is to transfer these ways of dealing with risk to other countries. For instance, it has been difficult to transfer Dutch technological solutions to Britain, which has recently experienced several floodings: one cannot simply 'cut and paste' solutions; the mindset is also important (Storr 2014). Another example: compared to the U.S., in the Netherlands it is easier to mobilize public resources to prevent disasters ahead of time, whereas in the U.S. the focus is on individual and local solutions and to disaster management rather than prevention (Higgins 2012).

Similarly, the Fukushima disaster and the responses it received can never be captured by means of a narrative of causes and objective measurements alone, since both the environmental health risk itself and the way people dealt with it have specific personal and cultural qualities. Stronger, one cannot strictly separate ('objective', 'natural' or 'technological') risk and ('cultural', 'human') coping with risk: both are at the same time objective and subjective, natural and cultural, technological and human. The terms being-vulnerable and being-at-risk include and go beyond these binaries. They communicate that experientially and existentially speaking, risk is all these things. There is neither an objective risk-in-itself that can be described separate from human experience and culture, nor a subjective risk that has nothing to do with what happens in reality. Risk is always personally and culturally mediated, and our experience and feelings with regard to risk are never merely 'mental' but always directed towards an object, a something that puts us at risk. And as a result of human interpretation and intervention (e.g. technological intervention), there is no such thing as natural risk: it is always also cultural. Nor does a merely personal or cultural risk exist; there is always a 'natural' something. Again, this is also true for environmental health risks, which are hybrids of human and non-human, natural and cultural, experiences and causes. Disasters such as that of Fukushima, for instance, are as much natural as they are cultural.

In the language of the social sciences one could say that such disasters are not only culturally interpreted but also culturally constructed. And the same is true for the interpretation and construction of historical disasters. Science and philosophy meet and met at the crossroads of risk and disaster. For instance, in response to the Lisbon earthquake and tsunami of 1755, which nearly destroyed the whole city and killed 10,000 or more people, there was a discussion among Enlightenment philosophers/scientists about whether it was due to natural causes or divine punishment. In his *Candide* (1759) Voltaire used the earthquake to challenge Leibniz's claim that we live in the best of all possible worlds. Rousseau responded to a poem on the earthquake by Voltaire and pointed to the role of humans – indeed to the *social-geographical* aspect of the disaster. He wrote in a letter to Voltaire: 'If the residents of this large city had been more evenly dispersed and less densely housed, the losses would have been fewer or perhaps none at all' (Rousseau 1756; see also Dynes 1999). And Kant ascribed the event to natural causes. He wrote three articles on the subject and formulated a theory of the causes of the earthquake that involved the shifting of large subterranean caves filled with hot, combustible gasses (Reinhardt and Oldroyd 1983). The earthquake was studied scientifically and led to earthquake engineering. At the same time, the earthquake also influenced Kant's notion of the sublime, developed in his *Critique of the Power of Judgment* (1790).

Thus, the modern habit to separate science from philosophy and religion, 'objective' research and 'subjective' culture, is a very specific way of viewing nature and risk, and actually needs what Latour called 'work of purification' (Latour 1993) in order to work: humans and non-humans, subjects and objects, nature and society, have to be conceptually separated. In reality, there is hybridity. For instance, the vulnerability of megacities depends on 'nature' but also on 'humans', on 'society', and on 'culture'. What needs to be explained is not that environmental health risk has a 'subjective' dimension as opposed to an 'objective' one, but how on earth we could ever have separated both given that our being-at-risk and our being-vulnerable is phenomenologically so hybrid. Let me therefore say more about modernity.

Risk alienation and risk distance

Environmental risk as modern risk

Modernity has a specific way of understanding and coping with risk. Sociologist Ulrich Beck famously used the notion of 'risk society' (Beck 1992) to describe how modern society responds to risk (see also the work of Anthony Giddens, e.g. Giddens 1999). Interestingly given the focus of this volume, Beck's point initially concerned specifically environmental risks: he argued that they had become the dominant product of industrial society rather than its unpleasant side effect. He was very interested in 'ecological disaster and atomic fallout', issues which concern global risks and which ignore social inequalities: 'Even the rich and powerful are not safe from them' (Beck 1992, 23). As a result of these new, modern risks, an entire risk assessment and risk management industry came into being. The political question, according to Beck, is no longer about distribution of wealth but 'How can the risks and hazards systematically produced as part of modernization be prevented, minimized, dramatized, or channelled? Where they do finally see the light of day in the shape of "latent side effects", how can they be limited and distributed away so that they neither hamper the modernization process nor exceed the limits of that which is "tolerable" – ecologically, medically, psychologically and socially?' (Beck 1992, 19). Moreover, because of the dominance of these risks, trust in for instance the nuclear industry has declined. All this means, according to Beck, that modernity has become more reflexive: 'it is becoming its own theme' (19) as questions regarding risk management take precedence.

I disagree with Beck's point that the social production of risks is something special for 'advanced' modernity or even for modernity *per se*. Instead I think that the production and transformation of risk and vulnerability is part of our existence (Coeckelbergh 2013), and that hence what Beck calls 'personal' risks (Beck 1992, 21) have always been connected with human (technological) action – although admittedly that action did not always have a global character and specific kinds of technologies (modern technologies) indeed have an enormous effect on society. Note also that Beck's claim assumes that we can strictly distinguish between the natural and the technological, natural risks and manufactured risks – an assumption which I question. Beck's thinking remains very modern. Yet taken as a whole, Beck's work shows once again how risk and responses to risks, how technology and society/culture, are very much interwoven. And it especially tells us something about modern risk and modern coping with risk: we are increasingly obsessed with risk management, that is, the management of risks which we humans have created.

But perhaps a better way of becoming aware of the specificity of the modern understanding of risk is to look at its opposite: so-called 'non-modern' – and if contemporary, 'less modern' – ways of dealing with risk. In the history of humankind, there have been very different attitudes to risk. For instance, ancient Greek tragedy suggests that we humans better accept that we lack full control, that we are in the hands of fate and should not challenge the gods (hubris). And in non-Western cultures we also find non-modern attitudes towards risk. For instance, in the Japanese context we find modernity but also Shinto and Buddhism, which also urge us to respect the forces and gods of nature which are more powerful than us, and which warn us not to think that we are the centre of everything: things happen, the universe is not interested in our desires and beliefs.

Such non-modern beliefs are not necessarily in contradiction to modern science. For instance, in response to the 2011 tsunami in Japan and the events at Fukushima, there were Shinto/Buddhist opinions that it was a divine punishment (see for example the reaction of the major of Tokyo) but also ideas that do not contradict Western science. Martin Palmer, director of the Alliance for Religions and Conservation (a secular body that helps faiths develop environmental programmes based on their own beliefs and practices), has been attributed the following descriptions of a Shinto perspective on the disaster:

> In Shinto, we are here by the grace of the gods, but we are not their main concern – we are not the centre of the story. We are not why the gods exist, we are not why creation exists, and we are not why these events exist. These natural disasters occur because this is just how nature is.
>
> (Palmer in Ivakhiv 2011)

In other words, Palmer argues here that according to Shinto beliefs, the disaster was not a divine punishment since nature is not concerned with us.

Moreover, traditional knowledge does not necessarily contradict modern science and technology either:

> the Shinto had been opposed to the nuclear power stations from day one as being not a good idea. If the stations had been built on sites that were chosen according to traditional Shinto rituals and understanding of the forces that live within the land, they would not be over dangerous cracks in the earth and easily attacked by nature. [Palmer] referred to 'a remarkable arrogance and disrespect for traditional understandings of the power and spiritual forces that reside in the land'.
>
> (Palmer in Ivakhiv 2011)

Thus, here Shinto ritual and understanding does not seem to be in contradiction to good science, which presumably also had discovered the dangerous cracks (but which perhaps were ignored by politicians and others involved in the planning and building of these nuclear power plants).

The modern attitude, however, is blind to such traditional understandings of risk and is obsessed with controlling and fighting nature. But this is often counterproductive. Combining Beck's insights and my point about technology creating new vulnerabilities (see below), one could say that our obsession with controlling nature and controlling risks has turned into its opposite: a techno-nature that gets out of control and new risks that are created and proliferate as a result of our science and technology. Let me say more about what I call 'vulnerability transformations'.

Vulnerability transformations

Another way of framing the problem of modernity with regard to risk is to focus on the term 'vulnerability': modernity is obsessed with fighting against vulnerability. Some even want to become immortal (for instance many so-called transhumanists). But as I have argued previously, these efforts to *reduce* risk and vulnerability always create new vulnerabilities. Vulnerability is transformed, not eradicated (Coeckelbergh 2013). Technology transforms human vulnerability and risk: perhaps it moves it to different areas, but the human condition remains a vulnerable and risky one, albeit often in different and new ways. For instance, nuclear power helps us to reduce dependence on other, older sources of energy. Our dependence on oil and gas gives us all kinds of vulnerabilities, for instance we become dependent on countries that have oil. With nuclear energy we decrease our vulnerability on such resources. But at the same time the solution – nuclear technology – creates new risks and vulnerabilities, related to radiation (radiation risk, for instance risk of a meltdown, and risks associated with nuclear waste and its disposal). And vulnerability to floodings is decreased by means of dikes and other water management technology, but creates new dependencies and vulnerabilities: we become entirely dependent on for instance dikes. Another example: when hunting we were dependent on the animal – will it appear or not, will we be able to catch it or not? – and farming and agricultural technologies have reduced this vulnerability. The plants are more under our control. The animals are now always available for slaughter and consumption. But this solution has generated its own problems: we eat too much meat and incur all kinds of health risks to the (non-human) animals and to humans, we are dependent on the weather and climate, toxic elements can get into the food chain and so on. Other examples: we used antibiotics to become less vulnerable to diseases, but became dependent on them and even resistant to them, which creates a new kind of vulnerability. We clean our houses in order to prevent infections, but if newborns are not exposed to dirt, germs and so on they might develop other problems (allergy for instance). Thus, each time there is a risk and vulnerability problem to which we respond with a technological solution, which then creates new risks and vulnerabilities.

Experiential distance and risk alienation

Perhaps one reason why we are so bad at dealing with risks in modernity has to do with the way we *experience* risk in modernity, in particular with our everyday experience of risk and with what I propose to call 'risk alienation'.

If we consider the phenomenology of modern technological-environmental risks, then it becomes clear that there is a kind of 'experiential distance' in risk situations. When I personally experience modern risk, I know that I am vulnerable to something out there, but I cannot see that, I cannot directly experience it. Moreover, I feel that this 'something out there' has nothing to do with me, with my actions, with my life. I neither produce the risk (or so it seems) nor can I directly cope with it. It is done by 'them', by others, by modern institutions and remote agents that are invisible to me. For instance, to stay in the area of energy production: electricity is produced somewhere else, not in my home. I only see the socket of the grid, I do not see the grid and I do not see the power plant (e.g. the nuclear power plant). Yet I am totally dependent on what I cannot see. There are invisible forces that control my life. There are invisible *people* that control my life. Experts deal with it, and with potential problems. The same is true for oil: I do not know or do not need to know where it comes from. I go to fill up at a petrol station. Again I am totally dependent on forces I cannot control. The oil is coming from somewhere else, somewhere far away, often a distant country. Water comes from the tap, but what if it suddenly stops? I am once again dependent on 'they' who produce the clean water, on the water distribution system (on 'it'), on everything and all that have to do with its production. But I am not part of that. I am a passive consumer, not a producer. Therefore, I am also a passive consumer of the risks and vulnerabilities. Others have to deal with the problems, others that are called 'experts'. And of course modern medicine is also a good example: I go to the doctor, I go to the hospital, and things are being given to me (e.g. medicines) and things are being done to me (e.g. an operation). But as a modern patient, I have a rather passive role – as the word patient already indicates. I am patient and I have to be patient. I have to wait until others solve the problem. I am once again entirely dependent on others and on 'the system'. I am also entirely vulnerable according to the vulnerabilities of the system. If 'they' make a mistake or something was wrong in 'the system', bad things may happen to me.

The result of this 'experiential distance' when it comes to risk, the result of this 'risk distance', is what I propose to call *risk alienation*: my being-at-risk and my being-vulnerable takes an alienated form. As a modern risk and vulnerability subject/object, I am vulnerable in an alienated and disempowered way. Modern risk and vulnerability are alienated from my own activities, feelings and experience. Modern risks, even those produced by human activities and technologies, feel increasingly like natural disasters: I cannot control them, I cannot do much about them, I am totally dependent on external events and people and processes 'out there'. I feel powerless, and families, groups, and communities feel powerless. Technological risks feels like what the gods might do to humans in an ancient Greek tragedy. Modern risk becomes tragic. Consider nuclear disasters, financial crises and computer viruses: they are like global floods or earthquakes. They are epidemic. The term 'epidemic' comes from the Greek *epi*, which means 'upon or above' and *demos*, which means 'people'. Modern risk is something upon and above the people. It 'befalls' us. It happens to us. It is up to the gods, the new gods which now seem to reside in nuclear power plants and computers. The analogy with religious experience is not coincidental, and it is worth further exploring the (quasi?) religious experience related to modern risk and vulnerability. Consider for instance invisibility and incomprehensibility (you cannot see the gods and you cannot comprehend their plans and motives), the sublime (the awesome), and indeed the tragic: are these aspects of religious-aesthetic experience not also relevant to modern risks? Paradoxically, it seems that our 'modern' experience of risk is remarkably similar to 'non-modern' religious and aesthetic experiences. This is an interesting topic in itself.

However, here I would like to emphasize the political consequences of modern risk, in particular disempowerment. Modern technologies take away power from me and give it to 'the system' and its experts. There is a hierarchical power structure. Modern risk politics takes away my chance to deal with the risks and vulnerabilities because it has already taken away my activity. I do not produce the energy and I can no longer produce energy. I do not heal and I can no longer heal. There is a loss of skill and know-how; we now lack direct engagement with our environment (see also Coeckelbergh 2015). We have delegated many activities to experts. We badly need and highly value health, energy, food and so on, but we have lost a direct relation to realizing these values. This implies a loss of power and a feeling of alienation. Both production of the goods and creation of the values themselves *and* the risks associated with their production have been outsourced. We are now vulnerable not to what we used to call 'nature', but to others and to 'the system', where the production and the power is centred. 'They' are the only ones who can and should deal with the risks.

Indeed, whereas my initial use of the phrase 'taken away' sounds like we have nothing to do with this risk modernization and (therefore) risk alienation process, the phrase 'we have delegated' is more appropriate, since we have everything to do with it. 'Modernity' is not a thing outside us; it is also inside us. We find it *convenient* and *comfortable* to give away the activity, know-how, etc. to others and to 'the system'. We have alienated ourselves and we have disempowered ourselves. We wanted to be consumers, babies, end-users clinging on to the socket. We wanted to decrease our vulnerability by inventing modern technologies and systems. We hoped that 'they' would make our lives more comfortable. And to some extent they have. But we also pay the price for this: we created new risks and vulnerabilities: new technological-environmental risks and vulnerabilities, and perhaps the greatest risk of all, the risk that we lose a direct relationship to the environment, and become totally dependent on systems that seem to have nothing to do with our lives. This is quite a paradox again: as moderns we wanted to gain full control (over 'nature'), but the result is that we have given away control (to 'technology', to experts). The new, modern, technologically transformed world we now live in does the same to us as the old 'wild' nature we were so afraid of: it scares us to death and makes us feel vulnerable and awesome in the face of whatever overpowers us: systems, technologies, institutions, nations and so on. In this sense, paradoxically again, risk experience is as non-modern as it has always has been.

Risk appropriation and re-empowerment

In response to this predicament, we could try to re-appropriate the production, technologies *and* the risks and vulnerabilities. For instance, we could produce our own energy, grow our own food, at least share some responsibility for dealing with health risks, create alternatives for nuclear energy, and so on. Such changes need not be anti-technological, and we need not and cannot go back to pre-modern times; perhaps new, smart technologies can help us. However, we have to make sure that the new vulnerabilities we create are not worse than the old ones. Maybe we have been too quick in setting up technological solutions, without considering the new risks and vulnerabilities these solutions might create. Maybe we should try to become a little less modern, and re-cultivate less modern virtuous such as patience (see also Buddhism again), acceptance of what happens beyond our control and so on.

That being said, modernity is a form of life, which cannot be changed that easily. Our efforts to re-appropriate and re-empower may well remain within the boundaries of Beck's 'reflexive modernity' – they will constitute reform and adaptation – or indeed constitute 'merely' a new kind of modernity. It is difficult for us moderns to imagine a significantly less modern form of life. All the same, with regard to risk and vulnerability, it would probably be best for us to accept that there is a tragic dimension to the human condition and to human vulnerability, and to keep in mind that since there is no clear separation between 'natural' risk and 'technological' risk, and between 'objective' risk and 'subjective' risk, modern methods of risk management and modern risk science (including psychology) have their limitations and risk hiding important dimensions of risk and vulnerability as existential and lived experience.

Conclusion

Let me conclude by saying more about the potential implications of this reflection on risk and vulnerability for coping with environmental health risks.

First, of course scientific expertise is needed, but we need to remain aware that it is a very specific form of human experience and human coping with risk, which is related to how we deal with risk and vulnerability in modernity, and which does not exhaust the spectrum of risk-coping possibilities. We need to admit at least more plurality when it comes to coping with risk. By looking at personal and cultural variation in the way people deal with risk we can also bring in other kinds of expertise and *wisdom*, and start to explore less modern ways of dealing with environmental health.

But plurality may suggest that risk scientists and risk experts can and should just continue their business as usual, *next* to what people do starting from other perspectives. This is probably not sufficient to deal with the challenges we face. Scientist and other 'experts' also need to re-think their role and activities. Perhaps they will need to become 'scientists plus something else', who are able to communicate with, say, local communities, are aware that modern ways of doing have their shadow sides, can critically reflect on the risks and vulnerabilities they might create, speak different languages than the scientific one, and maybe even transform their scientific practice.

To conceptualize the normative direction of such changes, we could say that subjects should not be turned into objects by means of language and measurement, that people should not be treated as a standing-reserve (Heidegger 1977). We could use discourse theory and hermeneutics (see for instance Habermas, Ricoeur and Gadamer) and/or Latour to further reflect on how we can create new kinds of dialogues and negotiations, perhaps including non-humans in the sense of Latour's *Politics of Nature* (2004). Different stakeholders may speak a different language, so we have to explore how they can talk to one another. After the risk of earthquakes of the past and those to come, we can look for common ground. Yet when we do so, we have to recognize that there will always be cultural-technological instabilities and there will be always impurities. We have to recognize that our risk problems are always about subjects and objects, technology and nature, humans and non-humans. And starting from different perspectives, we can reveal and disclose different worlds for one another, with or without language. This requires interdisciplinary and transdisciplinary efforts. Artists may also help to show new possibilities.

Second, however, it is not only the 'they' that need to change (the experts, the politicians, etc.). The gap between lay people and experts is likely to continue to exist as long as there is risk alienation: the way all of us — experts and lay people alike — do and organize things in modernity has implications for experience, knowledge and action, and for the way we live together. Modernity is not only a 'philosophical' or 'cultural' issue but also a personal and a political one. Therefore, exploring different ways of coping with risk and vulnerability also means exploring different ways of life and different social and institutional arrangements. This chapter suggests that if we care about a different, perhaps more inclusive and participatory risk politics, we need to change our entire way of doing things: we need to produce, work and live differently. We need to live together differently. Otherwise the appeal remains cosmetic and rhetoric, and we keep suffering from modern risk and modern risk alienation — a kind of 'meta' environmental health risk that does not go away when we have implemented the next emergency technological fix.

References

Beck U. (1992) *Risk Society: Towards a New Modernity*. Sage, London.

Coeckelbergh M. (2013) *Human Being @ Risk: Enhancement, Technology, and the Evaluation of Vulnerability Transformations*. Springer, Dordrecht.

Coeckelbergh M. (2015) *Environmental Skill*. Routledge, New York.

Douglas M. (1992) *Risk and Blame: Essays in Cultural Theory*. Routledge, London.

Dynes R.R. (1999) 'The dialogue between Voltaire and Rousseau on the Lisbon earthquake: The emergence of a social science view', University of Delaware Disaster Research Centre Preliminary Paper. http://udspace.udel.edu/bitstream/handle/19716/435/PP%20293.pdf?sequence=1 [Accessed 14 October 2015].

Figueroa P. (2013) 'Risk communication surrounding the Fukushima nuclear disaster: an anthropological approach', *Asia Europe Journal 11(1)*, 53–64.

Giddens A. (1999) 'Risk and responsibility', *The Modern Law Review 62(1)*, 1–10.

Heidegger M. (1977) *The Question Concerning Technology and Other Essays* (Trans. W. Lovitt). Harper & Row, New York.

Higgins A. (2012) 'Lessons for U.S. from a flood-prone land', *The New York Times*, 14 November 2012. www.nytimes.com/2012/11/15/world/europe/netherlands-sets-model-of-flood-prevention.html?_r=0 [Accessed 22 September 2015]

Ivakhiv A. J. (2011) 'Religion & the Japanese tragedy', *Immanence: Ecoculture, Geophilosophy, Mediapolitics*. https://blog.uvm.edu/aivakhiv/2011/03/16/religion-the-japanese-tragedy/ [Accessed 22 September 2015].

Kant I. (1790) *Critique of the Power of Judgment* (Trans. P. Guyer and E. Matthews). Cambridge University Press, Cambridge, 2000.

Kinsella W.J. (2013) 'Negotiating nuclear safety: responses to the Fukushima disaster by the U.S. nuclear community', An STS Forum on the East Japan Disaster. https://fukushimaforum.wordpress.com/workshops/sts-forum-on-the-2011-fukushima-east-japan-disaster/manuscripts/session-3-radiation-information-and-control/negotiating-nuclear-safety-responses-to-the-fukushima-disaster-by-the-u-s-nuclear-community/ [Accessed 22 September 2015].

Latour B. (1993) *We Have Never Been Modern*. Harvard University Press, Cambridge, MA.

Latour B. (2004) *Politics of Nature: How to Bring the Sciences into Democracy*. Harvard University Press, Cambridge, MA.

Latour B. (2005) *Reassembling the Social: An Introduction to Actor-Network Theory*. Oxford University Press, Oxford.

Marioka R. (2014) 'Gender difference in the health risk perception of radiation from Fukushima in Japan: the role of hegemonic masculinity', *Social Science & Medicine 107*, 105–12.

Morita A., Blok A. and Kimura S. (2012) 'Environmental infrastructures of emergency: the formation of a Civic Radiation Monitoring Map during the Fukushima disaster' in Hindmarsh R. (ed), *Nuclear Disaster at Fukushima Daiichi: Social, Political and Environmental Issues*. Routledge, London, 78–96.

Nelkin D. (1989) 'Communicating technological risk: the social construction of risk perception', *Annual Review of Public Health 10*, 95–113.

Niggemeier J. (2015) 'Sayonara nukes: development, mobilization strategies and organization of anti-nuclear protest in Japan after the 2011 Fukushima Accident', Working Paper No 48, Centre for East and South-East Asian Studies Lund University, Lund.

Ogawa A. (2013) 'Young precariat at the forefront: anti-nuclear rallies in post-Fukushima Japan', *Inter-Asia Cultural Studies 14(2)*, 317–26.

Reinhardt O. and Oldroyd D. R. (1983) 'Kant's theory of earthquakes and volcanic action', *Annals of Science 40*, 247–72.

Rousseau J.-J. (1756) 'Rousseau's letter to Voltaire regarding the poem on the Lisbon earthquake', http://geophysics-old.tau.ac.il/personal/shmulik/LisbonEq-letters.htm [Accessed 22 September 2015].

Slovic P. (ed.) (2000) *The Perception of Risk*. Earthscan, Virginia.

Sternsdorff Cistema N. (2013) 'Safe and trustworthy? Food safety after Fukushima', An STS Forum on the East Japan Disaster. https://fukushimaforum.wordpress.com/workshops/ sts-forum-on-the-2011-fukushima-east-japan-disaster/manuscripts/session-4a-when-disasters-end-part-i/safe-and-trustworthy-food-safety-after-fukushima/   [Accessed   22 September 2015].

Storr W. (2014) 'Flooded Britain: how can Holland help?' *The Telegraph*, 26 April 2014. www.telegraph.co.uk/culture/art/architecture/10769974/Flooded-Britain-how-can-Holland-help.html [Accessed 22 September 2015].

Strickland E. (2011) 'Explainer: what went wrong in Japan's nuclear reactors', *IEEE Spectrum*, 16   March   2011.   http://spectrum.ieee.org/tech-talk/energy/nuclear/explainer-what-went-wrong-in-japans-nuclear-reactors [Accessed 14 October 2015].

Voltaire (1759) *Candide, ou l'optimisme* (Trans T. Cuffe, *Candide, or Optimism*, 2005). Penguin, London.

Wikipedia. 'Fukushima Daiichi nuclear disaster', https://en.wikipedia.org/wiki/Fukushima_ Daiichi_nuclear_disaster [Accessed 21 September 2015].

8 Taking public opinion seriously in post-Fukushima Japan

Michio Miyasaka

Introduction

It has been sometimes pointed out that increasing transparency or accountability is important in nuclear policy-making. After the Fukushima accident, the notion of transparency appears to be feeling the pressure of ethical concerns that require ensuring broad participation in decision-making, at least by those heavily affected by the policy (Gardiner 2015). However, the argument becomes uncertain when it comes to increasing the size of the circle involved in nuclear policy-making, for example, how far we should include electricity consumers benefitting from nuclear power plants (NPPs) that stand at a distant area in planning post-accident actions of the plant. In this chapter, I will provide an overview of how the Japanese public changed (and did not change) their views on nuclear policies after the accident, and how they acted in elections and other opportunities to participate in nuclear policy-making, and will discuss the ethical challenges of its representative democracy at national and local levels.

Decommissioning dependent on currently unavailable methods

Actions that are to be taken once a nuclear accident occurs are categorized into two phases (ICRP 2009). The emergency phase, or emergency exposure situation in ICRP terminology, refers to the very moment during and/or soon after the accident when emergent actions are needed, such as sheltering, evacuation and distribution of iodine tablets. The post-accident phase, or existing exposure situation, indicates the period that comes after the emergency phase, during which the focus should be on management actions, such as resettlement, food restriction and decontamination. In the case of the Fukushima accident, the transition of phases took place in December 2011 (TEPCO 2011a), eight months after the outbreak of the accident. However, the transition was marked by the uncertainty of the post-accident phase, during which an essential part of the management's envisioned actions were beyond the current technological feasibility.

During the four years after the disaster at Fukushima Daiichi Nuclear Power Station (FDNPS), the Japanese government and the Tokyo Electric Power Company (TEPCO), the owner of FDNPS, disclosed plans that correspond with the emergency and post-accident phases. The emergency phase plan, published on April 17, 2011, targeted two objectives: (1) the steady decline of the radiation dose, and (2) bringing the release of radioactive materials under control and ensuring that the radiation dose is significantly held down. They considered the first objective to have been achieved in September and the second in December 2011, stating 'in addition to the reactors of TEPCO Fukushima Daiichi nuclear power station reaching a stable state, the impact of radiation beyond the plant site has been adequately reduced' (TEPCO 2011a, 1). In 2011, the Ministry of Economy, Trade and Industry (METI) declared that the reactors were in a condition of 'cold shutdown', which was defined according to the following criteria: (1) the temperature of the bottom of the reactor pressure vessels (RPVs) was maintained below approximately 100 °C; (2) the steam generation and the release of radioactive materials from the primary containment vessels (PCVs) were suppressed by controlling water injections, so that the radiation exposure at the site boundaries due to the release of radioactive materials from the PCVs was down to 0.1 mSv/y; and (3) the mid-term safety of the circulating water cooling system was secured (Nuclear Emergency Response Headquarters Government-TEPCO Integrated Response Office 2011).

The post-accident phase plan, published at the end of 2011, sketched a transition of efforts toward decommissioning, which included the removal of fuel from the spent fuel pools and that of fuel debris from the RPVs and PCVs (TEPCO 2011b). The removal of fuel assemblies stored in Unit 4 started in November 2013 and was completed in December 2014. TEPCO expressed their understanding of the fact that the removal of fuel debris could not be accomplished with 'conventional measures' and that it would take 'over the next 30 to 40 years' (TEPCO 2014a) to complete. Because a portion of the debris was flowing out from the RPVs and into the PCVs, the coolant that was being injected into the reactor cores was leaking into the RPVs and PCVs, and 'neither the status of the fuel debris nor the exact outflow locations are known' (TEPCO 2011b, 1). At the same time, the contaminated water management was regarded as one of the major initiatives during the mid- and long-term stages. TEPCO estimated that approximately 400 tons/day of groundwater was running naturally from the mountainside flow into the reactor buildings, and as such, became newly contaminated water (TEPCO 2014b). This suggests that their circulating water-cooling system is not a closed circuit, but will continuously contaminate the hydrosphere unless the leakage is fixed or the contaminated water is stocked and decontaminated before being released into the Pacific Ocean. Furthermore, TEPCO outlined the 'necessary deliberations' that would need to be made in the future: (1) radical countermeasures against flow of groundwater into reactor buildings, (2) measures to raise the decontamination capacity of the water purification facilities and (3) further installation of land-based facilities for contaminated water management (TEPCO 2011b, 6). TEPCO installed on-site tanks to hold 800,000 m³ of effluent, pledging that they would filter all water kept in tanks by March 31, 2015. They attempted the 'Ice Wall' method to create a 1,500 m × 30 m wall of frozen soil surrounding units 1–4 by circulating a calcium-chloride refrigerant of −30 °C (TEPCO 2014c). In reality, the contaminated water repeatedly leaked from the tanks and pressure hoses, and the soil did not freeze as it was expected to (TEPCO 2013a, TEPCO 2013b). They simultaneously attempted the 'groundwater bypass system' to pump up groundwater from the upper stream, bypassing the reactor/turbine buildings, after confirming that the temporarily stored water met the standard, and deposited it into the ocean (TEPCO 2013c). TEPCO estimated that the system could lower the groundwater level by 100 tons/day, and the Federations of Fishery Cooperatives in Fukushima approved the plan under certain conditions including adherence to the standard and the measures of deposit water management and the continuation of compensation for those concerned with the fishing industry (TEPCO 2015, Japan Times 2015).

A technoethical question can be raised regarding the post-accident phase of the Fukushima accident, during which the accomplishment of major actions was not achievable with the currently available methods: how could we justify running a nuclear power plant (NPP) that needs currently unavailable methods in case of a severe accident? As the Precautionary Principle requires us to take measures when an activity raises threats of harm to human health or the environment, the proportionality of twin technological assessments necessarily needs to be taken into account, as do the foreseeability of the threats and the availability of their countermeasures. The more evident the foreseeability of threats is, the more indispensable the countermeasures are. Serious accidents at Three Mile Island and Chernobyl have provided lessons about the fact that the removal of fuel debris is hardly feasible. The Fukushima accident again leaves that task to future generations, and leaves another one on top of that. The circulating water-cooling system of FDNPS, which is essential to maintain the crippled reactors in the state of 'cold shutdown', is continuously contaminating the hydrosphere at a relatively low level, and this will continue for an undefined period of time, until we have some effective measures to counter it, which are not currently available.

Governance and institutional reform and criticism

It has been repeatedly pointed out that the promotion and regulation of nuclear power had been integrally administered, which led to the incomplete regulation of electric power utilities in Japan. The Nuclear Safety Commission (NSC), which was in charge of the government's nuclear regulations at the time of the accident, was simultaneously an institution of the Agency of Natural Resources and Energy (ANRE), which has been promoting the use of nuclear power since 1970s. The NSC was therefore not competent to investigate or punish the utilities, and their lack of independence had created 'a situation in which information about the risk of nuclear reactors, conceived as a potential obstacle to nuclear promotion, was tactically manipulated' (National Diet of Japan Fukushima Nuclear Accident Independent Investigation Commission 2012, 54). At the same time, the Japanese electric power utilities were granted a monopoly to operate within their respective areas. Ten major electric power companies (EPCOs) were entrusted with power generation, transmission and marketing functions within specific regions. The ANRE reported in 2013 that only 3.6 per cent of the total power was produced and supplied by smaller, non-EPCO electric facilities, and only 0.6 per cent of the total retail market sales was transacted between EPCOs (Yamazaki 2013). This monopoly was demonstrated to form the backdrop of a moral hazard, whereby EPCOs supply local industries with electricity at prices free of competitive pressure and bear the costs of an accident only up to the fire-sale value of their net assets (Ramseyer 2012). The weakness of the regulatory system of Japan's nuclear power policy was pointed out by the committee that investigated the accident (National Diet of Japan Fukushima Nuclear Accident Independent Investigation Commission 2012).

To redefine the standard and the review process of regulatory clearance for restarting commercial reactors, the Nuclear Regulation Authority (NRA) was established as a branch of the Ministry of Environment to replace the NSC in September 2012. The NRA defines its mission as 'to protect the general public and the environment through rigorous and reliable regulations of nuclear activities'. According to its Chairman, Shunichi Tanaka, 'we should be careful not to consort with electric utilities and other interest groups; and we will be tireless in our efforts to improve our regulatory measures so that Japan's nuclear regulation standards will be among the world's highest' (Tanaka 2012). The Electricity Business Act was revised in 2013 to liberalize retail electricity sales and to separate electric power generation from power distribution and transmission. The gist of the revision was to promote the cross-regional coordination of transmission operators, to establish full retail competition and to unbundle the transmission/distribution sectors (Electricity System Reform Expert Subcommittee 2013). According to the METI, the reform program should be executed in three stages and the last stage should be finished during 2018 to 2020.

However, their reforms have already drawn criticism. Critics of the governance reform include officials from local governments, who are in charge of resident evacuation and call the attitude of the NRA to concentrate on regulatory measures into question. They have accused the NRA of focusing on the mechanical safety of NPPs and the geologic safety of the soil and the stratum while paying less attention to issues of post-accident situations. Niigata Governor Hirohiko Izumida criticized the NRA for ignoring level 5 from the IAEA's concept of 'defense in depth', during which off-site emergency response should be given in order to mitigate radiological consequences of significant releases of radioactive materials (International Atomic Energy Agency 1996, 6), because the NRA allegedly regarded it beyond their jurisdiction to verify (Izumida 2015). In regard to the liberalization of electricity sales, the slow speed and inconclusiveness of the reforms have been questioned. Although the 10 big EPCOs are to be separated into transmission/distribution companies, the law approves their capital alliance. No guarantee is yet established by law for free and fair competition between EPCO-based and non-EPCO companies.

Public opinion in post-Fukushima Japan

Before calling Japanese public opinion on nuclear power generation into question, we need to understand its political backdrop. When the Fukushima accident occurred in 2011, the Democratic Party of Japan (DPJ) was in the Cabinet, not the Liberal Democratic Party (LDP), which had been in power for more than half a century since 1955. The DPJ won political power in 2009 by holding up 'political leadership' as a reinforcement of control for bureaucrats. Their policy of nuclear energy constituted '[w]hile placing safety first and gaining the understanding and confidence of the people, take steady steps towards the use of nuclear power' (Democratic Party of Japan 2009, 26).

Yukio Hatoyama, the first Prime Minister of the DPJ, proposed an environmental policy that aimed for 25 per cent decrease in CO_2 and other greenhouse gas emissions by 2020. This was hardly an attainable goal, and some suspected that Hatoyama regarded nuclear power generation as a measure to realize his goal. After Hatoyama lost his position in June 2010, as the result of mishandling a diplomatic issue (the issue regarding a U.S. military base relocation that is unresolved to date) and a financing scandal (Kushida and Lipscy 2013, 14), Naoto Kan succeeded as Prime Minister and introduced the 'Green Innovation' policy, in which he emphasized the promotion of renewable energy, while no word was given on nuclear energy. When the Fukushima accident occurred in March 2011, Kan's government was blamed for its 'chaotic' initial response to the accident. As approval rates dropped sharply, Kan resigned as Prime Minister after the enactment of a specific law (Act on Special Measures Concerning Procurement of Electricity from Renewable Energy Sources by Electricity Utilities) in August 2011, which obliges electric power utilities to produce or purchase electricity with renewable energy sources – the enactment of this law was allegedly his condition for giving his resignation. The third Prime Minister, Yoshihiko Noda, used the slogan 'to achieve zero dependence on nuclear power by the decade of the 2030s' (Democratic Party of Japan 2012, 8), but his decision to compete against the LDP in the lower house election during their term of office ended in a terrible defeat.

Polls, elections, referendums and lawsuits

Polls conducted by news agencies have repeatedly shown that the majority of Japanese citizens are opposed to restarting NPPs. According to a public opinion poll of NHK, 20 per cent to 30 per cent of people were of the opinion that NPPs should be increased or made to meet the status quo, while approximately 70 per cent thought that they should be reduced or totally abolished (NHK Broadcasting Culture Research Institute 2015). This proportion of pro and con has not changed since the first investigations were conducted in June 2011. This marked a reversal of public opinion surveyed from 1978 to 2009 by the government, in which the proportion of pro and con had been 63 per cent to 80 per cent and 5 per cent to 22 per cent, respectively (Naikaku fu daijin kanbo seifu kohoshitsu 2015), which suggests that the majority of Japanese public lost their trust in nuclear power generation after the Fukushima disaster.

National and local elections have also suggested that the Japanese public prefer politicians who advocate for a gradual reduction of dependence on nuclear power over those who support an immediate and complete halt to nuclear power generation. In the 2012 lower house election, the LDP's manifesto proposed to establish economic and social structures that do not necessarily depend on nuclear power, to prioritize expertise through an independent regulatory committee about the safety of NPPs, to judge the possibility of restarting every NPP within 3 years, and to establish 'the best mix of energy sources' within at least 10 years (Jiminto 2012, 54). Their energy policy was vaguely comparable to that of the DPJ, who used the slogan 'Zero nuclear energy by 2030' (Democratic Party of Japan 2012), but the result was a triumph for the LDP. Rather more complicated results were observed in the local elections of prefectures with NPPs and in their neighbouring prefectures. In the 2015 gubernatorial elections of Fukui Prefecture, which holds the largest number of NPPs at 13, and of Aomori Prefecture, which has Higashidori Nuclear Power Station and a nuclear plant project (Oma Nuclear Power Plant), incumbent governors who did not define their position regarding the future of NPPs in their prefectures defeated their opponents, who had developed a campaign against NPPs. However, in the elections for the heads of local governments in Shiga Prefecture (in 2014), which does not have any NPP but is adjacent to Fukui Prefecture, and in Hakodate City (in 2015), which also has no NPPs but is adjacent to Aomori Prefecture by a small strait, candidates who clarified their position against NPPs fought a successful election campaign.

The Japanese public called for more direct participation, which required specific referendums regarding nuclear energy production. In 2013, the Prefectural Assembly of Niigata denied a petition by residents, which had collected 68,353 signatures, to pass a public referendum ordinance on restarting TEPCO's Kashiwazaki-Kariwa Nuclear Power Station (seven boiling water reactors with a total output capacity of 8212 MW), which is currently under safety examination. The LDP, the largest party, opposed the ordinance, claiming that the national nuclear energy policy should be under the control of the central government, and that it was not the right issue for a local referendum. Their concern about referendums can be traced back to 1996, when the nation's first and only referendum was held, which suspended the construction of an NPP by Tohoku EPCO in Maki, a town in Niigata Prefecture with a population of 23,222. Sixty-one per cent of voters (12,478) refused the construction plan, and Tohoku EPCO announced that it would abandon the plan in 2003.

In 2014, the Fukui District Court ruled that it would not allow the restart of reactors at Kansai EPCO's Ohi Nuclear Power Station (four pressurized water reactors with a maximum output capacity of 4710 MW), which is currently under safety examination. The court remarked on the superiority of personal rights over the EPCO's right to operate an NPP: 'The operation of an NPP legally belongs to the freedom of economic activity (defined in Article 22 of Constitution), and therefore, should constitutionally be regarded inferior to the core components of personal rights'. This is a departure from the Supreme Court's ruling in 1992: 'Given global environmental pollution due to coal-fired power generation, there is no other way but to promote nuclear power generation while increasing its safety'. Lawsuits by plaintiffs who demanded the shutdown of NPPs had been repeatedly refused by Japanese courts, because those who were entitled to sue should be limited to residents living in areas close to an NPP – within a distance of 50 km, according to the Supreme Court – and/or because the power utilities that bore the burden of proof regarding safety should be limited to basic design only (Sato 1993).

It is not clear whether the ruling by Fukui District Court is the first case that illustrates a shift in the standards of judgement for Japanese courts. The decision of the lower court can often be upset by the higher court, and it takes a long time before the Supreme Court presents its decisions.

As an interim conclusion of this section, two incompatible hypotheses can be formulated. First, the conventional system of parliamentary democracy in Japan functions effectively in reflecting public opinion, which prefers a gradual reduction of dependence on nuclear power rather than a drastic denuclearization. Second, the current political system insufficiently enables public participation, because Japanese public opinion is heard in very limited ways. People are presented with indirect and unfocused ways of nuclear policy-making, such as that evident from national and local elections, but they are often denied direct participation through referendums and lawsuits. In the last section, we shall look into these hypotheses in order to clarify the ethical challenges of representative democracy after Fukushima.

Public involvement in nuclear power policy-making

People's participation in policy-making has been argued for, on one hand, in the context of civil rights, as an essential part of the universal rights of a person living in a civil society, and in the context of consumer rights, on the other hand, as a more specified topic of the rights of a person living in an industrialized society. A *civil right* has been regarded as an enforceable right or privilege that, if interfered with by another, gives rise to action for injury. In general, freedom of speech/press/ assembly, the right to vote, the freedom from involuntary servitude, and the right to equality in public places are listed as civil rights. In contrast, *consumer rights* have been conceptualized in relation to the actual products and services that a company sells to consumers and to corporate business practices that directly affect consumers. Since John F. Kennedy's statement about the four basic consumer rights in 1962, including the right to safety, the right to a choice, the right to know and the right to be heard (Kennedy 1962), the list of consumer rights has been expanded by various groups, most notably the United Nations, to include the right to consumer education, the right to redress, the right to a healthy and sustainable environment, the right to basic needs, and the right to access (Bugnitz 2008). The public's role as stakeholder in designing the nation's nuclear energy policy needs to be discussed as a whole regarding the decision-making process of the establishment for the decommissioning of an individual NPP and regarding the development of plans of action in case of an accident involving an NPP. However, this would constitute a grand scheme, and we shall here focus on some aspects of *consumer rights* with regard to electric utilities' practices of running an NPP that directly affects residents and consumers. Issues in relation to the electricity that an electric utility sells to consumers will be omitted.

The right to a choice, the right to know

In the emergency phase of the Fukushima disaster, the insufficient disclosure of information by the government and TEPCO was harshly criticized. The government did not disclose information from the perspective of ensuring the residents' safety, namely to protect them from the potential progression of events into the worst-case scenario (National Diet of Japan 2012, Chapter 3, 80), while TEPCO would only disclose what was required by law and what was already confirmed by either them or other parties, but would not disclose any additional information, 'especially detrimental information' (National Diet of Japan 2012, Chapter 5, 41). The government and TEPCO used euphemistic and indecisive expressions for their explanations. They even regarded the term 'melt-down' and related terms as overly straightforward for describing the situation of the crippled reactors at FDNPS. At press conferences about the impact of the release of radioactive materials, Chief Cabinet Secretary Yukio Edano repeatedly used expressions that were arguably chosen to provide a sense of comfort, such as 'there will be no immediate impact on health'. However, these phrases were vague and residents did not receive sufficient information to judge the necessity of evacuation and the impact on their health (National Diet of Japan 2012, Chapter 3, 83).

As I have previously argued (Miyasaka 2013), the government and TEPCO adopted a paternalistic approach to information disclosure and the associated evacuation response during the emergency phase of the Fukushima disaster. Such a paternalistic approach is more likely to be justified in the emergency phase than in the post-accident phase, considering that the government must issue its evacuation orders and recommendations as soon as possible within the highly confusing environment that emerges at such a time. In the post-accident phase, however, scientists and politicians would hardly find morally justifiable reasons to withdraw information from those inflicted for an extended period, because the less pressing environment would allow them to spare time to share information with a wide range of stakeholders. The *Mid-and-Long-Term Roadmap* was created as one of the four basic policies to '[m]ove forward while maintaining transparent communications with local and national citizens to gain their understanding and respect', and promised that TEPCO, the Agency for Natural Resources and Energy, and the Nuclear and Industrial Safety Agency would take appropriate actions, including to 'maintain transparency by periodically reviewing this plan and publishing the status of work in the mid-and-long term' (TEPCO 2011b, 3). Their emphasis on transparency seems to be based on the standpoint of paternalism, whereby specialists assess the information and decide what the residents need to know. They promise 'to gain their understanding through the provision of necessary information to community residents and the parties concerned'. Their objective is to gain the community residents' understanding for what they have decided, but not to respect their right to a choice or their right to know, and the roadmap stated no principle or standard for information was to be disclosed to residents. However, the Fukushima disaster provided lessons on how the paternalistic perspective harbours conflicts of interest even in describing what happened during the accident, in inferring accident causes, and in estimating human cost. Respecting the consumer rights to know and the right to a choice would require the government and TEPCO to make a drastic shift of standpoint toward the autonomous option of information disclosure, which entails disclosing all information to all stakeholders who could be affected by that disclosure. The post-accident phase requires the legal system to enforce the electric utilities to disclose any information, including that which is scientifically ambiguous and open to interpretation, and allowing the recipients to decide on their own.

The right to be heard

To discuss the rights of the public in the post-accident phase of the Fukushima accident, we need to turn to the two hypotheses that we obtained from examining the relationship between public opinion and the political system in Japan in light of *spatial injustice*, or the spatial imbalance of risk and benefit. NPPs are often located in under-populated rural areas; hence, they provide benefits to urban residents while putting rural residents at risk. The imbalance has been politically compensated by several subsidies in Japan. According to the model case illustrated by the Agency for Natural Resources and Energy of the METI, if an NPP with an output capacity of 1350 MW is established, the area (prefecture, city, town or villages) where the plant is located will gain a total of 124 billion yen (approximately 1 billion U.S. dollars) from the National budget (Keizai Sangyo Sho Shigen Energy Cho 2010). The result of local elections from the last two years can be understood in light of this benefit-risk-subsidy scheme. The results of local elections in prefectures with NPPs, such as Fukui, Aomori, Hokkaido and Shimane, indicated that residents preferred governors who were relatively supportive of maintaining the status quo of nuclear power generation. A similar result was observed in the 2014 gubernatorial elections in Tokyo, which is one of the typical urban beneficiary areas with a large amount of electricity consumption, while there is no functioning NPP in it or in its neighbouring prefectures. It can be inferred that both the residents in prefectures with NPPs and those in distant prefectures with substantial electricity consumption have benefitted from NPPs by means of subsidies and their electricity production, respectively, and that they both would tolerate nuclear power generation. However, those living in areas that are neither near nor far from an NPP with less electricity consumption, and who therefore receive no subsidy from the National budget, might consider themselves at risk from NPPs while receiving little benefit. This is illustrated by the results of local elections in Shiga and Hakodate, where voters preferred anti-nuclear leaders.

Now the two incompatible hypotheses formulated in the previous section can be integrated into one: the differences between residents' preferences might reflect their sense of being *heard*, rather than their distance from NPPs. The right to be heard entitles a consumer to find someone who will respond to legitimate complaints about abuse that takes place in the market environment and about products that do not meet expectations (Buchholz 2008). If this is the case, insight is required to answer ethical questions about public participation in policy-making regarding individual NPPs, from their construction to decommission: Who should be entitled to be a stakeholder? How should we limit their right to participation? Should they be given a direct way to participate, such as an appointment as member of an NPP's Management Committee? Before the Fukushima accident, the conventional estimation of radioactive pollution caused by an accident relied on the geographical distance from an NPP. In addition, post-accident off-site actions, including evacuation and decontamination, the implementation of level 5 of defense in depth, in the IAEA's terminology, had been put in the hands of prefectural governments. In reality, however, radioactive substances were dispersed across prefectural borders and created hot spots with high doses of contamination, up to 200 km away from FDNPS (e.g. Kashiwa City and Kawaba Village). Although this imbalance was politically compensated by subsidies, the fixation of the situation can contribute to moral hazards on both sides: urban residents as beneficiaries of NPPs can become indifferent to the risk taken by others who are distant from them, and rural communities as risk-takers can become dependent on the subsidies and business activities of an NPP and its affiliated companies. To establish transparency and co-construction principles for nuclear power businesses, it is necessary to take the right to be heard seriously and to consider governance reforms to enforce electric utilities and regulatory bodies to enable effective consumer participation in nuclear power businesses beyond prefectural and even national boundaries.

Conclusion

We have viewed the technological and political situations in post-Fukushima Japan. The weakness of plans and actions made by the government and the electric utility raises a fundamental technoethical question on running a nuclear power plant that needs currently unavailable methods in case of a severe accident. Polls and elections suggested that on one hand the majority of Japanese citizens negatively changed their view on NPPs, and on the other hand they prefer gradual reduction of dependence on nuclear power to immediate denuclearization.

In the last section, I attempted to develop an argument ensuring public participation in nuclear policy-making relying on consumer rights. While the right to a choice and the right to know appear to be acknowledged widely because of the insufficient disclosure of information essential in the Fukushima accident, the political situation in post-Fukushima Japan suggests that the right to be heard needs more attention. The right to be heard needs to be addressed in justifying spatial imbalance of risk and benefit (or the conventional benefit-risk-subsidy scheme in Japan), and in considering governance reforms of nuclear power businesses beyond prefectural and national boundaries.

References

Buchholz R. A. (2008) 'Consumer's bill of rights' in Kolb R. W. (ed), *Encyclopedia of Business Ethics and Society*. SAGE Publications, Thousand Oaks, 438–39.
Bugnitz T. (2008) 'Consumer rights' in Kolb R. W. (ed), *Encyclopedia of Business Ethics and Society*. SAGE Publications, Thousand Oaks, 434–38.
Democratic Party of Japan (2009) *The Democratic Party of Japan's Platform for Government: Putting People's Lives First.* www.dpj.or.jp/english/manifesto/manifesto2009.html [Accessed 1 September 2015].
Democratic Party of Japan (2012) *Making Decisions to Get Things Moving. The Democratic Party of Japan's Manifesto: Our Responsibilities for Now and the Future.* www.dpj.or.jp/english/manifesto/manifesto2012.pdf [Accessed 1 September 2015].

Electricity System Reform Expert Subcommittee (Electricity Market Reform Office, Agency for Natural Resource and Energy, Ministry of Economy, Trade and Industry) (2013) *2013 Report of the Electricity System Reform Expert Subcommittee.* www.meti.go.jp/english/policy/energy_environment/electricity_system_reform/pdf/201302Report_of_Expert_Subcommittee.pdf [Accessed 1 September 2015].

Gardiner S. M. (2015). 'The need for a public "explosion" in the ethics of radiological protection, especially for nuclear power' in Taebi B. and Roeser S. (eds), *The Ethics of Nuclear Energy: Risk, Justice, and Democracy in the Post-Fukushima era.* Cambridge University Press, Cambridge, 87–118.

International Atomic Energy Agency (1996) *Defence in Depth in Nuclear Safety: A Report by the International Nuclear Safety Advisory Group (INSAG-10).* International Atomic Energy Agency, Vienna.

International Commission on Radiological Protection (2009) 'Application of the Commission's Recommendations for the protection of people in emergency exposure situations', ICRP Publication 109, *Annals of the ICRP 37(2–4).*

Izumida H. (2015) 'Fukushima go no mirai wo tsukuru' (in Japanese), *Weekly Economist,* 1 September, 82–84.

Japan Times (2015) 'Fishermen OK Tepco plan to dump water from wrecked Fukushima nuclear plant into sea', www.japantimes.co.jp/news/2015/08/26/national/fishermen-ok-tepcos-plan-dump-fukushima-plant-water-sea/#.VgyQf7TtlBc [Accessed 1 September 2015].

Jiminto (2012) *J-file 2012 Sogo seisakushu.* http://jimin.ncss.nifty.com/pdf/j_file2012.pdf [Accessed 1 September 2015].

Keizai Sangyo Sho Shigen Energy Cho (2010) *Dengen ricchi no gaiyo: chiiki no yume wo ookiku sodateru* (in Japanese). Dengen Chiiki Shinko Center, Tokyo, 3–4.

Kennedy J. F. (1962) "Special message to the Congress on protecting the consumer interest" *Public papers of the presidents of the United States* 93 236.

Kushida K. E. and Lipscy P. Y. (2013) *The Rise and Fall of the Democratic Party of Japan. Japan under the DPJ: The Politics of Transition and Governance.* Brookings Institution Press, Washington DC.

Miyasaka M. (2013) 'Lessons from the Fukushima Daiichi nuclear disaster' in Oughton D. and Hansson S. O. (eds), *Social and Ethical Aspects of Radiation Risk Management (Radioactivity in the Environment Vol. 19).* Elsevier, Oxford, 177–95.

Naikaku fu daijin kanbo seifu kohoshitsu (2015) Yoron chosa (in Japanese). http://survey.gov-online.go.jp/ [Accessed 1 September 2015].

National Diet of Japan Fukushima Nuclear Accident Independent Investigation Commission (2012) Main report. http://warp.da.ndl.go.jp/info:ndljp/pid/3856371/naiic.go.jp/en/index.html [Accessed 1 September 2015].

NHK Broadcasting Culture Research Institute (2015) Shakai ya seiji nikansuru yoronchosa (in Japanese). www.nhk.or.jp/bunken/yoron/social/index.html [Accessed 1 September 2015].

Nuclear Emergency Response Headquarters Government-TEPCO Integrated Response Office (2011) *Summary of Step 2 Completion of 'Roadmap towards Settlement of the Accident at Fukushima Daiichi Nuclear Power Station, TEPCO':* Genshiryoku saigai taisaku honbu seifu-tokyo denryoku togo taisakushitsu 2011 *Tokyo denryoku fukushima daiichi genshiryoku hatsudensho jiko no shusoku ni muketa michisuji step 2 kanryo hokokusho* (Full version, in Japanese). http://www.tepco.co.jp/en/press/corp-com/release/betu11_e/images/111216e3.pdf [Accessed 1 September 2015]

Ramseyer J. M. (2012) 'Why power companies build nuclear reactors on fault lines: the case of Japan', *Theoretical Inquiries in Law 13,* 457–86.

Sato H. (1993) 'Ikata/Fukushima daini genpatsu sosho saikosai hanketsu no ronten', *Jurist 1017,* 36–42 (in Japanese).

Tanaka S. (2012) *2012 Message.* www.nsr.go.jp/english/e_nra/outline/02.html [Accessed 1 September 2015].

TEPCO (2011a) *Roadmap towards Restoration from the Accident at Fukushima Daiichi Nuclear Power Station*. www.tepco.co.jp/en/press/corp-com/release/betu11_e/images/110417e12.pdf [Accessed 1 September 2015].

TEPCO (2011b) *Mid-and-Long-Term Roadmap towards the Decommissioning of Fukushima Daiichi Nuclear Power Units 1–4*. www.tepco.co.jp/en/press/corp-com/release/11122107-e.html [Accessed 1 September 2015].

TEPCO (2013a) *Leakage from B Area South Tank*. www.tepco.co.jp/en/nu/fukushima-np/handouts/2013/images/handouts_131003_01-e.pdf [Accessed 1 September 2015].

TEPCO (2013b) *Water Leak at a Tank in the H4 Area in Fukushima Daiichi Nuclear Power Station*. www.tepco.co.jp/en/nu/fukushima-np/handouts/2013/images/handouts_130819_04-e.pdf [Accessed 1 September 2015].

TEPCO (2013c) *The Groundwater Bypass System*. www.tepco.co.jp/en/nu/fukushima-np/water/13062501-e.html [Accessed 1 September 2015].

TEPCO (2014a) *Fuel Removal*. www.tepco.co.jp/en/decommision/planaction/removal-e.html [Accessed 1 September 2015].

TEPCO (2014b) *Status of the Fukushima Daiichi Status of the Fukushima Daiichi Nuclear Power Station Nuclear Power Station: With Focus on Countermeasures for Contaminated Water*. www.tepco.co.jp/en/decommision/planaction/images/140127_01.pdf [Accessed 1 September 2015]

TEPCO (2014c) *Measure of Reduction of Groundwater Inflow into Buildings of Units 1 to 4 Using Land-Side Impermeable Wall* ("Ice Wall"). www.tepco.co.jp/en/nu/fukushima-np/handouts/2014/images/handouts_140703_04-e.pdf [Accessed 1 September 2015].

TEPCO (2015) *Tokyo denryoku fukushima daiichi genshiryoku hatsudensho no sub-drain sui tou no haisui nitaisuru yobosho ni taisuru kaito nitsuite* (in Japanese). www.tepco.co.jp/news/2015/images/150825a.pdf [Accessed 1 September 2015]

Yamazaki T. (2013) *Electricity Market Reform Electricity Market Reform in Japan*. www.eu-japan.eu/sites/eu-japan.eu/files/Session2_Yamazaki.pdf [Accessed 1 September 2015].

9 Better living (in a complex world)

An ethics of care for our modern co-existence

Gaston Meskens

The bigger picture: the idea of a fair dealing with complexity

Living in a complex world

It has now become trivial to say that we live in a complex world. Industrialization, technological advancement, population growth and globalization have brought 'new challenges', and the global political agenda is now set by issues that burden both our natural environment and human well-being. Sketching what goes wrong in our world today, the picture does not look very bright: structural poverty; expanding industrialization and urbanization and consequent environmental degradation; waste of precious resources, water, food and products; adverse manifestations of technological risk; economic exploitation; anticipated overpopulation; and derailed financial markets. All of this adds up to old and new forms of social, political and religious oppression and conflict, and makes the world a difficult place to live for many people. The stakes are high and the need to take action is manifest.

What do we mean when we say that we live in a complex world? The need to tackle the problems listed above is clear, even so as the picture of the world we want: we envision a world free from poverty and conflict and in which humans live in a healthy relation with their natural environment. Humans, whether in their private life or as 'citizens' share interests that are self-evident in their practical necessity (food, water and shelter) or in their universal desirability (happiness, well-being). And 'in between' the practical concern of survival and the universal desire for happiness and well-being are a variety of things we find important and a variety of visions on how to organize our coexistence accordingly. While happiness may have a rather 'relative' character, the question of survival is a fairly absolute one. And many of the injustices in that respect seem to be rather absurd. As an example: today, about one in nine people on earth does not have enough food to lead a healthy active life[1] but the Food and Agricultural Organization of the United Nations tells us that even today there is actually enough food to feed everyone adequately. Is it only a matter of a proper distribution and of reducing waste in production and consumption or is the problem more complex than that? Theoretical perspectives such as the World Systems Theory (see, among others Wallerstein 2004) or that of the Earth Systems Governance project[2] may give the impression that the challenge we face is that of a proper organization of our society, in the sense of a complex engineering problem. There is indeed some logic in the claim that, in the interest of making sense of fair and effective global governance, it is important to first try to understand and assess 'the system' of the interlinked social practices and their relations with the natural and technological environment. The reasoning is that, once we acquire this understanding, it would be possible to 'fix the system' and to 'get the balance right'. The problem however is that this 'earth-society system' is not a neutral given 'out there'. It is not only subject to interpretation, it is also and essentially 'unimaginable', and this can be understood by taking a closer look at the character of the problems we face.

A neutral but imperative characterization of complexity (of complex social problems)

Whether we speak of clearly observable unacceptable situations (e.g. extreme poverty), perceived worrisome situations or developments (e.g. climate change or population growth), or practices or proposed policy measures with a potential controversial character (e.g. the use of nuclear energy, genetically modified organisms, or a tax on wealth), the idea discussed in the following is that we can characterize them all as 'complex social problems' with the same set of characteristics. If science has a role to play in making sense of these problems, it will typically face the fact that it has to deal with factual uncertainties and unknowns, which implies that its challenge in a socio-political context is not the production of 'credible proofs', but rather the construction of credible hypotheses. Besides, we know that our judgements on situations, developments, practices and proposed policy measures not only rely on available knowledge about them, but that they are first and foremost influenced by how we value them in relation to things we find important (nature, freedom, equality, protection, etc.).

Taking that into account, I want to propose a specific characterization of complexity of complex social problems that, I believe, will support the insight that fair and effective governance is initially not a matter of proper organization, but essentially that of a fair dealing with its complexity. The complexity of a complex social problem, such as combating climate change, the provision of affordable access to healthy food for all, or evaluation of the possible use of nuclear energy, may in this sense be described with seven characteristics (see the text box that begins on p. 117).

Characteristics 1, 2 and 3 are characteristics of a 'factual complexity' and 5, 6 and 7 refer to a complexity of interpretation as a consequence of that factual complexity. Number 4 (relative responsibilities) might be described as a 'combination' of a factual complexity and a complexity of interpretation: the fact that a concerned actor does (not) act according to his responsibility may have practical consequences for other actors, also in terms of their own ability to act responsibly. On the other hand, the actor's motivation to act according to his responsibility is of course also dependent on his interpretation of the situation and of arguments of others with respect to his responsibility. Due to their factual complexity, complex social problems are social problems that 'create themselves' uncertainty and ambiguity when interpreting what is at stake and what is to be done. The complexity of interpretation may thus be understood as a complexity of making sense of the problem. As this complexity

A neutral characterization of complexity: seven characteristics of a complex social problem

1   Diversified impact

- Individuals and/or groups are affected by the problem in diverse ways (benefit vs. adverse consequence, diverse 'degrees' of benefits or adverse consequences).
- The impact can be economic or related to physical or psychic health, or individual or collective social well-being.
- The character and degree of impact may evolve or vary in a contingent way in time.
- The impact may also manifest later in time (with the possibility that it manifests after or during several generations).

2   Interdependence

- The problem is caused and/or influenced by multiple factors (social, economic, technical, natural) and relates itself to other problems.
- Interdependence can change in time.
- The context of concern becomes global.

3   The need for a 'broader' coherent approach (organizational complexity)

Due to diversified impact and interdependence, problems need to be tackled 'together' in a coherent, systematic and 'holistic' approach. This approach needs to take into account the following four additional characteristics of complexity:

4   Relative responsibilities

Due to diversified impact, interdependence and the organizational complexity, responsibility cannot be assigned to one specific actor. Responsibilities are relative in two ways:

1   Mutual: the possibility for one actor to take responsibility can depend on whether another actor takes responsibility or not.
2   Collective: our collective responsibility is relative in the sense that it will need to be 'handed over' to a next 'collective' (a new government, next generations).

5   Knowledge-related uncertainty (knowledge problem)

Analysis of the problem is complicated by uncertainty due to speculative, incomplete or contradictory knowledge, with respect to the character and evolution of impact and interdependence, and with respect to the effects of the coherent and holistic approach.

6   Value pluralism (evaluation problem)

Evaluation of diversified impact, interdependence and organizational complexity and of subsequent relative responsibilities is complicated due to

- The knowledge problem
- The existence of different visions based on different specific values and world views

(continued)

(continued)

- The existence of different interests of concerned actors
- The fact that it is therefore impossible to determine in consensus what would be the 'real' problem or the 'root' of the problem
- The fact that 'meta-values' such as 'equality', 'freedom' and 'sustainability' cannot be translated unambiguously into practical responsibilities or actions

7   Relative authorities (authority problem)

The authority of actors who evaluate and judge the problem and rationalize their interests and responsibilities related to it in a future-oriented perspective is relative in two ways:

- The 'individual' authority of concerned actors is relative in the sense that, due to the knowledge and evaluation problem, authority cannot be 'demonstrated' or 'enforced' purely on the basis of knowledge or judgement. As a consequence, that authority needs to lean on 'external' references (the mandate of the elected politician, the diplomas and experience of the scientific expert, the commercial success of the entrepreneur, the social status of the spiritual leader, the appeal to justice of the activist, etc.).
- The 'collective' authority of concerned actors who operate within the traditional governing modes of politics, science and the market is relative, as these governing modes cannot rely on an objective 'authority of method': the systems of representative democracy (through party politics and elections) and the market both lean on the principle of competition, while science is faced with the fact that it needs to deal with future-oriented hypotheses.

As such, concerned actors have the opportunity to reject or question the relevance and credibility of the judgement of other actors, and consequently to question the legitimacy of their authority.

---

also includes 'the authority problem', the complexity of interpretation of a complex social problem can be understood as a complexity that is, in principle, experienced by all concerned actors 'together', and not only by each actor individually.

Reflexivity and intellectual solidarity as ethical attitudes or virtues 'in face of complexity'

This text does not want to propose a manual, procedure or instrument to solve complex social problems. Rather, the characterization of complexity is meant as an incentive and a basis for ethical thinking, as it opens the possibility to reflect on what it would imply to 'deal fairly with the complexity' of those specific social problems, and of the organization of our society accordingly. The *possibility* of doing so lies in the fact that the characterization of complexity in the form of the seven proposed characteristics can be called a 'neutral' characterization, in the sense that it does not specify wrongdoers and victims as such (which, of course, does not mean there cannot be any). Representing the complexity as a complexity of interpretation enables the responsibility to be described 'in face of that complexity' as a *joint responsibility* that is, as such, not divisive, which means that, *in principle*, it provides the possibility of rapprochement.

This joint responsibility 'in face of complexity' has, at the same time, a binding and a liberating character for all concerned. Regarding the binding character, although nobody is blamed or suspected of reckless behaviour or of escaping responsibility, one could say that the characterization of complexity is imperative for all concerned. First of all, any reflection on what it would imply to deal fairly with the complexity of the problem at stake would imply the need for each concerned actor to transcend the usual thinking in terms of their own interests, and the preparedness to become 'confronted' with the way he/she rationalizes their own interests within the bigger picture. At the same time, due to the knowledge and evaluation problem, every concerned actor would need to acknowledge his/her specific 'authority problem' in making sense of the complexity of that problem, taking into account that not only the way he/she rationalizes the problem as such, but also the way he/she rationalizes his/her own interests, the interests of others, and the general interest in relation to that problem is simply relative. That relativity is *reciprocal*, in the sense that nobody can claim higher authority based on a deeper understanding of the problem that would lead to a view on the 'solution' that all others concerned would simply need to accept. Finally, this reasoning provides us now with the possibility to argue that joint responsibility is not only binding but also liberating: as the authority of all concerned actors is relative in relation to the authority of others, it implies that all actors have the right to participate in making sense of the problem, and the right to co-decide on possible solutions to that problem.

One more thought on the idea of being jointly responsible 'in face of complexity' is relevant here. The fact that we are all jointly and equally responsible 'in face of complexity' does not necessarily require us to 'deconstruct' the political landscape down to the level of the individual citizen, in the sense that it would be meaningless or unethical for an interest group to gather around a jointly determined shared interest. In other words: the fact that specific authorities are *relative* does not mean that they cannot be *relevant*. The voice of science is relevant because of the scientific method used to formulate a specific factual finding or hypothesis. The voice of a group that gathers in order to stand stronger in its defence of a specific interest in the context of a specific problem is relevant because of that interest and because of the very fact of their gathering around it (and this counts as well for groups that represent business and industry, for groups that want to advocate the importance of a specific value [freedom, the value of nature, gender equity, …] as for citizens who, as an example, gather to protect their village against the construction of a large dam). Finally, the voice of a single citizen is relevant because of that person's right to be recognized as a citizen.[3] In other words: although, as a joint responsibility, we all would need to acknowledge the relativity of authority of our voice in face of the complexity of a complex social problem, the relevance of our specific stance, interest and argument connected to that problem would not be affected by that relativity.[4]

Recalling the previous considerations on what it would imply to 'deal fairly' with the complexity of complex social problems, we could now say that the joint responsibility of all concerned can be rephrased as the joint preparedness to adopt a specific responsible attitude or to foster a specific virtue 'in face of complexity'. That responsible attitude or virtue is identical for all concerned actors (be it the scientist, the politician, the engineer, the manager, the entrepreneur, the expert,[5] the civil society representative, the activist or the citizen), and can be described in a three-fold manner:

1   The preparedness to acknowledge the complexity of complex social problems and of the organization of our society as a whole
2   (Following 1) The preparedness to acknowledge the imperative character of that complexity, or thus to acknowledge the own authority problem (in addition to the knowledge and evaluation problem) in making sense of that complexity; for each concerned actor, that preparedness can be reformulated as the preparedness to see 'the bigger picture and oneself in it', each with his/her specific interests, hopes, hypotheses, beliefs and concerns
3   (Following 2) The preparedness to seek rapprochement with other concerned actors, and this especially through specific advanced formal interaction methods in research, politics and education that would enable sense to be made of that complexity.

The three-fold preparedness suggested here can be considered as a 'concession' to the complexity as sketched above, and it may be clear that, with these reflections, we now enter the area of ethics. A first simple but powerful insight in that sense is the idea that if nobody has the authority to make sense of a specific problem and of consequent solutions, then concerned actors have nothing other than each other as equal references in deliberating that problem. In his book *The Ethical Project*, the philosopher Philip Kitcher makes a similar reflection by saying that 'there are no ethical experts' and that, therefore, authority can only be the authority of the conversation among the concerned actors (Kitcher 2014). From the perspective of normative ethics, we can now (in a metaphorical way) interpret the idea of responsibility towards complexity as if that complexity puts an 'ethical demand' on every concerned actor, in the sense of an appeal to adopt a *reflexive attitude* in face of that complexity. That reflexive attitude would not only concern the way each actor rationalizes the problem as such, but also the way he/she rationalizes his/her own interests, the interests of others, and the general interest in relation to that problem.

For all concerned actors, as a concession towards that complexity, that reflexive attitude in face of complexity can now also be called an *ethical attitude* or *virtue*. However, given that the responsibility as suggested above would also imply rapprochement among concerned actors, one can understand that, in practice, this ethical attitude needs to be adopted in public, and that one needs specific formal interaction methods to make that possible. The joint preparedness for 'public reflexivity' of all concerned actors would enable a dialogue that, unavoidably, will also have a confrontational character, as every actor would need to be prepared to give account of his/her interests, hopes, hypotheses, beliefs and concerns with respect to the problem at stake. That joint preparedness can be described as a form of 'intellectual solidarity' as, in arguing about observable unacceptable situations (e.g. extreme poverty), perceived worrisome situations or evolutions (e.g. climate change or population growth), or practices or proposed policy measures with a potential controversial character (e.g. the use of nuclear energy, genetically modified organisms or a tax on wealth), concerned actors would need to be prepared to reflect openly towards each other and towards 'the outside world' about the way they not only rationalize the problem as such, but also their own interests, the interests of others, and the general interest in relation to that problem. Similar to understanding reflexivity as an ethical attitude or virtue, one can understand *the sense of intellectual solidarity* as an ethical attitude or virtue, and one could say that the second should and could be 'stimulated' by the first. In other words, a sense of intellectual solidarity requires reflexivity as an ethical attitude with respect to the own position, interests, hopes, hypotheses, beliefs and concerns, and this in any formal role or social position (as scientist, politician, engineer, manager, entrepreneur, expert, civil society representative, activist, citizen, etc.).

As a conclusion to the reasoning developed here, three more thoughts on the meaning of reflexivity and a sense of intellectual solidarity as ethical attitudes or virtues 'in face of complexity' need to be made.

First, it is important to stress that reflexivity as ethical attitude or virtue should not be understood as a 'psychological state of being' of concerned individuals. The idea is that, if a sense of intellectual solidarity requires reflexivity as an ethical attitude, one may also understand that the ability to adopt this attitude requires reflexivity as an 'intellectual skill', seeing the bigger picture and yourself in it (with your interests, hopes, hypotheses, beliefs and concerns). The important thing is that reflexivity as an intellectual skill may benefit from solitary reflection but it cannot be 'instructed' or 'taught'. Neither can it be 'enforced' or 'stretched' in the same way as one can do with transparency in a negotiation or deliberation setting. For all of us, reflexivity as an intellectual skill essentially emerges as an *ethical experience* in interaction with others. That interaction may be informal, but it may be clear that the meaningful and 'logical' interactions in this sense are those of the formal methods of knowledge generation and decision making we use to make sense of our co-existence and social organization: political deliberation, scientific research and education. I will briefly comment on what this would imply for these interaction modes in the last part of the text.

Second, if reflexivity and a sense of intellectual solidarity as ethical attitudes in face of that complexity would motivate advanced methods for knowledge generation and decision making that would enable a fair dealing with that complexity, one could of course wonder in which way our traditional methods of democracy and science would (not) be able to take up that role. And why would the market system not be able to fairly deal with the complexity of social organization in its own way? In the following part, I will briefly sketch in which way, I believe, our traditional workings of politics, science and the market are unable to fairly deal with the complexity of complex social problems today. In conclusion, I will elaborate an understanding of reflexivity and intellectual solidarity as ethical attitudes in relation to the governing modes of democratic politics, science and education on the one hand and in relation to the market on the other hand and argue what, in that sense, the consequences would be for each of them.

Third, it is important to emphasize that intellectual solidarity is not some high-brow elite form of intellectual cooperation. It simply denotes our joint prepared-ness to accept the complexity of co-existence in general and of specific complex social problems in particular, and the fact that no one has a privileged position to make sense of it all. Intellectual solidarity, as an *ethical commitment*, is the joint pre-paredness to accept that we have no reference other than each other.

The comfort of polarization: postmodernity and the denial of complexity

In somewhat abstract terms, one could understand modern representative democ-racy (within the nation state), science and the market as the three formal governing methods to produce meaning for our modern society. Representative democracy can be seen as the governance of our collective and personal interests, executed by an authority that received its mandate through elections in which different political-ideological parties competed, and the policy pursued by that authority can be seen as the produced meaning for society. Science is the governance of knowl-edge generation, and its intended meaning consists of the fundamental and general knowledge at the benefit of society on the one hand and the applicable knowledge at the service of politics and the market on the other hand. The market, in turn, can be understood as the governance of the production and consumption of products and services, and the functional and aesthetical benefits that come with these prod-ucts and services can be considered as the intended meaning.

All three governing methods as we know them today are typical products of enlightenment and modernity, and we can say that their emergence and formation *in modernity* was, for each in its own specific way, the result of an emancipation process characterized *as modernity*. As emancipation processes, all three of them have developed a system with an 'internal logic' to produce their meaning for society, and the basic principles of those systems can be called essential accomplishments of the enlightenment and modernity: for politics, these are the principles of represen-tative democracy, being the formal possibility to elect our political representatives, the formal possibility of negotiations among different and equally valuable political visions and the formal possibility of a mandated authority and its opposition; for science, it concerns the necessity of independence and objectivity in the generation of knowledge meant to inspire and direct our coexistence and social organization; for the market, it concerns the possibility of innovation and of the variation and quality of products and services thanks to the freedom and competitiveness of that market. However, because of their emergence through emancipation processes, one can understand that the actors in (and protagonists of) representative democracy, science and the market were not concerned with their own 'problem of authority' in generating that meaning, in the sense that they saw no reason *to give account to society* with respect to their own working in producing that meaning. The simple idea was that the internal logic of their system – in the sense of their own *method of evaluation* with the production of their meaning – was *self-corrective* and that, in this way, their produced meaning was societally *relevant, credible* and *justified* and therefore also 'authoritative'. For representative democracy, that self-corrective internal logic is the idea that it is the formally organized and legitimized 'battle of opinions' between representatives of the distinct ideological parties that determines what is societally relevant, credible and justified policy; for independent and objective science, that logic is the idea that it is the scientific method and the system of 'peer review' that determines what is societally relevant, credible and justified knowledge for policy; for the market, that logic is the idea that, while the market is the motor for innovation, society will in the end decide for itself which products and services are desirable and which not.[6]

The idea, however, is that, taking into account the character of complexity of our contemporary complex social problems, that internal logic is bound to fail today: the traditional internal logics of representative democracy, science and the market are, each in their own way, no longer able to 'grasp' the complexity of those problems and, as a result, they cannot work self-correctively. Therefore, their governing methods are no longer able to generate relevant, credible and justified meaning for society. For each of them, this idea can be made more explicit in the following way:

Representative democracy within the nation state

The working of representative democracy inspired by the ideology of 'democracy as organized conflict' and practiced through the system of elections and party politics hinders a deliberate analysis of (the complexity of) complex social problems as it is unable to represent the diversity of visions and interests in relation to those problems. Analysis of complex problems is strategically prepared (to match party ideologies) and causes polarization. In addition, the system tends to stimulate populism and political self-protection and allows strategic interpretation of the possibility and necessity of public participation.

In the case of complex problems that require deliberation on a global level, formal democracy remains restricted within the nation state while nation states profile themselves internationally according to the national political vision that happens to be in power in that moment. As interests of nation states with respect to a specific complex problem that requires the global as the context of concern do not essentially differ with respect to the nature of that problem, in global politics, the proclaimed central value of nation state sovereignty tends to rather hinder than facilitate global governance of that problem.

Science

Science that aims to foster 'objectivity' when dealing with complex social problems sees itself confronted with the necessity to work with future oriented hypotheses that cannot be proven.

(continued)

(*continued*)

Given that situation, and taking into account an enduring spirit of positivism in the academy that now also tends to affect the social sciences, one can notice that political and commercial pressure on science to deliver 'usable evidence' tends to stimulate tailor-made knowledge brokerage and scientific consultancy, expertise adapted to political preferences, political 'science shopping' and thin interpretations of the 'knowledge economy'.

The market

A 'self-corrective' and 'innovative' free and competitive market is apparently not able to determine its own ethics, in the sense that its internal market logic is unable to

- Determine the limits to economic growth
- Prevent conflicts of interest with politics
- Deal with the justification of controversial products or services
- Rule out labour exploitation
- Prevent environmental pollution
- Justify the relevance of financial speculation
- Determine what would be a correct 'use' of animals
- Care for the needs of next generations

In evaluating the working of politics, science and the market, there is one criterion that is identical for all three of them and of which the legitimacy is supported by the critics as well as their subjects of critique: societal trust. Trust of citizens in politics, of laypersons in scientific expertise and of consumers in the market is seen by politicians, scientists and entrepreneurs respectively as the ultimate criterion to evaluate their working. While society perceives this criterion of trust as a way to judge whether those politicians, scientists and entrepreneurs do not misuse the 'authority' it 'delegates' to them, those same politicians, scientists and entrepreneurs are today still convinced that trust is automatically guaranteed by the so-called self-corrective internal logic of the systems wherein they function. Not only consistent critical analysis from academia and civil society, but also the daily news feed about detached and populist politics, conflicts of interest among politics and the private sector, contradictory scientific advice on controversial risk-inherent technologies such as genetically modified food and nuclear energy, child labour and horrible working conditions in sweatshops, unbridled financial speculation, indecent CEO bonuses, etc. may serve as support for the observation that politics, science and the market are no longer able to generate trust based on their own internal logic.

In the previous chapter, I argued that, in the interest of a fair dealing with the complexity of our complex social problems, concerned actors would need to be prepared to adopt reflexivity and a sense of intellectual solidarity as public ethical attitudes in face of that complexity. In practice, this would require them to openly reflect towards each other and towards 'the outside world' about the way they not only rationalize the problem as such, but also their own interests, the interests of others and the general interest in relation to that problem. The previous considerations may support the argument that the traditional methods of representative democracy, science and the market do not (or at least not sufficiently) stimulate and enable reflexivity and intellectual solidarity as described above. Their internal logic is not self-corrective but self-protective, and this leads us to a conclusion. By emphasizing the problem of authority and adding it as a third dimension to 'the complexity of interpretation' (and thus to the classical knowledge–values problem), the idea of a fair dealing with complexity of complex social problems *informs in itself the need of critique* towards any 'rational' attempt to make sense of that complexity. In other words: if there are no privileged positions to make sense of complexity or thus to 'rationalize' complexity (no specific political-ideological positions, no specific scientific positions, no market logic), then a fair dealing with complexity would simply be a 'joint' making sense of complexity among all those concerned. If the legitimacy of the basic principles of democracy, science and the market remain unquestioned but the relevance, credibility and justification of the meaning they produce at the service of society cannot be tested any longer by the internal logic of their method, then the only way to generate societal trust with the meaning they produce is by opening up these methods for the possibility of critique by society, and by ensuring the capacity of society to engage in that critique. And from this point, the similarity between politics and science on the one hand and the market on the other hand disappears. While politics and science that open up their method towards society would become reflexive and thus more responsible forms of politics and science, a market cannot become 'reflexive', as it needs to follow its rigid logic of creating profit as return on investment. Obviously an entrepreneur in the clothing business can become reflexive with respect to the miserable working conditions in his sweatshops in Bangladesh, but with his eventual individual decision to raise the salaries and improve the working conditions, he would put himself outside of the market logic and his business would decline if there were no rigid political regulation forcing his competitors to do the same. So for the market, the preparedness to open up its method can be understood as 'only' the preparedness to create transparency in its internal working and to accept that the rules of the game are set by politics and science in agreement with society.

This conclusion brings us to the end of this part. The idea of reflexivity and a sense of intellectual solidarity as proposed ethical attitudes needed to fairly deal with the complexity of complex social problems, together with the critique that our traditional methods of representative democracy, science and the market do not stimulate or enable that reflexivity and intellectual solidarity, provide us now with the necessary elements to sketch an ethical framework that would follow from the general and neutral characterization of complexity of complex social problems. The idea is that this framework can consequently inspire new governance methods that would, as previously emphasized, enable a fair dealing with the complexity of our co-existence in general and with the complexity of our complex social problems in particular.

An ethics of care for our modern coexistence

Seeking reference: a short reflection on Western philosophy normative ethical theories

What do we talk about when we talk about ethics? Ethics are about being concerned with questions of right and wrong, but there are different 'levels' of thinking about these questions. Philosophy identifies 'meta-ethics' as that discipline or perspective that deals with concepts of right and wrong (What is rightness? What is goodness?). Next to that, philosophers speak of 'normative ethics' as the discipline or perspective that considers the references that can be used to evaluate a specific practice or conduct. In that sense, normative ethics thus refer to 'what ought to be' in absence of 'evidence' that would facilitate straightforward judgement, consensus and consequent action. That absence of evidence can also relate to knowledge as to the values we may want to use to evaluate that specific practice or conduct. However, absence of evidence does of course not exclude the possibility of some type of normative reference to assist that judgement. Throughout history, philosophers have tried to formulate specific rationales to defend possible references, and one can distinguish four categories of normative ethical theories in Western philosophy in that sense.[7] Since their emergence at various moments in history, all theories have been subject to academic critique with respect to their attempt to 'universalize' their approach. The theories and their critiques are summarized in the table below and briefly discussed hereafter.

Contemporary overviews of normative ethics theories – at least in the tradition of Western philosophy – recognize three general approaches to normative ethics that have a longer historical tradition: deontological ethics, emphasizing the importance of duties and rules to evaluate ethical practice; consequentialism, stating that actions need to be judged on the basis of their consequences; and virtue

Western philosophy normative ethical theories	*Danger/problem*
→ Theories that seek reference in 'universally applicable principles' *(Kantian) deontology, consequentialism (utilitarianism)*	Danger: risk of overlooking the particular of specific situations
→ Theories that seek reference in evaluating particular situations *'Particularism'*	Danger: risk of self-protective relativism (cultural, social, political)
→ Theories that seek reference in virtues ('being good') *Virtue ethics (Aristoteles)*	Problem: virtues do not always unambiguously translate into concrete action
→ theories that seek reference in the care for human relationships *Ethics of care*	Problem: works for close relations with known people; unclear how it could work for distant relations with strangers

ethics, emphasizing the importance of virtues as qualities of the 'moral character' of the human (see, among others, Driver, 'Normative ethics', in Jackson and Smith 2008, 31; Furrow 2005; Hursthouse 2013). The most important interpretations of deontological ethics thereby are (neo)Kantian deontology and contractarianism[8] or social contract theory (with, in the case of the latter, the interpretation of John Rawls in particular). Utilitarianism remains the most important theoretical interpretation of consequentialism, as well in Jeremy Bentham's original interpretation, stating that *'it is the greatest happiness of the greatest number that is the measure of right and wrong'* (Bentham 1977) as in more recent interpretations.[9] The fact that utilitarianism, Kantian deontology and contractarianism remain to seek reference for ethical behaviour in 'objective' criteria has been the subject of academic inquiry since their origin, and the idea of objective reference has been both defended and criticized since then. However, the general agreement today is that they all 'fail' in their ambition as separate theories. As Julia Driver puts it:

> Normative ethical theory has undergone a transformation in the last generation. Challenges have been made to normative ethical theory – particularly to the commitment to impartiality and the view that there is a single moral principle sufficient to guide action. Greater focus on relationships, virtues, and less abstract issues have transformed the major theories. (Driver, 'Normative ethics', in Jackson and Smith 2008, 58)

In his particular approach to the theory of ethics, the philosopher Dwight Furrow discusses the so-called 'ethical flaws' of utilitarianism, Kantian deontology and contractarianism that emerge in formulations of practical meaning of moral duty and motivation in concrete situations. However, he insists that both their historical development and practical meaning are still relevant and meaningful today:

> The strength of utilitarian, Kantian and social contract theories is that they give us a way of conceptualizing the intuition that all human beings are worthy of equal respect and concern. Historically, proponents and supporters of these theories have done much to promote the expansion of human rights. [...] If there is such a thing as moral progress in history, the expansion of human rights and the centrality of concerns about social justice that have occurred over the past 300 years qualifies as an example. (Furrow 2005, 95)

The academic debate around virtue ethics is known to be more recent, although it has an early origin. In general terms, one could say that since Aristotle, the importance of virtues to inspire how to 'be good' and to 'lead a good life' has been emphasized mainly in the context of religion, at least in the Western historical context. From the same perspective, it is understood that their value diminished during the Enlightenment in favour of the more 'objective criteria' of deontological ethics and, later, those of consequentialism. The 'revival' of virtue ethics came with the formulation of the 'anti-codifiability' thesis as reaction to the general theoretical vision that it is the 'task' of normative ethics to draw up a 'code' of universal rules and principles, formulated so that any non-virtuous person would be able to understand and correctly apply them (Hursthouse 2013).

In 1953, in her well-known paper *Modern Moral Philosophy*, Elizabeth Anscombe criticized modern philosophy's focus on abstract principles with potential universal character, and proposed to replace the concept of 'moral obligation' by the concept of a 'virtue' as a reference for action. In addition, she argued that it remains useless to practice moral philosophy without an adequate 'philosophy of psychology' that would be able to provide us with a better understanding of virtues (Anscombe 1958). According to Julia Driver, since then, many philosophers relied on this view to underline the importance of a virtue ethics approach to the moral judgement, and she claims that research has now gathered around the following thesis:

> Virtue ethics treats virtue evaluation as the 'primary' mode of evaluation; thus, any account of right action that is virtue-ethical needs to define right action in terms of virtue. (Driver, 'Normative ethics' in Jackson and Smith 2008, 55)

However, the essential problem with virtue ethics remains the fact that virtues cannot always be unambiguously translated into 'correct' practical action, and that the cases in which it is possible are very often of trivial nature. Next to this 'application problem', Hursthouse highlights the problem of the cultural-relative character of virtues and the problem of conflicting virtues in moral dilemmas, and concludes that virtue ethics, similar to utilitarianism and deontology, continues to struggle with the problem of justification of moral belief and action: it is not always clear which qualities of our moral character can be considered 'real' virtues, and the question remains open whether it is possible (and needed) to reduce reference in moral issues to a set of 'essential' virtues (Hursthouse 2013).

In a somewhat simplified way, one can understand the academic research and debate today as situated 'in' and 'in between' the three traditional approaches to normative ethics discussed above. The fact that the alternative 'ethics of care' theory, being the theory that grounds reference for moral judgement and ethical behaviour in the care for human interpersonal relationships, emerged from feminist philosophy may be understood as characteristic for recent history. In her famous (and still controversial) book *In a Different Voice*, the philosopher Carol Gilligan relied on her research in psychology to suggest the existence of gender differences in ethical thinking and behaviour, and she claimed that these differences are already observable from childhood on (Gilligan 1982). The idea was that 'female ethical experiences' emerge from a typical concern with the specific of the situation and from out of a 'care' for the relationships with relatives (Driver, 'Normative ethics' in F. Jackson and Smith 2008, 57). This 'ethics of care' perspective was developed further by Nel Noddings. Her book, *Care: A Feminine Approach to Ethics and Moral Education*, from 1984 characterized the 'justice approach' as rigid, cold and emotionless (Noddings 2003). To the extreme, feminist ethics did not criticize deontology and consequentialism for their ambition to ground reference for moral judgement and ethical behaviour in 'reason and rationality' *as such*, but rather because of the typical male character of that ambition (Driver, 'Normative ethics' in Jackson and Smith 2008, 57).

The context of this text does not allow further elaboration on the four main theories of Western normative ethics. The overview is presented here as a reference for the formulation of a specific ethics of care theory that could guide evaluation and action 'in face of complexity' in the context of complex social problems as characterized above. In other words, my argument is that the essence of the theory and practice of moral judgement and ethical behaviour is to be found in a perspective of ethics of care, and this not only for our personal life, but also and essentially for the organization of our co-existence. Although feminist philosophy has done important work in developing the idea of human relationships as reference for moral judgement and ethical behaviour, the argument is that it is possible to formulate an 'ethics of care for our modern co-existence' that has nothing to do with feminism as such (obviously this argument should not be understood as a judgement on the importance of the original feminist approach in the first place). The basic idea of an ethics of care approach has actually a strong consequentialist character as such: the idea that we would need to judge our actions based on the (potential) direct or indirect effect on our relations with other people, and this based on the understanding that these relations are essential for our existence, which means that we need to 'care' for them. In this sense, the ethics of care theory will not only give reflexivity and intellectual solidarity (the 'virtues' formulated in the first part of this text) a more concrete meaning but also inspire in what way the advanced methods for knowledge generation and decision making would differ from the traditional ones.[10] This will be further elaborated in the next paragraph.

An ethics of care, 'bound in complexity'

The previous section elaborated on the meaning of reflexivity and (a sense of) intellectual solidarity as ethical attitudes or virtues, and on the need to adopt these attitudes or to foster these virtues *because* of complexity. In addition to that, it is possible to develop an ethical theory on how to deal fairly with the complexity of complex social problems based on the simple insight that we are all *bound in* that complexity. The idea that 'we are all in it together' informs the view that we should care for our relations with each other, not only in the sense that we need to be reflexive with respect to how our complex relations 'emerge' and 'work', but also in the sense that we *need* each other to make sense of complex social problems such as climate change, and to tackle them.

In short, the characterization of complexity as sketched above enables a formulation of an ethics of care that could work for our distant relationships with strangers. The basic idea is that the 'fact of complexity' brings along three new characteristics of modern co-existence that can be named 'connectedness', 'vulnerability', and 'sense of engagement'. Their meaning in relation to the complexity of complex social problems can be summarized as follows:

Connectedness

We are connected with each other 'in complexity'. We cannot any longer escape or avoid it. Fair dealing with each other implies fair dealing with the complexity that binds us. Given the character of the social problems we face, that connectedness has now a global 'dimension'.

Vulnerability

In complexity, we are intellectually dependent on each other while we face our own and each other's 'authority problem'. We should care for the vulnerability of the ignorant and the confused, but also for that of 'mandated authority' (such as that of 'the scientific expert', the 'teacher' or 'the elected political representative'). Last but not least, we should care for the vulnerability of those who cannot be involved in joint reflection and deliberation at all. Obviously, without wanting to make evaluative comparisons between them, these can be identified as the next generations, but also as those among us who are intellectually incapable to join (animals, children and humans with serious mental disabilities).

(Sense of) Engagement

Our experiences now extend from the local to the global. As intelligent reflective beings, becoming involved in deliberating issues of general societal concern became a new source of meaning and moral motivation for each one of us. As citizens, we want to enjoy the right to be responsible in the complexity that binds us, although not only in our own interest. The idea I want to present here is that, for contemporary humans, the will to contribute to making sense of the complexity of our co-existence can be understood as driven by an *intellectual need* and as *a form of 'intellectual' altruism*. The contemporary human becomes frustrated and unhappy if she/he is unable to put that social engagement into practice in one way or another. According to the Buddhist thinker Matthieu Ricard, 'real' altruism is a mental attitude, motivation and intention (Ricard 2015).[11] However, one can understand that acting upon that attitude, motivation and intention will only have limited and temporal effect if at the same time the traditional governing modes of politics, science, the market and education systematically and strategically curtail our possibility to engage in practice.

We can now connect this ethics of care perspective with the idea of reflexivity, and intellectual solidarity as ethical attitudes or virtues, as elaborated above. Connectedness, vulnerability and a sense of engagement, identified as new characteristics of co-existence, imply the need for 'intellectual solidarity' with each other in the way we make sense of complexity of co-existence and of our relations in that co-existence. This can be represented as having a sense for interaction modes that are 'confronting' or 'enabling' at the same time.

	Connectedness, vulnerability and a sense for engagement inspire 'intellectual solidarity as a joint ethical commitment', in the sense of
Connectedness	The joint preparedness to enable and participate in intellectual confrontation with respect to the rationales we use
	• To defend our interests, hopes, hypotheses, believes and concerns • To relativize our uncertainties and doubts
	The joint preparedness to recognize that the practical limitations to participation in deliberation cannot be used to question the principle of participation as such
Vulnerability	The joint preparedness
	• To acknowledge that we are intellectually dependent on each other • To respect each other's authority problem and the vulnerability of those who cannot participate
(Sense for) engagement	The joint preparedness to enable and support 'intellectual emancipation' of others with the aim of providing every human being with the possibility of developing 'reflexivity as an intellectual skill', or thus to develop a (self-)critical sense and to be a (self-)critical actor in society

Trust by method: intellectual solidarity in science, democracy and education

Moving now from normative ethical thinking to applied ethical thinking, the advanced formal interaction modes to enable reflexivity and a sense of intellectual solidarity referred to above can be given a name and a practical meaning. Taking into account the knowledge problem and the evaluation problem as the central characteristics of the complexity of complex social problems, reflexivity and a sense of intellectual solidarity as public ethical attitudes or virtues would need to inspire the method used to generate knowledge about these problems, and the method used to negotiate and make decisions related to them accordingly. So the question becomes, in what way could these virtues inspire the practice of research and decision making?

With the presentation of virtue ethics as one of the four traditional theories of ethics (of Western philosophy), it was noted that the problem with virtue ethics as a theory of normative reference is that virtues do not always translate unambiguously into concrete action. First of all, virtues such as being 'good', 'honest', or 'prudent' obviously need to be considered in a practical context or situation in order to understand their practical meaning. However, even then, different virtues can come into conflict with each other, or acting from the perspective of one virtue can be complicated because of the existence of conflicting values to take into account. In the same perspective, it is true that neither reflexivity nor a sense of intellectual solidarity can unambiguously inspire concrete action of concerned actors but, perceived in the ethics of care perspective presented here, they can inspire interaction methods that would *enable and enforce* them as virtues in the interest of meaningful dialogue. The following reasoning may clarify this. In the first part, it was said that reflexivity as an intellectual skill may benefit from solitary reflection but also that it cannot be 'instructed' or 'thought'. Neither can it be 'enforced' or 'stretched' in the same way as one can do with transparency in a negotiation or deliberation setting. For all of us, reflexivity as an intellectual skill essentially emerges as an *ethical experience* in interaction with others. That interaction may be informal, but it may now be clear that, from a joint concern to make intellectual solidarity and thus that experience for everyone possible, meaningful interactions in this sense are to be organized in (what I would call) the three formal and 'neutral' methods[12] we use to give meaning to our co-existence: scientific research, political deliberation and education.[13] In the interest of keeping this text concise, I will briefly comment on how this can be understood for all three of them.

As the challenge of science in making sense of complex social problems is no longer the production of credible proof but the construction of credible hypotheses, reflexivity and intellectual solidarity as ethical attitudes inspire the need to engage in advanced methods that are self-critical and open to visions from outside the traditional disciplines of science. In other words, in an advanced method of science, knowledge to advise policy is generated in a 'transdisciplinary' and 'inclusive' way, or thus as a joint exercise of problem definition and problem solving with input from the natural and social sciences and the humanities as well as from citizens and informed civil society.

An advanced method of political negotiation and decision making inspired by the ethical attitudes of reflexivity and intellectual solidarity would be a form of 'deliberative democracy' that sees deliberation as a collective self-critical reflection and learning process among all concerned, rather than as a competition between conflicting views driven by self-interest. Political deliberation liberated from the confinement of political parties and nation states, and enriched with opinions from civil society and citizens, and with well-considered and (self-) critical scientific advice would have the potential to be fair in the way it would enforce actors to give account of how they rationalize their interests from out of strategic positions, but also in the way it would enable actors to do so from out of vulnerable positions. It would be effective as it would have the potential to generate societal trust based on its method instead of on promised outcomes. While the utopian picture sketched here would imply a total political reform on all levels, intellectual solidarity can already open up old political methods for the good of society. At both local and global levels, politicians could organize public participation and deliberation around concrete issues, and engage in taking the outcome of that deliberation seriously.

Last but not least, there is the need for a new vision on education. Fair dealing with complex social problems needs an education that cares for 'critical-intellectual capacity building'. It would be naïve to think that scientists, politicians, engineers, entrepreneurs, managers, experts, activists or citizens will adopt the ethical attitudes of reflexivity and intellectual solidarity simply on request. The preparedness of someone to be reflexive about her/his own position and related interests, hopes, hypotheses, beliefs and concerns can be called a moral responsibility, but it essentially leans on the capability to do so. Insight into the complexity of our co-existence in general and into our complex social problems in particular, and an understanding of the ethical consequences for politics, science, the market and education itself, need to be stimulated and fostered in basic and higher education. Education should move beyond the nineteenth-century disciplinary approaches and cultural and religious comfort zones, and should become pluralist, critical and reflexive in itself. Instead of educating young people to function optimally in the strategic political, cultural and economic orders of today, they should be given the possibility to develop as a cosmopolitan citizen with a (self-)critical mind and a sense for ethics in general and for intellectual solidarity in particular.

An ethics of care perspective on our modern co-existence 'bound in complexity' provides a powerful reference to defend the value of (and the need for) these advanced interaction methods. Recognizing the meaningful relations between the advanced approaches to education, research and political decision making presented above, together they not only enable and stimulate reflexivity and intellectual solidarity based on their discursive potential, but also provide the possibility to generate societal trust with their working. That societal trust considered here is not the trust that the outcome of deliberation will be the 'correct one', but that its method has the potential to be judged as fair by everyone involved, given the complexity of the problem.

So what is the real problem with living in a complex world? Whether we speak of clearly observable unacceptable situations (such as extreme poverty), perceived worrisome situations or evolutions (such as climate change or population growth), or practices or proposed policy measures with a potential controversial character (such as the use of nuclear energy, genetically modified organisms, or a tax on wealth), we can say that our social challenges became more complex. The real trouble with these challenges is not their complexity as such, but the traditional governance methods we use to make sense of them in politics, science and the market. Inherited from modernity, the idea is that these methods are no longer able to 'grasp' the complexity of these social problems. In this text, I argued, in depth why and how these traditional governance methods are not inspired by reflexivity as an ethical attitude and intellectual solidarity as an ethical commitment, driven as they still are by the doctrine of scientific truth and the strategies of political 'positionism' and economic profit. On the other hand, it may be clear that we do not need deep utopian reform of our society to make research transdisciplinary and inclusive, and to make education pluralist, critical and reflexive. Even in the old modes of political conflict, steered and limited by party politics and nation state sovereignty, it is possible in principle to organize public and civil society participation in deliberation around concrete issues, and to take the outcome of that deliberation seriously. So although we do not live in a society inspired by intellectual solidarity, we have the capacity to foster it and to put it in practice.

Notes

1 Source: The World Food Programme (www.wfp.org/).
2 See www.earthsystemgovernance.org/.
3 Note that the meaning of 'citizenship' remains open to interpretation and that, as characterized in Howard-Hassmann and Walton-Roberts (2015), the 'human right to citizenship' remains a 'slippery concept'. The Universal Declaration on Human Rights states in its Article 15 that 'Everyone has the right to a nationality' and in its Article 21 that 'Everyone has the right to take part in the government of his country, directly or through freely chosen representatives' (United Nations 1948) but makes no mentioning of the notion of citizenship as such. The general understanding of the meaning of citizenship is 'the status of a person recognized under the custom or law as being a member of a state' (Wikipedia 2015) but the term is also used in broader political, social and cultural contexts.
4 Also the 'relevance' of a specific joint political interest is a concept open to interpretation. It can be 'officialized', as in the case of an NGO officially accredited to the United Nations or become 'established', as in the case of Greenpeace, but in many other cases it needs to be defended as such, as in the case of ad-hoc citizens' movements and pressure groups.
5 In the context of this text, 'expert' denotes any person with a special expertise compared with others involved. This could be a scientist in an advisory role towards a political authority, or someone who works for a regulatory commission, but also a medical doctor in relation to a patient.
6 Note that also 'education' can be considered as a formal governing method to produce meaning for society (the systematic and programmatic way to provide humans with 'capabilities', and this by way of teaching them general and specialized knowledge, skills and competences). However, in the reasoning developed here, education is not considered in the same way as representative democracy, science and the market. Obviously what is 'taught' in our education programmes today has been influenced by modernity as an emancipation process, but the method of education itself is not a result of that emancipation process, and neither was it ever set up with the aim to work 'self-corrective'. Obviously the role of education is crucial in a reasoning on a better dealing with the complexity of our social problems, so I will highlight that role later in the text. Also 'culture' in its different expressions can be considered a method to produce meaning for society (with possible meanings such as aesthetics and social critique, but also the feeling of connectedness or alienation). What can be said, written, done and shown in culture today has of course in various ways been determined by modernity as an emancipation process, but, similar to education, culture itself is, as 'method', not a result of that modernity as emancipation process. In the same sense, it has never been set up to work 'self-corrective'. Last but not least, I need to note that the idea of a self-corrective logic does of course not apply to the human sciences, as their statements about reality do not necessarily need to be empirically tested.
7 The focus on 'Western philosophy' has no other meaning than to provide a 'pragmatic' framework for the reasoning developed here. Obviously thought from 'Eastern philosophy' may be relevant here too. I see the major differences between them mainly in an historical evolutionary perspective and not caused by different ideologies or deeper insights.
8 Recent academic philosophy distincts 'contractarianism' from 'contractualism'. Contractarianism considers moral principles as those principles that emerge from deliberation among 'reasonable' people. The problem is that this can still lead to arbitrary principles (e.g. the decision to kill the weakest person of the group). Contractualism situates moral authority in deliberation as well, but, in addition, follows Kant in the vision that only those principles can be legitimate that could be accepted by free and equal persons in deliberation based on mutual respect (Driver, 'Normative ethics', in Jackson and Smith 2008).

9 See for example Peter Singer's recent development of his concept of 'effective altruism', based on the idea that an ethical life is a life instructed by the principle of 'doing the most good you can do' (Singer 2015).

10 In addition, from a philosophical perspective, the idea is that both the vision on virtue ethics and ethics of care formulated here do not face the traditional problems formulated above, as they do not aim to instruct concrete practical action of concerned actors, but rather inspire specific modes of reflective and deliberative interaction among them. A further discussion on this philosophical problem falls outside of the scope of this text.

11 Altruism as a 'mental attitude' is of course not a typical Buddhist perspective. Since the concept was proposed by the French philosopher Auguste Comte, the meaning of altruism and the motivations for altruism as an 'attitude' have been the topic of study in philosophy as well as in (evolutionary) psychology and evolutionary biology. For the latter, see, among others, Wilson (2015).

12 The specification of 'formal' and 'neutral' methods is important here, in the sense that it denotes interactions that happen according to specific rules and guidelines to be agreed upon jointly in the interest of the meaning they aim to produce. This marks the difference with the other interaction modes we use to give meaning to life and our co-existence, being (in the broadest sense) 'culture' (including art), 'play', spirituality and religion. See also the next endnote.

13 Previously, I have characterized representative democracy, science and the market as the three formal governing methods that, each in their own way, create meaning for our society. I also said that education, despite the fact that it can be understood as another method to create meaning for our society, is not to be seen in the same perspective, as its method itself is not a result of modernity as an emancipation process, and neither was it ever set up with the aim to work 'self-corrective'. The difference between creating meaning for our society as organization and giving meaning to our society as co-existence is subtle but important. The second refers to interaction methods that give meaning via 'discursive interaction' using specific 'languages'. This is the reason why democracy, science and education belong to this category and the market not. On the other hand, culture can also be understood as an interaction method to give meaning via specific languages (literary fiction, poetry, visual art, dance, theatre, …). However, culture is not taken into account here for the simple reason that its 'methods' are obviously not determined by formal agreements, rules and laws (rather, on the contrary, cultural expression should be 'free'). Also organized religion can be understood as a way to give meaning to our society as co-existence. However, given that the 'separation of church and state' is now widely recognized as a criterion for democracy, similar to 'culture', religion is not taken up in the category of 'advanced formal methods' here. Of course religious thought has the right to be taken into account in political deliberation and education (and even in science), but the idea is that it may not influence the methods of democracy, science and education. This is of course theory, as we know that this influence exists in many ways today (although not necessarily in more problematic ways than from out of a positivist approach to science). Because of practical reasons, a further discussion of these matters falls outside of the scope of this text.

References

Anscombe G. E. M. (1958) 'Modern moral philosophy', *Philosophy 33*, 124.

Bentham J. (1977) *A Comment on the Commentaries*. J. H. Burns and H. L. A. Hart (eds). Continuum International Publishing Group Ltd., London, Atlantic Highlands, NJ.

Furrow, D. (2005) *Ethics: Key Concepts in Philosophy*. Bloomsbury Academic, New York.

Gilligan C. (1982) *In a Different Voice: Psychological Theory and Women's Development*. Harvard University Press, Cambridge, MA.

Howard-Hassmann R. E. and Walton-Roberts M. (eds) (2015) *The Human Right to Citizenship: A Slippery Concept*. University of Pennsylvania Press, Philadelphia.

Hursthouse R. (2013) 'Virtue ethics' in Zalta E. N. (ed), *The Stanford Encyclopedia of Philosophy*. http://plato.stanford.edu/archives/fall2013/entries/ethics-virtue/ [Accessed 15 June 2016].

Jackson F. and Smith M. (eds) (2008) *The Oxford Handbook of Contemporary Philosophy*, First Edition. Oxford University Press, Oxford.

Kitcher P. (2014) *The Ethical Project*. Harvard University Press, Cambridge, MA.

Noddings N. (2003) *Caring: A Feminine Approach to Ethics and Moral Education* Second Edition. University of California Press, Berkeley.

Ricard M. (2015) *Altruism: The Power of Compassion to Change Yourself and the World*. Little, Brown and Company, New York.

Singer P. (2015) *The Most Good You Can Do: How Effective Altruism Is Changing Ideas About Living Ethically*, First Edition. Yale University Press, New Haven, London.

United Nations (1948) *The Universal Declaration of Human Rights*. www.un.org/en/universal-declaration-human-rights/ [Accessed 15 June 2016]

Wallerstein I. (2004) *World-Systems Analysis: An Introduction*. Duke University Press, Durham, NC.

Wikipedia (2015) 'Citizenship' *Wikipedia, the Free Encyclopedia*. https://en.wikipedia.org/w/index.php?title=Citizenship&oldid=695640571 [Accessed 15 June 2016].

Wilson D. S. (2015) *Does Altruism Exist? Culture, Genes, and the Welfare of Others*. Yale University Press, New Haven, London.

Part IV

Ethics of radiological protection

10 Considerations on medical radiation usage

Jürgen Kiefer

Introduction

From the point of view of radiation protection, the medical use of radiation is a very special case. It is the only situation in which humans are intentionally exposed to ionizing radiation (excluding emergencies and criminal actions). The justification is based on the possibility of diagnostic and therapeutic benefits. Diseases may be detected earlier and the chances for effective cures increased. It has to be kept in mind, however, that radiation always represents a health hazard, irrespective of the source, and it may still harm the patient, even if it is delivered by a medical doctor. The number of radiological procedures has increased enormously over the years (Figure 10.1), and medical exposures contribute substantially to the global population radiation load (Figure 10.2). In developed countries ('Health Care Level I' in the terminology of UNSCEAR) they amount to about half of the total, only surpassed by the natural background radiation. On the other hand these

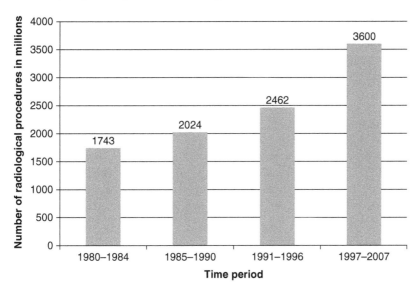

Figure 10.1 Number of radiological procedures worldwide (in millions). Data from UNSCEAR (2010).

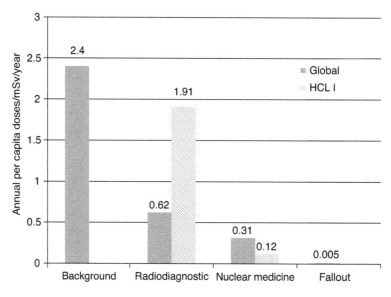

Figure 10.2 Annual per capita doses as global averages and in 'Health Care
         Level I' countries. Data from UNSCEAR (2010).

are mean values, and in some countries the situation may be drastically different.
Technological sources (e.g. nuclear energy which is widely discussed in the general
public) play only a minor role.

Physicians who prescribe radiological procedures are confronted with a great
responsibility; they are bound by the Hippocratic Oath (in its modern version): 'I
will apply, for the benefit of the sick, all measures which are required, *avoiding those
twin traps of overtreatment and therapeutic nihilism*' (italics by the author). This is clearly
an ethical challenge which has been extensively discussed by many authors. It is
not intended and also not possible to give a comprehensive review here. A short
overview of the questions involved was given by Malone (2009). Also the European
Union (EU) addressed the issue in the SENTINEL-Project 'Safety and Efficacy
for New Techniques and Imaging using New Equipment to Support European
Legislation' (Malone et al. 2009) detailed on the SENTINEL website (www.
dimond3.org/). A special workshop on ethical questions was also organized in
Dublin in 2006, (www.dimond3.org/Dublin%202006/WP6_RP_Ethics_Intern_
Meeting.pdf). The International Atomic Energy Agency (IAEA) also addressed this
issue in a special workshop (IAEA 2011, see also Malone et al. 2012).

Frequencies and doses

It is clear from the foregoing and also to be expected that the frequencies of radiological medical procedures are higher in so-called 'developed' countries than in
the rest of the world but one finds surprising differences even between European
countries, Japan and the United States, as demonstrated in Figure 10.3.

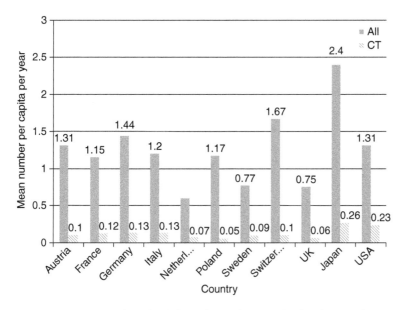

Figure 10.3 Mean number of radiological procedures per head and year and
mean number of CT scans per head and year. Data for Europe from
EU (2014), for Japan from UNSCEAR (2010), for the United States
from Mettler et al. (2009).

The highest values are found in Japan (2.4) followed by Switzerland (1.67), while
on the other side of the scale are the UK (0.75) and the Netherlands (0.6). The
ratio between maximum and minimum amounts to an astonishing four, although
all countries belong to 'Health Care Level I' and consider themselves as possessing
a highly developed health care system. The average citizen in Japan sees his radiologist four times more than his Dutch counterpart. This difference is not reflected in
the mortality rates: 8.57 per 1000 a year for the Netherlands, and 9.38 per 1000
a year for Japan (www.laenderdaten.de/bevoelkerung/sterberate.aspx). These are
raw figures not taking into account the different age structure but they illustrate
that the frequency of radiological examinations does not necessarily improve the
population's health status. Mettler et al. (1987, 1990) suggested that the number of
radiological examinations correlated with the number of physicians in a country
which led to the definition of 'Health Care Levels' by UNSCEAR. With more data
available it is now possible to take a closer look. In Figure 10.4 the frequencies of
CT scans as shown in Figure 10.3 is plotted versus the number of CT scanners per
million inhabitants. A good correlation is seen ($R^2 = 0.72$) which suggests that the
availability of machines represents an important parameter for examination frequencies in different countries. This does not necessarily mean that economic interests (e.g. amortization of capital) are involved but that they also cannot be excluded.

More important in terms of risk estimation are population doses which are
depicted in Figure 10.5. They essentially mirror the distribution of frequencies

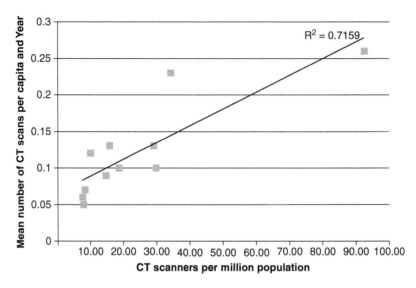

Figure 10.4 Correlation between the frequency of CT scans and the number of CT scanners per million population in different countries as listed in Figure 10.3. CT frequencies are from Figure 10.3, numbers of equipment (year 2006) were taken from OECD (2007).

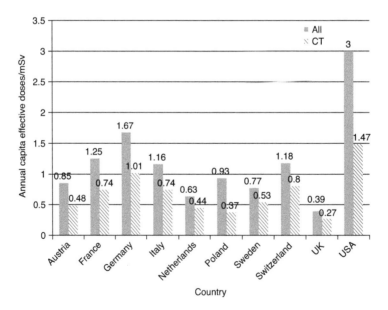

Figure 10.5 Average annual per capita effective doses by radiodiagnostic examinations. Data sources as in Figure 10.3.

(Figure 10.3). The role of computed tomography (CT) is noteworthy: while CT scans comprise only about 10 per cent of all radiodiagnostic procedures they contribute about 60 per cent to the dose with little differences between countries. This is a relatively new development related to the proliferation of CT scanners in recent years. For example, while there were 702 scanners in Germany in 1995 the number grew to 1340 in 2007, i.e. it nearly doubled in only 12 years (OECD 2007). There is no doubt that computed tomography produces very good images, superior to those obtained by plain radiography, but one may ask whether the diagnostic goal cannot often be reached by less sophisticated and less dose-intensive means.

Risk considerations

Members of the general public are normally not interested in doses but in risk. Both are, of course, related but the connection is not an easy one. The problem starts with the quantities used. In discussions on radiation risk 'effective dose' is the most used term. It is quite useful in general radiation protection but one has to bear in mind that it is not a measurable quantity but a construct, to great extent based on judgement. The value is obtained by multiplying organ doses with 'tissue weighting factors' and summing up over all exposed organs. The tissue weighting factors are recommended by the International Commission of Radiological Protection (ICRP) and are part of the legislation of most countries. They are based on risk estimates for genetic effects and cancer ('stochastic effects'). From time to time the factors are changed whenever new research results indicate this to be necessary. This does not happen too often but it means that effective doses may be quite different depending on the time when they were determined, even if the physical dose distribution was identical. Table 10.1 displays the old (ICRP 26) (ICRP 1977), current (ICRP 60) (ICRP 1991) and the new values (ICRP 103) (ICRP 2007a) to be introduced into national legislation.

Table 10.1 Tissue weighting factors as recommended by ICRP.

	ICRP 26 (1977)	ICRP 60 (1991)	ICRP 103 (2007a)
Gonads	0.25	0.2	0.08
Bone marrow	0.12	0.12	0.12
Colon		0.12	0.12
Lung	0.12	0.12	0.12
Stomach		0.12	0.12
Urinary bladder		0.05	0.04
Breast	0.15	0.05	0.12

(continued)

Table 10.1 Tissue weighting factors as recommended by ICRP. (*continued*)

	ICRP 26 (1977)	ICRP 60 (1991)	ICRP 103 (2007a)
Liver		0.05	0.04
Oesophagus		0.05	0.04
Thyroid	0.03	0.05	0.04
Brain			0.01
Skin		0.01	0.01
Bone surfaces	0.03	0.01	0.01
Salivary glands			0.01
Remainder	0.3	0.05	0.12

The concept of 'effective dose' has been introduced mainly for planning purposes in radiation protection, to serve as a guideline in the establishment of regulations, e.g. the definition of dose limits. The 'tissue weighting factors' apply to the average population, irrespective of age and gender. Effective dose must only be used with regard to stochastic effects, i.e. hereditary effects and cancer. The reason why the gonads were placed at a prominent position is not their particular sensitivity with regard to cancer induction but because of the danger of mutations in the germline which could be transmitted to the progeny. There currently seems to be widespread agreement that this risk, although undoubtedly real, plays a lesser role than the possibility of radiation-caused cancer initiation as extensively discussed by UNSCEAR (UNSCEAR 2001). Consequently, the tissue weighting factor was substantially reduced in ICRP 103 (ICRP 2007a).

In medicine effective dose may be used to compare different scenarios (as also done here) but it is completely inappropriate for discussing the risks of specific procedures or estimating the health impairment at the population level as also clearly pointed out by the ICRP (ICRP 2007a). Effective dose is unfortunately and inappropriately also frequently used to compare the 'hazardousness' of different types of radiological examinations. An example is shown in Figure 10.6 taken from a compilation of the European Union (EU 2014). One can see that the highest values are found when the lower part of the body is exposed (Ba enema, CT abdomen). This is due to the fact that the gonads, which have the highest weighting factor, lie in the beam path. If the new factors of ICRP 103 are introduced, the values as given in Figure 10.6 will be substantially changed and an abdominal CT will be 'less hazardous' from one day to the other.

The use of effective dose in medicine has been critically discussed by several organizations (see for example UNSCEAR 2010; ICRP 2007a; ICRP 2007b) and many authors. A comprehensive review is outside the scope of this contribution.

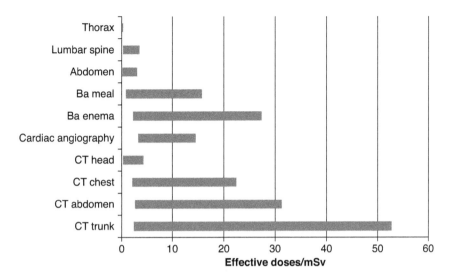

Figure 10.6 Ranges of effective doses for various X-ray examinations in European
countries (EU 2014).

Brenner (2008), to cite just one example, described the concept as 'flawed' and
suggested an alternative approach based on BEIR VII (NRC 2006).

Effective dose has it merits in operational radiation protection but it was never
intended to be used to estimate individual radiation risks as for example in radiodiagnostics. The ICRP has clearly stated that '*it should not be used to assess risks of
stochastic effects in retrospective situations for exposures in identified individuals, nor should it
be used in epidemiological evaluations of human exposure*' (ICRP 2007b). This excludes
the calculation of cancer rates in populations as a result of medical radiation exposures based on data given (for instance in Figure 10.5). Also the effective doses for
different types of examinations (Figure 10.6) are not related to the actual risk of
the exposed patient because he or she do not represent 'reference persons' used by
the ICRP to define effective doses. A better approach is to start from organ doses
and organ-specific risk estimates taking into account age and sex. This method was
applied by the NRC's committee on the 'Biological Effects of Ionizing Radiations'
(BEIR). In Report VII (NRC 2006) the issue is discussed in great detail, and a list
of estimated risk factors is given. Figure 10.7 shows an excerpt from this extensive
tabulation. The calculations are based on physical organ doses, measured in J/kg
with the special name 'Gray' (Gy).

It is obvious that the very young in particular are considerably more at risk than
adults while for the older population it is comparatively low. This clearly has relevance for the justification of radiological examinations.

To examine the cancer risks of radiological procedures at a population level,
Berrington de Gonzales and Darby (2004) compared data from 14 countries,
appropriately using organ doses for every type of examination, and came to the

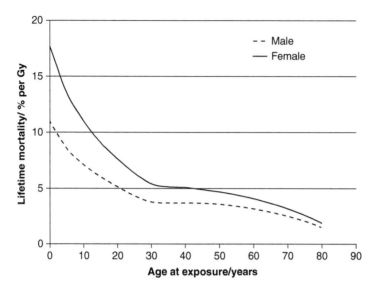

Figure 10.7 Lifetime mortality cancer risk per Gray as a function of age at exposure (NRC 2006).

conclusion that the attributable cancer risks lie between 0.6 and 3.2 per cent. Taking into account that about one quarter to one third of people in western countries will eventually die of cancer (www.cancerresearchuk.org/health-professional/cancer-statistics/mortality) these are low rates if weighted against the proven benefit. This, however, does not override the necessity of careful justification in each single case.

The majority of radiological examinations are connected with comparatively low doses where risk estimations are difficult and complicated by large uncertainties. They are based on epidemiological studies of exposed people, the most important of which being the Life Span Studies of the Japanese atomic bomb survivors. They are frequently updated, the most recent compilations for mortality being Ozasa et al. (2012, 2013), for solid cancer incidence Preston et al. (2007) and for leukaemia (and other cancers of haematological origin) incidence Hsu et al. (2013). Statistically significant excess rates are found at doses above about 100 mSv, i.e. considerably higher than commonly experienced in radiological examinations and also than with occupationally exposed workers. As the dose response is (for solid cancers) compatible with a linear relationship without a threshold, the 'linear no threshold' (LNT) dependence is used in radiation protection (i.e. the effect of low doses is extrapolated from the known action of higher doses). This is a working hypothesis and not a proven fact. LNT has been heavily criticized particularly in recent years (see Doss 2013 as an example). The debate continues, and radiological examinations figure prominently in the discussions. While Brenner and Hall, both highly estimated and experienced radiobiologists, issued a clear warning against uncritical prescriptions of CT scans (Brenner and Hall 2007) seeing a danger to the population's health (see also Picano 2004), others (Tubiana et al. 2009) point out that low radiation doses may be much less harmful than suggested by LNT. They go as far as to state '*It is unethical to fuel anxiety with debatable hypotheses*' suggesting that CT scans not performed may be a greater risk than the 'doubtful' radiation hazard. Uncertainties provoke speculations. One hypothesis, contrary to LNT, is 'radiation hormesis', the assumptions that low radiation doses stimulate repair processes thus providing a health benefit (Kaiser 2003, Doss 2013).

There is very little epidemiological data on the effects of radiodiagnostic examinations. In children it has been shown that multiple CT scans increase the probability of leukaemia and brain tumours with organ doses around 50 mGy (Pearce et al. 2012). Similar results were reported in a large Australian study (Mathews et al. 2013); the conclusions of both publications were heavily criticized by Boice (2015). Recent studies in Germany (Krille et al. 2015) and France (Journy et al. 2015) did not confirm the findings of elevated cancer risks in young people after CT scans.

There is obviously not yet a final answer about the risk of very low doses. However, while this statement is scientifically true it does not absolutely exclude the possibility of cancer induction by multiple CT scans. The LNT hypothesis has its shortcomings but prudency and professional responsibility do not allow it to be lightly dismissed as 'unfounded'.

Application of the principles of radiation protection

The ICRP defined the essence of radiation protection in three simple sentences (ICRP 1977) which are worth reiterating:

> *No practice shall be adopted unless its introduction produces a positive net benefit.*
> *All exposures should be kept as low as reasonably achievable, economic and social factors taken into account.*
> *The dose equivalent to individuals shall not exceed the limits recommended for the appropriate circumstances by the Commission*

These lines may be condensed into three catchwords: **justification, optimization, limitation.** Justification is at the heart of medical radiation usage. More is detailed below.

Optimization

The 'ALARA principle' (as low as reasonably achievable) does not mean to keep the dose as low as possible by all means but to choose the exposure in such a way that the diagnostic goal is reached. Underexposed images are in most cases useless. In adult patients the images are quite often blurred because of X-ray scattering the influence of which can be substantially reduced by using a grid. As the grid also absorbs a part of the useful radiation the exposure has to be increased proportionately. Not to use the grid because of the ALARA principle, accepting a loss in diagnostic conclusiveness, is by no means 'reasonable'.

On the other hand, optimization requires not performing a CT scan if the same diagnosis can be obtained by a plain radiograph. It always has to be kept in mind that the goal of a radiological examination is not an impressive image but a reliable diagnosis. There is no doubt that CT images display more details and better contrast; the question is whether this is indispensable to help the patient. In radiation therapy optimization means to select a sufficient dose for the tumour while at the same time sparing the surrounding healthy tissue. This is a demanding task which nowadays requires very sophisticated methods and machinery.

Limitation

There are no legally fixed dose limits for patients. This sounds strange and does, of course, not imply that limitation does not play a role in medical radiation usage. The radiologist is responsible for choosing the right exposure taking into account what was just said about optimization. The ICRP suggested the introduction of 'diagnostic reference levels' (DRL), today used in many countries, which should not be misinterpreted as dose limits. They are guidelines for good practice and quite often have to be adjusted to fit the individual patient's conditions. Nevertheless, they constitute a great help for everyday work.

Justification

Radiation exposure to humans has to be justified and is only permitted if the expected benefit exceeds the possible harm. In medicine this very general statement requires more detailed specifications. The ICRP (ICRP 2007b) distinguishes here three levels of justification (ICRP 2007b, Holmberg 2011).

> Level 1: Generic justification: Use of radiation in medicine. This is taken for granted as it is accepted that there are in principle clear benefits for the patient.
> Level 2: Justification of a specific procedure to deal with a specific medical objective.
> Level 3: Justification of the chosen type of examination for a specific patient, taking into account health status, age and gender.

Justification has to be documented specifying the underlying reasoning in detail. The general rule is that procedures involving ionizing radiation are only justified if the diagnostic goal cannot be reached by other methods, for example clinical observation, ultrasound or magnetic resonance imaging (MRI). But even if the necessity of a radiological examination is clearly indicated, one must still justify the appropriateness of the specific procedure chosen (by applying the optimization principle in detail), whether a CT scan is necessary, and why the result cannot be obtained by plain radiography. This should be part of the justification documentation.

For certain patient groups (such as children, pregnant women and women who might be pregnant) justification is particularly important and must be exercised with special care. Radiation risk depends on age at exposure (Figure 10.7), and infants and children are among the most sensitive human beings who deserve our greatest attention. Unjustified radiation exposures are never compatible with ethical standards but in the case of children they are just plain criminal.

Pregnant women constitute another critical group. The growing embryo, as rapidly dividing tissue, is very radiosensitive. Exposures particularly in very early stages of gravidity (week 2 to 6) can cause malformations, especially of the central nervous system and the skull. Although these are threshold effects one has to bear in mind that the thresholds are rather low, 50–100 mSv, which may reach the uterus through multiple abdominal CT scans. Prenatal exposures may also initiate cancer manifested in early childhood. This used to be a controversial issue as no significant results were found in the Japanese bomb survivors but it seems to be clear now, on the basis of extended research efforts, that the embryo is very sensitive also in terms of radiation induced cancer (Wakeford 2013).

Another issue related to justification is the examination of 'asymptomatic patients', i.e. of people who wish to have a precautionary check of their health. The European Union states very clearly:

> Any medical radiological procedure on an asymptomatic individual, to be performed for the early detection of disease, shall be part of a health screening programme, or shall require specific documented justification for that individual by the practitioner, in consultation with the referrer, following guidelines from relevant professional bodies and competent authorities. (EU 2013)

There are screening programmes in various countries, such as those for the early detection of breast cancer by mammography authorized by the regulating bodies. Apart from these a 'grey market' has developed to include whole-body CT scans as part of a general health check ('manager check'). A quick search on the internet produces quite a number of offers, mainly by private institutions with prices indicated. A random example (Accessed September 22, 2015) sounds like this:

> The most detailed health check we offer. It includes all the CT scans and blood tests from the Key Essential Check with the addition of two specialist blood profiles.

To be at least formally in line with the regulations prospective customers are told that it has to be ascertained whether or not they comply with the 'clinical referral criteria', so that the law is satisfied. One might wonder whether the enormous increase of CT scans in non-hospital institutions in the US (1996: 2.2 million, 2007: 11 million, data from NCRP 2009) is related to examinations with no clear medical justification. Unjustified exposures of humans by ionizing radiations constitute an offence, as ruled by a German High Court in 1997 (BGH 1997).

There is very little data about the extent of unjustified procedures. A systematic review was performed in Sweden (Leitz et al. 2011). Nearly all institutions in the country performing CT scans were examined on a particular day and the quality of justifications evaluated. Overall, 80 per cent of all examinations were found to be justified but the results varied considerably between the hospitals and primary care centres and also between the anatomical regions examined. Although the result of this study appears to be satisfactory, the authors conclude that there is still a need for improvement.

Unjustified CT scans are particularly critical if performed in younger people. Oikarinen et al. (2009) conducted a retrospective study in Finland on 200 patients under the age of 35, chosen at random from more than 2000 cases. Results are depicted in Figure 10.8.

Although it is unclear how representative this study may be, its startling results still clearly call for further investigation.

CT scans are without doubt superior in terms of image quality compared to plain radiography. It is thus tempting to use this technique even if it is not necessarily required for diagnosis. It must also be considered that the decision may be influenced by economical considerations if a machine is readily available in the department. As long as CT scans deliver higher doses by about a factor of ten compared to conventional radiography, however, the justification must be extremely careful, particularly with young patients. It should be mandatory to document the reasons not only for a radiological examination but also for a high dose procedure specifically.

The ICRP rule quoted above postulates 'a positive net benefit' for a procedure to be justified. This sounds like a simple arithmetic calculation but the situation is much more complicated. There is neither just a number for risk nor for benefit, and the evaluation is hampered by all the uncertainties mentioned above. This leaves

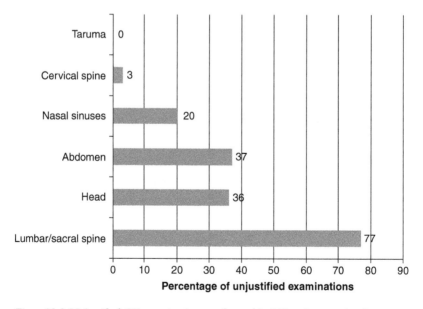

Figure 10.8 Unjustified CT examinations performed in 200 patients under the age of 35 (Oikarinen et al. 2009)

the radiologist alone with his conscience to decide on ethical standards and how to treat the patient to the best of his knowledge. In other words, even with all available scientific data, justification is still an ethical challenge. This excludes the influence of economical arguments on the outcome.

Communication

In an ideal setting patient and doctor meet as partners discussing jointly the best approach to solve the medical problem. The situation in real life is quite different, not only in radiology but almost every time a patient enters the doctor's office. After some discussion the physician 'prescribes' a medicine, a treatment or a diagnostic procedure. The revealing wording suggests a relationship between a master and an uninformed counterpart. Nevertheless 'informed consent' is nearly always required and puts the doctor in an ethically difficult position, as well as requiring balanced (and time consuming) communication. The doctor has to consider not only the present medical problem but also the patient's personal situation and his ability to comprehend the issues involved. This limits the range of 'patients' autonomy' which is considered a key element in decision finding (Sia 2011, Hofmann and Lysdahl 2008). It should go without saying that benefits and risk are extensively discussed in a form which should be comprehensible to the patient. Unfortunately this is frequently not sufficient because the patient has his own views influenced by the media, the internet, and the experiences of friends and relatives. The social environment plays also an important role which varies considerably from country and country. In a society where 'radiation fear' is widespread (as for example in Germany) it may require quite some effort to convince a patient that a particular procedure offers real benefits. It is not uncommon for a possibly lifesaving radiation therapy on a tumour to be declined because 'radiation is dangerous and may cause cancer'. On the other hand, consent may be guided by 'consumerism' (Hofmann and Lysdahl 2008). As the radiological techniques are highly developed it is felt that one has the 'right to get the best', resulting in self-referrals and patients requesting CT scans when conventional radiography would be sufficient.

The situations described above put the radiologist in a difficult position. He must be able to convince the patient that what he recommends is the best available approach. Trust is the key in the patient–doctor relationship. It has to be built up and must be based on convincing scientific expertise.

Unfortunately, paternalism (treating the patient like a child under age) is still widespread. Paternalism can in some cases be used to disguise insufficient knowledge. It is not uncommon for a patient's question about the radiation risk of a CT scan to be answered by 'you get more during a flight to Mallorca' (this applies to Germany, other countries may have different destinations). A chest CT dose is about 3 mSv, and a four-hour flight at cruising altitude causes an exposure of about 25 microSievert. In other words, one would have to fly sixty times to the island and back to make up the exposure of one CT scan.

The ignorance of many members of the medical profession concerning radiation doses and related risks constitutes a major problem in patient communication, undermining the build-up of trust. There is not much data about the extent of this deficiency. The few surveys available (cited in Picano 2011) produced startling results. Even in well-established teaching centres a large fraction of doctors were not familiar with referral guidelines and a great majority misjudged doses and risks. These findings are supported by a recent German study (Heyer et al. 2010). Even basic facts were often missing, for example that ultrasounds and MRI scanning do not use ionizing radiations. These problems have been recognized, and improvements in medical education are demanded. The ICRP published a report 'Radiological protection education and training for healthcare staff and students' (Vano et al. 2009, see also Mettler 2009) outlining a possible curriculum and giving useful advice on how to implement it.

It must be stressed that communication between patient and doctor should help to build up trust so that the best decision for both parties can be reached. This requires a comprehensible explanation of benefits and risks which is only possible if the physician possesses extensive knowledge of the medical and scientific questions involved. It is clear from this that the radiologist has to see the patient before the radiological examination. Self-referrals and referrals by non-specialists must be very critically scrutinized.

Conclusions and final remarks

Radiological examinations contribute significantly to the radiation burden of the general population, particularly in highly developed countries ('Health Care Level I' according to UNSCEAR). There is no doubt that this technique carries a great benefit for the detection of diseases and may lead the way to effective cures. There is, therefore, no reason to diabolize radiology in a general way as one sometimes finds in popular media. On the other hand, risks must not be overlooked. Both aspects must be carefully assessed. The patient has the right to be fully informed, and the discussion has to proceed in a way comprehensible to him or her. This postulate implies that the physician possesses extensive knowledge of the medical and scientific background. There are often clear deficits in the syllabus of medical faculties, especially with regard to radiation protection, which ought to rectified.

The last years have seen impressive developments: CT scanners producing high quality images with considerably less radiation doses are being developed (Kalender 2014), and magnetic resonance tomography has been established as a powerful complement to X-ray-based techniques. Both CT and MRT have their special merits and cannot replace each other. Radiodiagnostics is here to stay, but so are the problems discussed in his contribution.

Radiology is a science, maybe an art, but it must never degenerate into a business!

References

Berrington de González A. and Darby S. (2004) 'Risk of cancer from diagnostic X-rays: estimates for the UK and 14 other countries', *Lancet 363*, 345–51.
BGH (1997) Bundesgerichtshof, Federal Republic of Germany, Ruling of December 3, 1997, Az.: 2 StR 397/97.

Boice J. D. Jr. (2015) 'Radiation epidemiology and recent paediatric computed tomography studies', *Ann ICRP 44(1 Suppl)*, 236–48.

Brenner D. J. (2008) 'Effective dose: a flawed concept that could and should be replaced" *Brit. J. Radiol 81*, 521–23.

Brenner D. J. and Hall E. J. (2007) 'Computed tomography – An increasing source of radiation exposure', *New Engl. J. Med. 357*, 2277–84.

Doss M. (2013) 'Linear no-threshold model versus radiation hormesis', *Dose Response 24*, 480–97.

European Union (EU) (2013), Council Directive 2013/59/EURATOM of 5 December 2013 laying down basic safety standards for protection against the dangers arising from exposure to ionising radiation, and repealing Directives 89/618/Euratom, 90/641/Euratom, 96/29/Euratom, 97/43/Euratom and 2003/122/Euratom. http://eur-lex.europa.eu/JOHtml.do?uri=OJ:L:2014:013:SOM:EN:HTML [Accessed 10 Oct. 2015].

European Union (EU) (2014) Medical Radiation Exposure of the European Population, EU Report RP 180, European Union.

Heyer C. M., Hansmann J., Peters S. A., and Lemburg S. P. (2010) 'Paediatrician awareness of radiation dose and inherent risks in chest imaging studies – a questionnaire study', *Eur J Radiol 76*, 288–93.

Hofmann B. and Lysdahl K. B. (2008) 'Moral principles and medical practice: the role of patient autonomy in the extensive use of radiological services', *J Med Ethics 34*, 446–49.

Holmberg O. (2011) 'Justification: the IAEA initiative', *IAEA* 13–16.

Hsu W. L., Preston D. L., Soda M., Sugiyama H., Funamoto S., Kodama K., Kimura A., Kamada N., Dohy H., Tomonaga M., Iwanaga M., Miyazaki Y., Cullings H. M., Suyama A., Ozasa K., Shore R. E. and Mabuchi K. (2013) 'The incidence of leukemia, lymphoma and multiple myeloma among atomic bomb survivors: 1950–2001', *Radiat Res 179*, 361–82.

IAEA (2011) *Justification of Medical Exposure in Diagnostic Imaging*. International Atomic Energy Agency, Vienna.

ICRP (1977) Recommendations of the ICRP, ICRP Publication 26, *Ann. ICRP 1(3)*.

ICRP (1991) 1990 Recommendations of the International Commission on Radiological Protection, ICRP Publication 60, *Ann. ICRP 21(1–3)*.

ICRP (2007a) The 2007 Recommendations of the International Commission on Radiological Protection, ICRP Publication 103, *Ann. ICRP 37(2–4)*.

ICRP (2007b) Radiological Protection in Medicine, ICRP Publication 105 *Ann. ICRP 37 (6)*.

Journy N., Rehel J. L., Ducou Le Pointe H., Lee C., Brisse H., Chateil J. F., Caer-Lorho S., Laurier D., and Bernier M. O. (2015) 'Are the studies on cancer risk from CT scans biased by indication? Elements of answer from a large-scale cohort study in France', *Br J Cancer 112*, 185–93.

Kaiser J. (2003) 'Hormesis: a healthful dab of radiation?' *Science 302*, 378.

Kalender W. A. (2014) 'Dose in x-ray computed tomography', *Phys Med Biol 59*, R129–50.

Krille L,. Dreger S., Schindel R., Albrecht T., Asmussen M., Barkhausen J., Berthold J. D., Chavan A., Claussen C., Forsting M., Gianicolo E. A., Jablonka K., Jahnen A., Langer M., Laniado M., Lotz J., Mentzel H. J., Queißer-Wahrendorf A., Rompel O., Schlick I., Schneider K., Schumacher M., Seidenbusch M., Spix C., Spors B., Staatz G., Vogl T., Wagner J., Weisser G., Zeeb H. and Blettner M. (2015) 'Risk of cancer incidence before the age of 15 years after exposure to ionising radiation from computed tomography: results from a German cohort study', *Radiat Environ Biophys 54*, 1–12.

Leitz, W., Almèn, A. and Richter S (2011) 'A study on justification of CT examinations in Sweden', *IAEA 2011*, 113–19.

Malone J. F. (2009) 'Radiation protection in medicine: ethical framework revisited' *Radiat Prot Dosimetry 135*, 71–78.

Malone J., Guleria R., Craven C., Horton P., Järvinen H., Mayo J., O'reilly G., Picano E., Remedios D., Le Heron J., Rehani M., Holmberg O and Czarwinski R. (2012) 'Justification of diagnostic medical exposures: some practical issues. Report of an International Atomic Energy Agency Consultation', *Br J Radiol 85*, 523–38.

Malone J., O'Connor U. and Faulkner K. (2009) 'SENTINEL Project special initiative: ethical and justification issues in medical radiation protection', *Radiat Prot Dosimetry 135*, 69–70.

Mathews J. D., Forsythe A. V., Brady Z., Butler M. W., Goergen S. K., Byrnes G. B., Giles G. G., Wallace A. B., Anderson P. R., Guiver T. A., McGale P., Cain T. M., Dowty J. G., Bickerstaffe A. C. and Darby S. C. (2013) 'Cancer risk in 680,000 people exposed to computed tomography scans in childhood or adolescence: data linkage study of 11 million Australians', *BMJ 346*, 23–60.

Mettler F. A. (2009) 'ICRP Publication 113. Radiological protection education in medicine: an essential but often missing element', *Ann ICRP 39(3–4)*.

Mettler F. A., Bhargavan M., Faulkner K., Gilley D. B., Gray J. E., Ibbott G. S., Lipoti J. A., Mahesh M., McCrohan J. L., Stabin M. G., Thomadsen B. R. and Yoshizumi T. T. (2009) 'Radiologic and nuclear medicine studies in the United States and worldwide: frequency, radiation dose, and comparison with other radiation sources – 1950–2007' *Radiology 253*, 520–31.

Mettler F. A., Davis M., Kelsey C. A., Rosenberg R. and Williams A. (1987) 'Analytical modeling of worldwide medical radiation use', *Health Phys 52*, 133–41.

Mettler F. A., Haygood T. M. and Meholic A. J. (1990) 'Diagnostic radiology around the world', *Radiology 175*, 577–79.

National Council on Radiation Protection and Measurements (NCRP) (2009) Ionizing radiation exposure of the population of the United States 2006. NCRP report no. 160. Bethesda, MD: National Council on Radiation Protection and Measurements.

NRC (2006) *NRC Health Risks from Exposure to Low Levels of Ionizing Radiation*. BEIR VII. The National Academies Press, Washington, DC

Oikarinen H., Meriläinen S., Pääkkö E., Karttunen A., Nieminen M. T. and Tervonen O. (2009) 'Unjustified CT examinations in young patients', *Eur Radiol 19*, 1161–65.

Organisation for Economic Co-operation and Development (OECD) (2007) Computed tomography (CT) and magnetic resonance imaging (MRI) census. Benchmark Report: IMV, Limited, Medical Information Division.

Ozasa K., Shimizu Y., Suyama A., Kasagi F., Soda M., Grant E. J., Sakata R., Sugiyama H. and Kodama K. (2012) 'Studies of the mortality of atomic bomb survivors, report 14, 1950–2003: an overview of cancer and noncancer diseases', *Radiat Res 177*, 229–43.

Ozasa K., Shimizu Y., Suyama A., Kasagi F., Soda M., Grant E. J., Sakata R., Sugiyama H. and Kodama K. (2013) 'ERRATA for Volume 177, number 3 (2012) in the article "Studies of the mortality of atomic bomb survivors, report 14, 1950–2003: an overview of cancer and noncancer diseases"', *Radiat Res 179*, e0040–e0041.

Pearce M. S., Salotti J. A., Little M. P., McHugh K., Lee C., Kim K. P., Howe N. L., Ronckers C. M., Rajaraman P., Sir Craft A. W., Parker L. and Berrington de González A. (2012) 'Radiation exposure from CT scans in childhood and subsequent risk of leukaemia and brain tumours: a retrospective cohort study' *Lancet 380*, 499–505.

Picano E. (2004) 'Sustainability of medical imaging', *BMJ 328*, 578–80.

Picano E. (2011) 'Communication, consent and the patient: unlocking the radiological chamber of secrets' *IAEA 2011*, 77–82.

Preston D. L., Ron E., Tokuoka S., Funamoto S., Nishi N., Soda M., Mabuchi K., and Kodama K. (2007) 'Solid cancer incidence in atomic bomb survivors: 1958–1998', *Radiat Res 168*, 1–64.

Sia S. (2011) 'Re-examining ethical issue: philosophical considerations', *IAEA 2011*, 25–30.

Tubiana M., Feinendegen L. E., Yang C., and Kaminski J. M. (2009) 'The linear no-threshold relationship is inconsistent with radiation biologic and experimental data', *Radiology 251*, 13–22.

United Nations Scientific Committee on the Effects of Atomic Radiation (UNSCEAR) (2001) Hereditary Effects of Radiation. Report to the General Assembly, with Scientific Annex. United Nations.

United Nations Scientific Committee on the Effects of Atomic Radiation (UNSCEAR) (2010) Sources and Effects of Ionizing Radiation, 2008 Report, Annex A: Medical Exposures. United Nations.

Vañó E., Rosenstein M., Liniecki J., Rehani M. M., Martin C. J., and Vetter R. J. (2009) ICRP Publication 113, 'Education and training in radiological protection for diagnostic and interventional procedures' *Ann ICRP 39*, 7–68.

Wakeford R. (2013) 'The risk of childhood leukaemia following exposure to ionising radiation – a review', *J Radiol Prot 33*, 1–25.

11 Social and ethical issues in remediation

Deborah H. Oughton

Introduction

Nuclear accidents and radiation protection measures can have far-reaching consequences for affected communities. These impacts go beyond the potential direct radiological health effects, and include a variety of social and economic effects. Remediation measures can do much to alleviate anxiety and restore the way of life. However, remediation is rarely without side effects: it can be expensive, socially disruptive, or damaging to the environment. While the primary objective of remediation is usually dose reduction, for an action to be justified, the benefits of dose reduction or averted dose should outweigh the costs of remediation (ICRP 2009). Remediation can also have benefits that go beyond dose reduction, such as increasing public understanding and control, restoring consumer confidence in a product, or securing the livelihood and social structure of affected populations (Oughton et al. 2004). The perceived success or feasibility of an environmental remediation process will depend not only on the technical process, dose reduction and direct economic costs of remediation, but also social and environmental consequences, as well as broader economic and political implications.

Controversy about the acceptability or justification of remediation measures can be technical: actors may disagree over the size of dose averted, the economic cost of the measures or the health effects resulting from exposure. However, many arguments are grounded in more ethical reasons: one might agree on what the size of doses and costs is, but still disagree over whether the benefits outweigh the remediation investment, or which is the most justified of alternatives. Valuing social and environmental consequences is inherently complex, and even more so when the likely size and type of outcomes is uncertain. Thus transparency in decision-making requires an open consideration of all factors impacting on the decision-making. It follows that an extended evaluation of a remediation strategy will need to consider a wide variety of criteria, including social factors such as the public perceptions of risk, and dialogue with affected communities, as well as ethical aspects such as informed consent and the fair distribution of costs and benefits (Oughton et al. 2004; Howard et al. 2002).

This paper reviews the main social and ethical issues associated with remediation. It starts by giving an overview of some of the consequences of the Chernobyl and Fukushima accidents, then summarizes some of the generic social and ethical aspects of remediation, concluding with a presentation of some of the remediation measures that are not primarily intended to reduce dose.

The social and ethical costs of nuclear accidents

The Chernobyl accident showed that consequences of a nuclear accident go far beyond health issues, and that there can be serious social, psychological and economic consequences, particularly with the breakdown in social infrastructure (Bay and Oughton 2005; UNDP 2002; IAEA 2006). Over 300,000 people were relocated, more than 5 million were living on areas classified as contaminated (>37 kBq/m²), and over 5000 childhood thyroid cancers have been associated with the accident (IAEA 2006). Resettlement and other remediation measures led to capital losses connected to labour and income, production from agricultural land and mineral resources, and decrease in product value. The largest economic losses were from the removal of agricultural land and forests from use, and the closure of agricultural and industrial facilities: 784,000 hectares of agricultural land and 694,000 hectares of forest were taken out of production in the three countries (UNDP 2002; IAEA 2006). In Belarus, 282 rural settlements were closed down due to resettlement. The agricultural effects were particularly strong in rural areas, which are vulnerable because of the great economic dependency on agriculture and forestry (UNDP 2002). People lost not only their main livelihood from forestry and agriculture, but also their secondary source of income, such as from hunting, fishing and collection of wild berries and mushrooms (Bay and Oughton 2005). Many families were facing additional financial stress from the economic crisis in the 1990s. Increases in alcoholism, depression, anaemia and drug use were reported in affected communities, along with increase risks of associated disease (UNDP 2002).

The amounts of radioactive material released from Fukushima were less than at Chernobyl, with much lower initial doses to the population and emergency workers. The high doses to firefighters at Chernobyl resulted in 28 casualties from radiation exposure as well as the death of the Red Forest surrounding the nuclear plant (IAEA 2006). These types of high dose effects were not experienced at Fukushima. However, environmental contamination caused severe societal upheaval. By June 2012, 164,000 people had been evacuated from the surrounding areas (DIET 2012), and a little over 50,000 had returned by the end of 2015. Of the remaining 110,000 people, about 50,000 are not expected to be able to return to their homes, 30,000 can expect more than 5 years before they can go back, and 30,000 are able or will be shortly able to return (IAEA 2015; Fukushima Prefecture 2016a). The societal and health consequences of evacuation after Fukushima have been significant. Increased stress, depression, obesity and psychological effects have been documented in evacuees (Shigemura et al. 2012; Ohtsuru et al. 2015), and more than 2000 are thought to have died as a consequence of the stress of long-term relocation (Tanigawa et al. 2012). People have lost their homes and livelihoods, and even non-evacuated areas suffered economical consequences from losses of consumer trust, decreasing product value and a reduction in tourism (IAEA 2015; Fukushima Prefecture 2016b). Despite areas being lifted from evacuation orders, many towns have a low return rate.

Resettlement and relocation after Chernobyl and Fukushima resulted in a wide range of social and economic consequences. Many resettlers lost their jobs, social network, and connection to places of particular community or historical value like graveyards or places where they played as children. Resettlement also changes the demographics of the areas. The Gomel region in Russia lost about 43 per cent of its population between 1986 and 2000, and demographic parameters, like mortality and birth rate have changed dramatically as elderly people in particular did not want to leave their villages, while young people did. The emigration of young people impeded the whole social and economical development of the region, including a shortage of teachers and doctors (UNDP 2002). Large demographic changes have been seen in the towns open for return in Fukushima, as well as other areas outside the evacuation zone, with young families being more likely to evacuate, and the elderly generation more likely to return (Fukushima Prefecture 2016b). For many people, the decision to return is impacted not only by anxiety about radiation levels; concerns about the availability of infrastructure such as medical services, schools, shops and employment score high, and sometimes higher than radiation doses (IAEA 2015).

The enormous societal consequences of the two accidents means that evaluating the accident and remediation measures only in terms of the doses will be insufficient. Work on emergency preparedness and management after the Chernobyl accident recognized this problem and produced a number of recommendations (Oughton et al. 2004; Howard et al. 2002). The next section looks at these recommendations and updates them in light of the Fukushima accident.

Multi-dimensional aspects of remediation

Acknowledgement of the multi-dimensional aspects of remediation has been an important part of European emergency preparedness projects, including STRATEGY – Sustainable Restoration and Long-Term Management of Contaminated Rural, Urban and Industrial Ecosystems (www.strategy-ec.org.uk) and EURANOS (www.euranos.fzk.de). These projects evaluated remediation against a number of criteria such as practicality and acceptability, socio-ethical aspects, environmental consequences and indirect side-effect costs (Howard et al. 2002; EURANOS 2006). Stakeholder evaluation of remediation measures suggested that many options were as likely to be rejected on socio-ethical grounds as technical and economic grounds (Nisbet 2002). Examples included a strong aversion to any measure that would bring about contamination of previously uncontaminated foods (e.g. mixing milk from different sources) or environments, and an awareness of the problems of contaminated foodstuffs appearing on the black market. Legal constraints also play an important role, particularly with respect to environmental legislation (e.g., habitat protection) and labour rights (Oughton et al. 2004).

Based on the experience of these projects, a summary of some of the most important social and ethical issues to consider in remediation is reproduced below and updated to reflect the Fukushima experience. The list is not exhaustive and can provide only an illustration of some of the issues that might be considered; hence descriptions and examples are rather general. Furthermore the cultural and political settings are likely to play a large role, and one would expect to see differences between different countries.

Self-help measures

"Self-help" considers the extent to which the affected persons themselves can implement actions, and their degree of control or choice over the situation. Voluntary actions that are carried out by the public or affected individuals themselves, or that increase personal understanding or control over the situation, are usually deemed positive as they respect the fundamental ethical values of autonomy, liberty and dignity. Concrete examples include the provision of counting equipment, dietary or drinking water advice, and certain gardening or agricultural procedures that could be carried out by the vegetable grower or farmer. The importance of this was seen in both Chernobyl and Fukushima (Hériard Dubreuil 1999; Hayano et al. 2013). Fukushima saw a high demand for personal dose measurements, whole body counting, and food measurements. Technological developments in access to personal dosimeters as well as sharing the information on social media (for example, Safecast maps available at http://blog.safecast.org/) played an important role. Many authors have reported successful projects such as BabyScan – a whole body counter for small children (Hayano et al. 2014) and D-Shuttle (dosimeters that can provide time readouts of doses and be connected to GPS) (Naito et al. 2014; Adachi et al. 2015).

Discrimination and community impacts

The averted dose and the calculated cost of remediation have direct consequences for the welfare of society and/or individuals, and are thus also important ethically relevant aspects. However, the costs of remediation can go beyond the economic costs of implementation. Negative economic side effects can arise from rural breakdown, and perceived stigma of affected communities (Flynn et al. 2001). Health effects are linked to more than the direct radiological impacts of radiation exposure. Many reports have noted concerns about stigma and discrimination in Fukushima:

> The most important health effect is on mental and social well-being, related to the enormous impact of the earthquake, tsunami and nuclear accident, and the fear and stigma related to the perceived risk of exposure to ionizing radiation. (UNSCEAR 2014, 10)

Other reports of discrimination include TEPCO workers (Shigemura et al. 2012) and schoolchildren (see discussion and references in IAEA 2015, 140). Parents concern for their children include worries about their being able to find marriage partners in later life, remembering the hardships and discrimination experienced by the hibakusha (victims of Hiroshima and Nagasaki). Discrimination can also result in consequences for a range of industries, particularly food or tourist industries where lack of consumer trust can impact on even non-contaminated materials, and for the local identities of people and groups. After the accident Fukushima saw drops of up to 50 per cent in prices of various agricultural products from the whole prefecture, and although prices have risen in recent years, markets prices of many products are still below those of the rest of Japan (Fukushima Prefecture 2016a). Remediation needs to address these issues by acting proactively to restore consumer trust, reduce discrimination, and also by providing adequate mental health support to the victims of stigma and discrimination.

Remediation can also be economically beneficial to communities, for example through generation of local employment opportunities, though it may also be possible that some sections of the population can make a profit from remediation (such as selling or hiring equipment), which can lead to social inequity. This has been reported in other disasters, including the aftermath of the foot and mouth outbreak in the UK, when a minority of the affected communities made a large profit from the disaster (DEFRA 2002) as well as after Hurricane Katrina (Sandel 2009).

Compensation and free informed consent

Although there are strong ethical grounds to compensate people for the hardships and losses experienced by nuclear accidents, compensation has raised problems at both Chernobyl and Fukushima. Experience from Chernobyl illustrates the problems of compensation in promoting the 'victimization' of affected populations, as well as the challenges with lifting compensation (UNDP 2002; Bay and Oughton 2005). In Fukushima, compensation was given not only to those ordered to evacuate, but also for impacts on livelihood and way of life, loss of profits due to both restrictions and consumer trust and, for those remaining, infrastructure changes. In addition, there were specific schemes for young families and pregnant women, including for voluntary evacuations (OECD 2012). However, the rules were complex, and many evacuees had difficulties in meeting the requirements for documentation (IAEA 2015). Compensation can result in divisions and conflicts within communities, for example due to differences in the way tsunami and radiation evacuees were assessed.

Compensation is also linked to the issue of higher wages paid to remediators, and is usually deemed important to ensure consent and autonomy. Employers have a duty to obtain the informed consent of any worker who may be exposed to chemical and/or radiation risk. This is particularly important if lower paid workers are employed to carry out the measure, as it has been suggested that the necessary conditions for free-informed consent are often violated for these groups (Shrader-Frechette 2012, 2013). The increased risk may justify some form of compensation via higher wage premiums, but compensation itself can raise questions of whether or not this may coerce people into taking risks they would otherwise not have (Shrader-Frechette 2013; Hannis and Rawles 2013).

Distribution of dose, costs and benefits

The way in which remediation impacts on distribution of costs, risks and benefits has significance due to the fundamental ethical values of equity, justice and fairness. Costs, benefits and risk may vary over both space and time, and between different members of a community. In many cases the poorest and most vulnerable parts of society are those most affected by any disaster (Bullard 1990, Shrader-Frechette 2012) Dose distribution is obviously a main consideration for radiation protection, and many remediation measures that reduce collective dose (manSv) may change the distribution of dose, for example, from consumers to workers or populations around waste facilities. Some remediation measures could result in an equitable distribution of cost and dose reduction, such as investment by taxpayers to reduce activity concentrations in a common food product; others are less equitable, for example, when a reduction of dose to the majority is only possible at the expense of a higher dose, cost or welfare burden, on a minority (e.g. banning all farm production in a small community). The question of who is paying the monetary and social costs of remediation and who will receive the benefits must also be addressed. Another question is whether the remediation has implications for vulnerable or already disadvantaged members of society (children, ethnic or cultural minorities)? Who is being affected? Who is paying?

Non-dose-reducing social remediation strategies

For certain remediation measures, reduction in dose need not be the only benefit, or even the main benefit. Choice, control, familiarity, closeness and numerous other social and psychological factors play an important role in shaping perceptions towards hazards. It follows that both communication policy and remediation that are sensitive to these factors may stand a greater chance of success. Some measures will tend to increase personal control or choice regarding the risks (i.e. information on actions that can be taken to reduce exposures), whilst others (i.e. state-controlled interventions) might provoke feelings of helplessness (MacGregor 1991). Also, actions need not be limited to those that reduce the exposure to radiation, for example, actions might include better medical attention to reduce all illnesses (Morrey and Allen 1996).

The STRATEGY and EURANOS projects suggested a number of remediation measures where dose reduction was not the primary aim (Table 11.1). These included measures such as compensation, provision of medical check-up, setting up a public information centre, instigating education programmes, stimulating the involvement of stakeholders in decision making, or provision of counting equipment (Howard et al. 2002; EURANOS 2006). A selection of these is presented below.

Table 11.1 Social remediation

Dietary advice	Provision of advice on ways to reduce dietary radionuclide intake. Examples might be advice to reduce consumption of specific foodstuffs (e.g. game, mushrooms etc.), to not drink water from private supplies, or to prepare food in ways that reduce contamination levels (e.g. washing and peeling vegetables and fruit, brining fish, cooking meat, etc.).
Provision of monitoring equipment or personal dosimeters	Providing counting equipment or local measurement stations so that the public can check habitats or foodstuffs for radionuclide content (particularly home grown or self-gathered). Personal dosimeters can help individuals gain understanding or control over their own exposure situation.
Changing intervention limits	Changing intervention limits in foodstuffs may be considered either in order to protect a particular producer/group or due to revision of dose-risk estimates. One example is the increase in limits in reindeer meat that was introduced in Norway in 1987, largely to protect the Sami reindeer herders (Skuterud and Thørring 2012). On the other hand, at Fukushima, levels were reduced in an attempt to increase consumer trust (IAEA 2015).
Food labelling	Food labelling involves provision of information on activity concentrations, and also possibly on the source of produce, and on any remedial treatment.
Information/advice bureau	This social measure involves the provision of information by advice or information centres. This will give an opportunity for specialized and specific provision of information and communication according to individual or local needs and requirements, and for people to have questions answered.
Education programme in schools	Revision of school curriculum to include education on radiological risks, radiation protection and appropriate actions is also important. After any incident, schools are likely to be an important source of information to children.
Health surveillance and medical check-up	Medical check-up can be introduced for exposed individuals or groups, with the aim of providing better health care in the case of radiation-related illnesses (i.e. early identification and treatment of cancer) and other non-radiation-related diseases. Measures should also be provided for psychiatric support. There should be specific schemes for pregnant women as experience shows that this group is one of the most likely to seek medical advice. Needs to be combined with training of medical and public health staff.
Stakeholder engagement	These are various procedures that can stimulate stakeholder engagement, ranging from dialogue to actual engagement in remediation activities. Authorities need to ensure that sufficient resources are allocated to professional support, including expert and laypersons dialogue and collaboration.

More information can be found in the STRATEGY and EURANOS project templates.[1]

Provision of counting equipment and independent monitoring are methods that have been successfully applied in Chernobyl affected communities. A study carried out in Belarusian villages concluded that the approach not only resulted in reducing exposures with minimal social and psychological side effects, but also was also more economically cost effective than the standard 'top-down' management procedures (Hériard Dubreuil et al. 1999). The demand for dosimeters and whole body measurements after Fukushima has been discussed above. Calls for independent monitoring following waste disposal are a common request from community decision. Ethically, intervention procedures that involve the populations themselves help promote the principle of informed personal control over radiation risks.

Conclusion

Any remediation strategy will be strengthened by a holistic approach to remediation, integrating economic, ecological and health measures; it is not sufficient to simply focus on the dose-reduction aspects of radiation protection. This is supported by multi-disciplinary research on long-term management of radioactive contamination carried out by the EU. All projects highlighted the importance of including the affected population with regard to self-help measures and involvement in decision-making processes. In addition to respecting people's fundamental right to shape their own future, and thereby increasing trust and compliance, such approaches can lead to significant improvements in the effectiveness and acceptability of remediation in communities, and in the long run are likely to improve cost-effectiveness.

Acknowledgement

This work was partly supported by the Research Council of Norway through its centres of excellence funding scheme (Project Number 223268/F50) and the Norwegian Research Council PREPARE project (Project Number 226135).

Note

1 www.strategy-ec.org.uk/cms/countermsrs.htm and www.euranos.fzk.de/index.php?action=euranos&title=products.

References

Adachi N., Adamovitch V., Adjovi Y., Aida K., Akamatsu H., Akiyama S., Akli A., Ando A., Andrault T., Antonietti H., et al. (2015) 'Measurement and comparison of individual external doses of high-school students living in Japan, France, Poland and Belarus – the "D-shuttle" project', *Journal of Radiological Protection 36*, 49–66.
Bay I. and Oughton D. H. (2005) 'Social and economic effects' in Smith J. and Beresford N. A. (eds), *Chernobyl, Catastrophe and Consequences*. Springer-Verlaug, Berlin, 239–62.
Bullard R. D. (1990). *Dumping in Dixie: Race, Class and Environmental Quality*. Westview Press, Boulder, CO.

DEFRA (2002) 'Surveys of the economic impact of foot and mouth disease in six districts', *Department for Environment, Food and Rural Affairs (DEFRA)*, London. www.defra.gov.uk/animalh/diseases/fmd/2001/index.htm [Accessed 31 May 2016].

DIET (2012) *National Diet of Japan Fukushima Nuclear Accident Independent Investigation Commission.* The official report of The Fukushima Nuclear Accident Independent Investigation Commission, The National Diet of Japan, Tokyo.

EURANOS (2006). *Generic handbook for assisting in the management of contaminated food productions systems in Europe following a radiological emergency.* Deliverable From the EURANOS Project. EURANOS (CAT1)-TN(06)-06. www.euranos.fzk.de/index.php?action=euranos&title=products [Accessed 31 May 2016].

Flynn J., Slovic P. and Kunreuther H. (2001) *Risk, Media and Stigma: Understanding Public Challenges to Science and Technology.* Earthscan, London.

Fukushima Prefecture (2016a) *Fukushima Revitalisation Status: Fukushima Prefecture Government.* www.pref.fukushima.lg.jp/site/portal-english/list385.html [Accessed 31 May 2016].

Fukushima Prefecture (2016b) *Steps for Revitalisation in Fukushima: Fukushima Prefecture Government.* www.pref.fukushima.lg.jp/site/portal-english/list385.html [Accessed 31 May 2016].

Hannis M. and Rawles K. (2013) 'Compensation or bribery? Ethical issues in relation to radwaste host communities' in Oughton D. H. and Hansson S. O. (eds) *Social and Ethical Aspects of Radiation Risk Management.* Elsevier, Oxford, 347–73.

Hayano R. S., Tsubokura M., Miyazaki M., Satou H., Sato K., Masaki S., Sakuma Y. (2013) 'Internal radiocesium contamination of adults and children in Fukushima 7 to 20 months after the Fukushima NPP accident as measured by extensive whole-body-counter surveys', *Proceedings of the Japan Academy, Series B 89*, 157–63. www.jstage.jst.go.jp/article/pjab/89/4/89_PJA8904B-01/_pdf [Accessed 31 May 2016].

Hayano R. S., Yamanaka S., Bronson F. R., Oginni B. and Muramatsu I. (2014) 'BABYSCAN: a whole body counter for small children in Fukushima', *J. Radiol. Prot. 34*, 645–53.

Hériard Dubreuil G. F., Lochard J., Girard P., Guyonnet J. F., Le Cardinal G., Lepicard S., Livolsi P., Monroy M., Ollagon H., Pena-Vega A., Pupin V., Rigby J., Rolevitch I. and Schneider T. (1999) 'Chernobyl post-accident management: The ETHOS project', *Health Physics 77*, 361–72.

Howard B. J., Andersson K. G., Beresford N. A., Crout N. M. J., Gil J. M., Hunt J., Liland A., Nisbet A., Oughton D. H., and Voigt G. (2002) 'Sustainable restoration and long-term management of contaminated rural, urban and industrial ecosystems', *Radioprotection – colloques 37(C1)*, 1067–72.

IAEA (2006) *Chernobyl's Legacy: Health, Environmental and Socio-Economic Impacts.* The Chernobyl Forum. International Atomic Energy Agency, Vienna, World Health Organisation (WHO). www.who.int/ionizing_radiation/chernobyl/chernobyl_digest_report_EN.pdf [Accessed 30 May 2016].

IAEA (2015) *The Fukushima Daiichi Nuclear Accident*, Technical Report, Volume 5. International Atomic Energy Agency, Vienna. http://www-pub.iaea.org/books/IAEABooks/10962/The-Fukushima-Daiichi-Accident [Accessed 30 May 2016].

ICRP (2009) 'Application of the Commission's recommendations to the protection of people living in long-term contaminated areas after a nuclear accident or a radiation emergency', International Commission on Radiological Protection (ICRP), Publication 111 *Annals of the ICRP 39(3)*.

MacGregor D. (1991) 'Worry over technological activities and life concerns', *Risk Analysis 11*, 315–24.

Morrey M. and Allen P. (1996) 'The role of social and psychological factors in radiation protection after accidents', *Radiation Protection Dosimetry 68*, 267–71.

Naito W., Uesaka M., Yamada C. and Ishii H. (2014) 'Evaluation of dose from external irradiation for individuals living in areas affected by the Fukushima Daiichi nuclear plant accident', *Radiation Protection Dosimetry 163*, 353–61.

Nisbet A. F. (2002) 'Management options for food production systems contaminated as a result of a nuclear accident', *Radioprotection-Colloques 37(C1)*, 115–20.

OECD (2012) *Japan's Compensation System for Nuclear Damage*. Organisation for Economic Cooperation and Development (OECD/NEA). www.oecd-nea.org/law/fukushima/7089-fukushima-compensation-system-pp.pdf [Accessed 31 May 2016].

Ohtsuru A., Tanigawa K., Kumagai A., Niwa O., Takamura N., Midorikawa S., Nollet K., Yamashita S., Ohto H., Chhem R. K. and Clarke M. 'Nuclear disasters and health: lessons learned, challenges, and proposals', *Lancet 2015 Aug 1; 386(9992)*, 489–97. doi: 10.1016/S0140-6736(15)60994-1.

Oughton D. H., Bay I., Forsberg E.-M., Kaiser M. and Howard B. (2004) 'An ethical dimension to sustainable restoration and long-term management of contaminated areas', *Journal of Environmental Radioactivity 74*, 171–83.

SAFECAST (2014) *Safecast Map*. http://blog.safecast.org/ [Accessed 31 May 2016].

Sandel M. J. (2009) *Justice: What's the Right Thing to Do*. Farrar, Straus, Giroux, New York.

Shigemura J., Tanigawa T., Saito I., Nomura S. (2012) 'Psychological distress in workers at the Fukushima nuclear power plants', *J. American Medical Association 308(7)*, 667–69.

Shrader-Frechette K. (2012) 'Nuclear catastrophe, disaster-related environmental injustice, and Fukushima: prima facie evidence for a Japanese "Katrina"', *Environmental Justice 5(3)*, 133–39.

Shrader-Frechette K. (2013) 'Environmental injustice inherent in radiation dose standards' in Oughton D. H. and Hansson S. O. (eds), *Social and Ethical Aspects of Radiation Risk Management*. Elsevier, Oxford, 197–211.

Skuterud L. and Thørring H. (2012) 'Averted doses to Norwegian Sami reindeer herders after the Chernobyl accident', *Health Phys. 102*, 208–16.

Tanigawa K., Hosoi Y., Hirohashi N., Iwasaki Y. and Kamiya K. (2012) 'Loss of life after evacuation: lessons learned from the Fukushima accident', *Lancet 2012 Mar 10;379(9819)*, 889–91. doi: 10.1016/S0140-6736(12)60384-5.

UNDP (2002) *The Human Consequences of the Chernobyl Nuclear Accident – A Strategy for Recovery*. United Nations Development Programme. http://chernobyl.undp.org/english/docs/strategy_for_recovery.pdf [Accessed 30 May 2016].

UNSCEAR (2014) 'Report to the General Assembly, Scientific Annex A: levels and effects of radiation exposure to the nuclear accident after the 2011 Great East-Japan earthquake and tsunami' in *Sources, Effects and Risk of Ionizing Radiation, vol. I*. United Nations Scientific Committee on the Effects of Atomic Radiation. Report to the 68th session of the United Nations General Assembly A/68/46, Vienna, 2 April 2014, 311.

12 Radioactive waste

Some ethical aspects of its disposal[1]

Christian Streffer

Introduction

The solution of long-term radioactive waste management (RWM) contains a technical and an ethical/social dimension. The concept and construction of the necessary repositories implies not only technically achievable measures but also legally and politically feasible aspects as well as publicly acceptable points on ethical and social grounds. The technical solutions have to ensure reasonably safe and secure containments of highly radioactive waste with long physical lifetimes for an indefinite/distant future in order to isolate to a high degree radioactivity from the biosphere, including humans, and to avoid undue burdens on future generations. The radiotoxicity of long-lived radionuclides has to be taken into account. The strong protests and debates in many countries (particularly Germany) about the management of radioactive waste and the finding of an adequate waste disposal strategy shows that a considerable potential for conflict has been built up. The emotionally charged positions and the passion with which arguments are put forward are frequently an external indicator. Often the discussion about the nuclear disposal facility masks deeper social debates about the significance of technological developments for the future shape of the economy, energy production and life in society.

The acrimony with which this conflict is carried out in public is also doubtlessly characteristic of the debate and is worthy of more careful attention, especially if one is interested not just in the theoretical development of problem solving strategies, but also in the practical resolution of the conflict. If a decision is to be brought about through the answering of factual questions, the social dimensions of the conflict will also have to be analysed in order to discover how the current polarized positions can be converted into a constructive discourse about rational strategies, which can be understood and tolerated by all parties. This is the only possible way to achieve an effectively legitimized decision on the site issue and the modalities of a final disposal facility for high-level waste.

Roeser (2011) has dealt with these problems very carefully and has come to the conclusion:

> A fruitful debate about nuclear energy should do justice to quantitative, empirical information as much as emotional, moral considerations. This approach

allows for a different way of dealing with risk emotions in public debates by avoiding both the technocratic pitfall and the populist pitfall alike. Instead, this alternative approach allows for what I would like to call an 'emotional deliberation approach to risk'. It allows the public a genuine voice in which their emotions and concerns are appreciated, listened to, and discussed, rather than ignored (technocratic pitfall) or taken as a given that makes discussion impossible (populist pitfall). By discussing the concerns underlying emotions, justified concerns can be distinguished from – morally or empirically – unjustified concerns. This approach means that debates about risky technologies include emotions and moral concerns that have to be taken into account in order to come to a well grounded ethical assessment. (200)

Such a procedure is desirable, if not necessary, and also appropriate in a democratic system to attain the acceptance or at least the tolerance of the people affected. The formation of opinions must occur in a democratic process that this is not in the line of technocratic decisions, but ultimately a democratic decision. Democracy requires argumentation, and publicity requires transparency. In the decision-making process regarding a disposal facility for high-level radioactive waste with long-term considerations, considerable importance is placed on the uncertainty of scientific knowledge and models, to possible ambiguity in the evaluation of a condition, and to possible contradictions in the statements of experts. As a consequence, the affected population feels insecure and frequently irritated. Unavoidable uncertainties in knowledge and scientific data, and the way these are presented and dealt with, are without doubt extremely difficult topics and substantial obstacles for the attempt to gain acceptance for disposal facilities of this kind. Statements must be made about long-term safety over periods of time so long that they reach the limits of the human capacity of imagination. Prognostic statements are then only possible by means of model calculations with correspondingly high levels of uncertainty. Reaching an understanding of these matters is no easy task (Streffer et al. 2011).

The very long time spans of the necessary prognoses clearly reinforce these effects considerably. The most recent developments in Fukushima, Japan, also show that exceptionally extreme events can occur which cannot always be expected even if all available data are used as a basis for planning. This situation shows that precautionary efforts must be undertaken because the consequences may be severe. Clearly this applies particularly to the planning of disposal facilities for high-level waste where considerations over very long time periods have to be made.

Geological processes of evolution occur over considerably longer periods of time than biological or social processes of evolution. Therefore prognostic statements about the possible nature/safety of the technical and geological barriers can be made for possible geological developments and their changes over longer time periods with sufficiently higher degrees of accuracy than prognoses about inhabitancy for the region of a disposal site. Such prognostic statements will be even more problematic for the lifestyles of those people who may possibly live at such a site in the future. But even the better geological prognostic values about the certainties/uncertainties do not justify ignoring the possible claims of future generations to adequate RWM, or dismissing these claims as irrelevant. On the contrary, in principle an adequate waste management strategy must – in keeping with the ethical principle of universalism – give the same consideration to members of future generations as it does to those of the present generation. These aspects have very often been discussed in context with technical installations and especially with repositories for high-level radioactive waste during the last decades (cf. Flowers 1976; SSK 1985, cit. in Streffer et al. 2011; ICRP 1998; Shrader-Frechette 2000; KASAM 2007; ICRP 2007; Taebi 2011; Roeser 2011; Streffer et al. 2011; ICRP 2013). Thus the same protection measures have to be granted for future generations as for the present.

The above discussion of these extreme complexities of the conflict is not intended to either accord a special status to the problem of RWM, or indicate scepticism about the likelihood of resolving this conflict; highly complex controversies, in which the debate over the appropriate or suitable solution to a problem throws up questions. The conflict should be clarified and the arguments should be valued with regard to both the available options and the existing normative (ethical) as well as psychological and social aspects (Roeser 2011; Streffer et al. 2011). An approach for the development of valid recommendations and strategy to deal with RWM may be:

1   The problem should be considered on the basis of its technical feasibility independent of its social effects and independent of the existing, sometimes irrational assumptions.
2   The problem should not solely be reduced to its technical aspects. The various conflict-generating differences in the evaluation have to be taken into account.

Objective problems with radioactive waste management (RWM)

In order to develop proposals and make corresponding recommendations for which problem-solving strategies could be proposed and hopefully be accepted – serving as a preparation of such a discourse – it may be helpful to first consider the problem causing the conflict on a rational basis, independent of its resonance in society and politics. Thus it is necessary to consider the technical and solid scientific facts. As already pointed out this does not mean, however, that the problem should be reconstructed as a merely technical issue – on the contrary. Such a reconstruction on the pure technical basis will certainly be considered a technocratic enthusiasm and a reductive interpretation of the problem, and therefore will not be supported by the public and might even be strongly opposed. It is therefore very important: there has to be transparency in the decision-making processes. The participation of stakeholders is both required and highly desirable.

The threat posed to humans and the environment by radioactive material results from the release of radioactive material from the repository, its migration into the biosphere, and as a further consequence exposure through ionizing radiation originating through the radioactive decay. If the radioactive material migrates from the repository into the biosphere such an exposure of the natural environment and the human population can take place through the external exposure pathway as well as through the internal exposure pathway by uptake of contaminated food and inhalation of radioactive material. It is therefore necessary to safely store radioactive waste for a long time period (particularly high-level waste from nuclear facilities). Based on the geological features granite, clay or salt rock are discussed as appropriate geological barriers and storage in several hundred meters up to thousand meters deep of these barriers is foreseen. The spent nuclear fuel (SNF) will be discharged from the nuclear reactor and kept in a cooling pond at the site of the reactor for some years so that the radionuclides with relatively short physical half lifetime can decay and the extreme heat producing processes connected with the radioactive decay have been terminated to a great extent during this time. Thereafter a conditioning of the fuel, emplacement in transport casks and further cooling for some decades (usually 40 years) will take place before the SNF is emplaced in the disposal facility to avoid the high temperatures of SNF by energy released during radioactive decay (Streffer et al. 2011).

The aim of the geological, deep-seated repository is to isolate the radioactive waste from the biosphere for very long time periods so that no or very little exposure to the environment and human population can occur. As some of the radionuclides of the highly radioactive waste have very long half lifetimes, e.g. ^{238}U: $4.47 \cdot 10^9$ years; ^{129}I: $1.57 \cdot 10^7$ years, it is necessary to choose a geological formation with stable conditions over very long time periods. Periods of several tens of thousands years were initially taken into consideration in Germany for considering the safety of the repository (SSK 1985). A key argument for such a period was that a new ice age can be expected in Europe within this time frame. However, on the basis of prognostic statements about the timescales of the stability and possible geological changes in the repositories and especially due to the prognosis of geologists about the possible migration of material through the geological barriers, assessments of the long-term safety of disposal facilities for radioactive waste have now been expanded to a range between several hundreds of thousands and one million years.

Therefore, in the models for repositories of radioactive waste from nuclear power stations, prognostic values are given for several hundred thousand to millions of years today. As shown above the physical half-life times of some radioisotopes range up to many millions of years and considering the mentioned prognostic time periods from the geological judgements it is accepted worldwide that the radioactive material needs to be confined in isolation from the biosphere for these very long periods of time (Streffer et al. 2011; ICRP 2013). A release of radioactive material can only occur when the solid containers of high-quality material are corroding. Then the radionuclides may migrate from the technical barrier of the repository to the geological barrier. Such a migration is possible especially for radionuclides in the gaseous state or for water-soluble radionuclides (like tritiated water or iodine-129) if water has entered the technical part of the repository. The radioactivity must migrate through the host rock (the 'near field') and the overlaying rock (the 'far field') before reaching the biosphere. This will take several thousand to several hundred thousand years.

Such a migration of radioactive material will occur with very high probability in smaller amounts and on a limited area above the location of the repository (Streffer et al. 2011). On principles of radiological protection it is claimed by the International Commission on Radiological Protection (ICRP 2013) that the resulting radiation dose (effective dose; ICRP 2007) should not be higher than 0.3 mSv per year. The German Government even proposes for the effective dose a reference value of 0.1 mSv per year (BMU 2010). This means radiation doses caused during the long term by releases of radioactive material from the repository should be within a range of 5 to 10 per cent of the average dose from natural sources (2.4 mSv per year in Germany). Different model calculations in salt and clay as host rocks come to the conclusion that the compliance with such reference levels of radiation dose can be achieved over the necessary time periods (Marivoet et al. 2008). An explosion and thus an accidental release, e.g. by occurrence of a criticality, should not occur at all in a repository with regular orientation of the cascades (Baltes et al. 2007). Therefore the conditions of release and migration of radioactive material through the host rock are such that an external exposure pathway with a notable, relevant radiation dose can be neglected or even excluded. Only a radiation dose from the internal exposure pathway will have some significance in the far future. Then the resulting radiation dose is in such a range that no health effects have been measured after such exposures until now (Streffer et al. 2004; UNSCEAR 2006; ICRP 2007; Streffer 2009). In these low dose ranges the causation of cancer may be possible under the assumption of the LNT concept (linear no threshold relation); however, in the dose range below 100 mSv no significant increase of cancer has been observed (BEIR 2005; UNSCEAR 2006; ICRP 2007).

An ethical framework for disposal of radioactive waste

Obligations to future generations are generally indefinitely valid. Management strategies for radioactive waste should nonetheless be developed for limited time spans. This has to be done under conditions of a 'sustainable development' which postulates a 'moral obligation towards future generations' (KASAM 2007). The Radioactive Waste Management Committee of the OECD/NEA (1995) has come to the conclusion that the achievements of 'intergenerational equity' considering future generations and of 'intragenerational equity' considering the present generations are necessary. This is discussed in a similar way by Shrader-Frechette (2000). Obligations which commit to prudent management of radioactive waste are in principle indefinitely valid and continue to exist towards the members of distant generations – though their binding force gradually decreases over time (Streffer et al. 2011). The complex sequences (the 'sequence spaces') which must be included in the development of waste management strategies must nonetheless have time limits set, to meet the rational requirements of planning and for reasons of efficiency. Such a time limit should be based on the foreseeable future effect of the consequences, and thus on the relative hazard potential of the contents of the disposal facility and of possible exposure in the biosphere, which can vary with the phases of the decay process and the chosen waste management strategy (Kern and Nida-Rümelin 1994; Streffer et al. 2011).

The present generation as the primary beneficiary of nuclear energy has the obligation to initiate the solution of the disposal problem. The demand for *immediate* disposal of high-level waste, however, imposes an unjustifiable burden on the present generation. From an ethical point of view, the utilization of moral principles which impose the entire burden of disposal on the present generation as a community of originators and beneficiaries is by no means self-evident. As long as – based on authoritative forecasts – reliable relations of exchange could be organized across generational or communal boundaries, without detriment to third parties, there could be no ethical objection to, for example, transferring the 'responsibility for disposal' in exchange for freely accepted compensation. The demand for an immediate solution to the problem is not self-evident and requires justification. If there may be an improvement of reducing the radiotoxic impact by a better scientific or technical knowledge, e.g. by transmutation, so that a generation of the near future has access to 'better' waste management strategies e.g. an improved design of a repository, then it may even be advisable to take this option. Considerations of justice do, however, impose a duty on the originator to offer adequate compensation. This also applies, mutatis mutandis, to international relations of exchange: for an adequate perception of long-term obligations, the relevant factors are not national borders – which can vary dramatically with time as historically views and experience show over centuries – but the availability of skills and resources (Streffer et al. 2011).

Processes to solve the question of disposal facilities must be designed in such a way that they do justice to everyone equally as far as possible, and in particular give adequate consideration to the claims of future generations. It is desirable that the legitimating procedures should be designed to respond to the claims and the local and technical knowledge of those alive today, where these are concerned by the conflict, but this must be weighed up against obligations towards those who are not involved in the consultations, in particular members of future generations. Thus the criterion for the decision must not be solely the agreement of members of the present generation, achieved through procedures. On the contrary, the decision must also be acceptable in the sense of a rationally presented justification based on universalist arguments (Kant 1903/1911). In the public debate, there must be an advocacy for those who cannot participate, or who have no incentives to stand up for their requirements. This responsibility cannot simply be claimed by individual stakeholders or groups of stakeholders; the transfer of this responsibility must be legitimated by some democratic mechanisms.

A categorical rejection of all proposed solutions for the disposal of high-level waste is incompatible with our obligations towards future generations. The management of radioactive waste is a collective duty shared by the society as a whole. This gives rise not only to the duty of care but also to the obligation to participate constructively in the development of suitable proposals, and/or to create or support structures which make this kind of participation possible. The right of veto held by those who base their arguments on the unsuitability of a proposed site or on the disposal concept per se is linked with the expectation that they will participate constructively in the development of alternative proposals. Promising projects and processes which aim at the development of alternative proposals must be supported with the necessary resources. A categorical rejection of all proposals ignores our obligations towards future generations.

Some further aspects to consider ethical principles for RWM under long-term conditions

Ethical justification of long-term responsibility

As a normative discipline, ethics has also dealt with problems in the future. Historically, however, the debate has been limited to the near future, inasmuch as this has been affected by problems of conflict resolution, and that primarily means conflicts that occur within a direct interaction. There was no recognizable need for solving long-term trans-generational conflicts in the far future to which ethical debates could have reacted. However, for such an obligation it seems necessary to set a range of time period. The time frame of a million years for the evaluation of the long-term safety of high-level waste repositories seems to be an appropriate compromise between the ethical requirements for long-term responsibility and the limits of practical reasons based on geological knowledge and judgement. The rationale behind this time frame of a million years is the ability to find sites in a geological environment which, according to current geo-scientific knowledge, are believed to conserve their favourable features for a period of that order of magnitude. Historically the productivity of the older generations was always perceived as benefiting later generations as well, so that Kant for instance could only recognize a question of 'trans-generational justice' in the opposite sense to that discussed today (Kant 1912). Very much in contrast to this, the modern debate is characterized by the opposite perception, that the legacy of the present generation may be an ecological and economic burden to the future generations (Streffer et al. 2011). Following Mittelstraß (2008) this modern debate actually began with the problem of radioactive waste.

Today, the concern for future generations is mostly formulated in terms of 'intergenerational justice' (Tremmel 2009) and – especially in the context of sustainable development – focuses on the problem of fair distribution of scarce resources between generations as it was first globally recognized when oil reserves were perceived to be scarce in the 1970s (from today's perspective this perception was skewed). Furthermore the problem was addressed theoretically in the book *A Theory of Justice* by J. Rawls (1971), which has been very influential for the actual debates on ethics and political philosophy with respect to problems of 'just distribution': Rawls' so-called 'difference principle' requires that social institutions are arranged in a way so that inequalities of wealth and income operate to the advantage of those who will be worst off. This arrangement of a fair intragenerational distribution immediately leads to a problem of trans-generational justice: what is to be distributed must be fixed so that just distribution in the first generation is not established at the expense of later generations.

The related term 'intergenerational justice' implies a set of problems evoking misleading connotations and producing pseudo-problems. The prefix 'inter' points to the idea of a mutual relationship that has to be brought into some kind of balance ('justice'). Such issues of justice between generations do exist. The universal use of the expression 'intergenerational justice', however, suggests that the ethical problems concerning remote future generations are basically of the same kind. And yet in the contexts in which long-term obligations are discussed, *inter*generational relationships soon cease to exist (almost certainly from generation G_{0+4} on). The future generations concerned here have no mutually interactive relationship with us: such far future generations will be confronted with the consequences of our technology-related actions, but conversely the actions of future generations are not relevant for us. Relationships between generations of the 'inter' type must therefore be clearly distinguished from those relationships to be dealt with in terms of long-term responsibility. But even if one does not misunderstand the problems at issue as problems of *inter*generational justice, and speaks more cautiously of, for example, problems of 'cross-generational justice', it is not self-evident that, from an ethical perspective, those are problems of justice at all. Contrary to the tacit assumption often made in the debate following Rawls' *Theory of Justice*, not all problems of moral obligation can be reformulated as problems of distributive justice. The converse does apply, however: all problems of distributive justice can be reformulated as problems of moral obligation. For example, we can consider whether the present generation is under an obligation to safeguard some parts of resources for remote future generations, to avoid or to limit particular risks. But problems of obligation can be discussed even where there are no issues of distribution regarding future generations. One example is the elementary, non-trivial question of whether the present generation is obliged to ensure the survival of the species *homo sapiens* with its reproductive behaviour, or whether a refusal to conceive is, in moral terms, at least permissible. It would be strangely artificial, however, to reconstruct this as the question of whether we are obliged to grant future generations the same access to a resource called 'life' as we demand for ourselves. Put it in a much simpler, more general way, the question is whether the members of a generation g_0 (e.g. our own generation) are under any obligation towards remote future generations. There is a whole range of ethical questions relating to the future which cannot always be (easily) reconstructed as problems of inter- or cross-generational distributive justice, e.g. those concerning a shrinking biodiversity (extinction of species), large-scale geological formation changes above and below ground which often go hand in hand with ground water lowering (*Ewigkeitslasten*, 'eternity burdens'), genetic changes in the human, animal or plant genome and so on. And it seems as if – at least when the long-term dimension of this problem is considered – the question of what to do with toxic or radioactive waste is another example of this kind (Gethmann 1993; Streffer et al. 2011). Thus there is no doubt that the present generation has obligations against the future generations. However, does the obligation finish at a generation k > i (e.g. i = 3 or 4)? Everyday experience seems to support the position taken by quite a number of people, namely that obligation has to end with some greater or lesser degree k, because knowledge about the needs of future generations decreases in proportion to temporal distance. When one tries to express this idea more precisely, however, it appears less plausible. If all obligations end with some degree of generation k, this would mean that there are no obligations at all towards the members of generation g_{i+1}, as opposed to g_i, just because they are members of a generation with a degree $k > i$. Restricting obligations like this would be incompatible with the methodological principle of ethical universalism (Streffer et al. 2011). Temporal particularism ('only the next three generations have rights') can of course be discussed with as much consistency as any other kind of particularism, linking moral rights to ethnic affiliation, religion, class, gender etc. If one grants entitlements to moral subjects at all, however, it seems quite arbitrary to set a temporal, spatial, racial or other limits on them. The decisive argument for not limiting the scope of obligation is not so much a universalistic ethical conception, but the ethical irrelevance of all reasons for such a limit.

Then the question follows: Are we obligated to members of the kth generation to the same degree as we are to those of the first generation after us? An affirmative answer to the foregoing question often leads to the conclusion that we must also answer this question in the affirmative mode. The conclusion should be that there is an obligation towards members of the generation g_k, just as for members of the generations $g_{k-1}, g_{k-2}, \dots g_1$. This does not necessarily follow. On the contrary, it is always essential to distinguish – regardless of the temporal distance between the obligated and the entitled parties – between the existence of an *obligation* on the one hand and the degree to which it is *binding* on the other (in the choice of words, if not in substance, the distinction follows Kant (1907/1914, AA VI MS:390ff).

For issues of long-term obligation, the assumption of an unchanging obligation for the individual leads to a paralysing pragmatic paradox: do we have obligations towards the 10,000th generation which are just as binding as those towards our children's generation? While we are sufficiently familiar with the 'lifeworld' of our children to determine the circumstances and consequences of actions, in material terms, with a fair degree of certainty, we can describe these only in the framework of an imagined 'lifeworld' for the 10,000th generation after us. Thus while we can anticipate the 'lifeworld' of our children enough to reach a moral judgement, for the 10,000th generation after us we would have only very vague ideas with tremendous uncertainty. This would mean that, taking long-term obligation into consideration, it would be wrong for us to either commit or omit actions which are currently under debate – even if not committing (not omitting) such actions may have disastrous consequences for our children's generation (Streffer et al. 2011).

Long-term obligation in the absence of knowledge

Given the consequences that would arise if we base our actions on the assumption of an equally binding obligation towards all future generations, regardless of how little we know about them, it is necessary for *ethical* reasons to distinguish between the obligation which exists universally, indefinitely, and a degree of binding force which decreases with spatial, social, and here especially, with temporal distance. However, when the claims must be rejected, that on the one hand obligations exist towards all future generations, and on the other hand the obligations remain equally binding for all distant future generations, then the question arises: how should the obligation towards future generations be qualified? The obvious answer is to apply a sort of 'constructive' procedure: it is taken into account that there is a difference between the obligation towards distant future generations ('future long-distance obligation') and the obligation towards our children and grandchildren ('future local obligation'). However, cases of local obligation allow us to reconstruct the rules upon which long-distance obligations are also constructed. The difference between local and long-distance obligations is that, in the case of long-distance obligation, we have obligations towards people (respectively they have claims on us) who will never, not even potentially, face us as partners in interaction and thus in conflict. Our rules for conflict resolution ('peace strategies') can thus only be 'projected' onto these generations. The following example may clarify and demonstrate that the gradation of binding force is entirely in agreement with our everyday moral experience and thinking: there is a general categorical obligation to help everybody in need. If, for example, someone faints during a flight, the obligation applies to everybody present to help the fainted person. The degree of binding force is, however, higher for professional flight attendants or for medical doctors who are present just by chance than for other present people. In the case of two random witnesses to the fainting attack, both have the obligation to help, but it is not necessarily equally binding for both. It is certainly more binding for the flight attendants and any doctors who may be present because of the delegation of obligation into professional hands (Streffer et al. 2011).

The particular requirements of long-term obligations become clearer when one bears in mind that regarding an obligation spanning 10,000 generations makes considerable use of the fact that our relationship to the future generations is characterized by decreasing levels of knowledge. If the ethical relevance of our lack of knowledge about the future were not considered, the qualification of moral obligations would be separated from important factors of judgement about actions and its consequences with roughly counterintuitive results. This should not, however, be misunderstood: one cannot assume a constantly existing correlation between the temporal distance and the degree of knowledge/ignorance with regard to any developments and then – in the manner of a fixed discount rate – allow the binding force to diminish along the time line. The degree of ignorance about temporally remote world conditions is not more a constant than knowledge about spatially remote conditions (e.g. in as yet unexplored continents) has been, throughout human history. In some areas at least, research and exploration make it possible to identify new conditions, to formulate parameter dependencies as well as laws for governing courses of events despite the existence of tremendous variability. Therefore it can be allowed to propose more or less proven hypotheses and reject other hypotheses as impossible.

As a general rule, obligations are not only universalistic, insofar as they exist towards every person who may in the future be affected by the consequences of decisions. They are also universalistic in the sense that every person is the addressee of the obligation. If – as might be the case for long-distance obligations – individual actors do not assume their obligation, or do not do so adequately, because they do not possess the requisite cognitive or the respective material resources, then in many cases the collective organization of the assumption of obligations allows a greater scope. On the basis of the present obligations it is absolutely necessary to improve the status of knowledge. Research is required in order to improve the knowledge with respect to the disposal of radioactive material (cf. studies of transmutation of radionuclides, of migration of radionuclides in the host-rock). Those actions by which the knowledge is improved should have the preference in the process of decisions and the results should be taken into account.

Thus the increase in the scope of our actions through technologization and collectivization is accompanied with the obligation to form organizations and equip them with the requisite resources. Then it will be lightened to organize society's long-term obligations on the basis of the knowledge gained, or of rationally founded suppositions, without being dependent on the resource constraints of the individual actors. The obligation towards future generations thus also includes the obligation of the individual actors to try to ensure an adequate supply of the resources necessary for this. In this process responsibility is transferred to organizations, by means of delegation of obligations, and the binding force applying to different people becomes differentiated. Nonetheless, the individual as the actual bearer of the obligation cannot completely release himself or herself from responsibility – on the contrary, in delegating the fulfilment of his or her obligations, the individual is at the same time assuming responsibility for monitoring the responsible organizations. This can in turn be partly organized through the division of labour, by creating further organized responsibilities, but ultimately it is up to the individual actor as moral subject to supervise and demand the exercise of delegated responsibility as part of the fulfilment of his duties. Participation of the actual bearers of obligation in consultation processes within and outside the organization is thus a key prerequisite for the adequate fulfilment of these duties.

However, the fulfilment of the duties towards the members of future generations responds to demands which cannot be directly raised. In relation to the time spans which are at stake in the management of high-level waste, the claims actually made by contemporaries in fact represent only a very narrow track of all claims which must be taken into consideration. First of all, we must make well-founded attributions about the claims of these future generations. Here we cannot assume a systematic coherence between the claim profiles of present-day parties to the conflict and the future generations who are to be included as parties to the conflict. The certainty with which such attributions can be made tends to decrease with temporal distance, as does the justifiability of the assertion that one can competently represent the claims of future generations. Thus for issues with a long-term perspective the decision-making burdens must be deferred to procedures: the rights to represent future generations must be transferred in a legitimized manner and require especially a procedural organization of measures for avoiding contingency. This transfer then also develops self-binding powers, with which the participant himself limits his rights of participation and control in order to guarantee the legitimacy of the procedure.

A lack of acceptance for decisions then no longer means that the process is inadequate (no more than widespread acceptance means that the process is adequate).

On the contrary, only the correct execution of a process which is in actual fact accepted as producing legitimation does produce legitimation (Luhmann 1969; Grunwald and Hocke 2006). The responsible representation of future claims thus requires a mandate which is legitimized by procedural organization, anchored in institutions, and controlled by society. Rights of representation cannot simply be claimed by declaring oneself to be competent, responsible, or personally affected.

In the context of temporal long-term considerations (in the range of million years) about the safety and possible risks of repositories for high-level radioactive waste it may be enlightening to remember the period of the lifetimes of 'Homo-Species' and its direct ancestors on earth.

Periods of evolution of Homo species (years before our time; times are estimated on findings of bones and respective analyses)

Homo erectus1.	9 Million until 100,000 years
Homo heidelbergensis	600,000 until 200,000 years
Homo neanderthalesis	250,000 until 28,000 years
Homo sapiens	150,000 years until now
1st script (incomplete)	since 5,000 to 6,000 years ago

These data show that the estimates about the safety and possible risk considerations go back to around the time of the first appearance of Homo erectus. The oldest bones of Homo sapiens were found in Africa around 150,000 years ago. Around 100,000 years ago Homo sapiens started to migrate from Africa to Europe (*New Scientist*, October 27, 2007, 36–41).

Conclusions

The solution of long-term radioactive waste management (RWM) contains a technical and an ethical/social dimension. The concept and construction of the necessary repositories implies not only technically achievable measures but also legally and politically feasible aspects as well as publicly acceptable points on ethical and social grounds. The prudent disposal/management of radioactive waste presupposes the development of an appropriate overall strategy with regard to safety, health protection and environmental protection over an extremely long time period.

The time frame of one million years and reference doses between 0.1 to 0.3 mSv per year for the evaluation of the long-term safety of high-level waste with radionuclides of long physical half-lives seems an appropriate compromise between the ethical requirements for long-term responsibility and the limits of practical reasons. Geological evolution occurs over considerably longer periods of time than biological or social processes of evolution. Therefore statements about the possible safety of the geological barriers can be made over longer time periods than prognoses about inhabitancy for the region of a disposal site. The technical solutions have to ensure beyond reasonable doubt safe and secure containment of long-lived highly radioactive waste for the indefinite/distant future and avoidance of undue burdens on future generations. Processes of legitimization to solve the question of disposal facilities must be designed in such a way that they do equally justice to everyone, and in particular give adequate consideration to the claims of future generations.

Obligations to future generations are generally valid indefinitely. Management strategies for radioactive waste must nonetheless be developed for limited time spans. The binding force of obligations decreases gradually with distant generations. The question must be considered: to which degree is the binding force qualified in its strength and coupled to the knowledge about the living conditions of distant future generations? In the absence of knowledge about the 10,000th generation the binding force is less evident to this generation than to our children's generation. The present generation as the primary beneficiary of nuclear energy has the obligation to initiate the solution of the disposal problem. The demand for *immediate* disposal of high-level waste, however, imposes an unjustifiable burden on the present generation. Further research is needed in order to improve the knowledge and under these conditions plausible research has the absolute priority in all decisions. For issues with a long-term perspective the decision-making burdens must be regulated by certain procedures: the rights to represent future generations must be transferred in a legitimized manner and require especially a procedural organization of measures for avoiding contingency.

A categorical rejection of all proposed solutions for the disposal of high-level waste is incompatible with our obligations towards future generations. A comprehensive supply of information to the public must be ensured. Transparency of the decision-making process as well as information about the fundamental foundations of the gained results is strongly required. Such a procedure is desirable, if not necessary, and also appropriate in a democratic system to attain the acceptance or at least the tolerance of the people affected. The formation of opinions must occur in a democratic process that this is not in the line of technocratic decisions, but ultimately a democratic decision. Democracy requires argumentation, and publicity requires transparency.

Note

1 This contribution is based on the project *Radioactive Waste – Technical and Normative Aspects of Its Disposal*. Springer-Verlag, Berlin, 2011 by Streffer C., Gethmann C. F., Kamp G., Kröger W., Rehbinder E., Renn O. and Röhlig K.-J.

References

Baltes B., Rohlig K. J. and Kindt A. (2007), Sicherheitsanforderungen an die Endlagerung hochradioaktiver Abfälle in tiefen geologischen Formationen, Entwurf der GRS', *Gesellschaft für Anlagen- und Reaktorsicherheit*, GRS-A 3358.
BEIR (2005) BEIR VII. *Health Effects of Exposure to Low Levels of Ionizing Radiation*. National Academy Press, Washington, DC.
BMU (Bundesministerium für Umwelt, Naturschutz und Reaktorsicherheit) (2010) *Sicherheitsanforderungen an die Endlagerung wärmeentwickelnder radioaktive Abfalle*. www .bmu.de/atomenergie_ver_und_entsorgung/downloads/doc/42047.php [Accessed 30 September 2010].

Flowers B. (1976) 'Nuclear power and the environment', *Royal Commission on Environmental Pollution* (ed), Sixth Report, London.

Gethmann C. F. (1993) 'Langzeitverantwortung als ethisches Problem im Umweltstaat' in Gethmann C. F., Kloepfer M. and Nutzinger H.G. (eds), *Langzeitverantwortung im Umweltstaat* Economica Verlag, Bonn, 1–21.

Grunwald A. and Hocke P. (2006), Die Endlagerung nuklearer Abfalle als ungelöstes Problem' in Hocke P and Grunwald A (eds), *Wohin mit dem radioaktiven Abfall? Perspektiven für eine sozialwissenschaftliche Endlagerforschung.* Nomos Verlagsgesellschaft, Berlin, 11–34.

ICRP (1998) 'Protection recommendations as applied to the disposal of long-lived solid radioactive waste', ICRP Publication 81, *Ann. ICRP 28(4)*.

ICRP (2007) 'Recommendations of the International Commission on Radiological Protection' ICRP Publication 103. Pergamon Press, Oxford, New York, Frankfurt, Seoul, Sydney, Tokyo.

ICRP (2013) 'Radiological protection in geological disposal of long-lived solid radioactive waste' ICRP Publication 122, *Ann. ICRP 42(3)*.

Jones D. (2007) 'Going global: how humans conquered the world', *New Scientist 2007*, 36–41.

Kant I. (1903/1911) [AA IV GMS] 'Grundlegung zur Metaphysik der Sitten' in *Gesammelte Schriften.* Bd. IV, Berlin.

Kant I. (1907/1914) [AA VI MS] 'Die Metaphysik der Sitten' in *Gesammelte Schriften.* Bd. VI, Berlin.

Kant I. (1912) [AA VIII Idee] 'Idee zu einer allgemeinen Geschichte in weltbürgerlicher Absicht' in *Gesammelte Schriften.* Bd. VIII, Berlin, 15–35.

KASAM (2007) 'Nuclear Waste – State-of-the-Art Report 2007 – responsibility of current generation, freedom of future generations', main report from the Swedish National Council for Nuclear Waste (KASAM).

Kern L. and Nida-Rumelin J. (1994) *Logik kollektiver Entscheidungen.* C. H. Beck, München.

Luhmann N. (1969) *Legitimation durch Verfahren.* Suhrkamp Verlag, Frankfurt/Main.

Marivoet J., Cunado M., Norris S. and Weetjens E. (2008) 'Impact of advanced fuel cycle scenarios on geological disposal', *Euradwaste '08* Conference, Luxembourg, 20–22 October 2008. http://ftp.cordis.europa.eu/pub/fp7/fission/docs/euradwaste08/papers/paper-10-impact-of-advanced-pt-j-marivoet_en.pdf.

Mittelstraß J. (2008), Vorwort' in Gethmann C. F. and Mittelstraß J. (eds), *Langzeitverantwortung. Ethik, Technik, Ökologie.* Wissenschaftliche Buchgesellschaft, Darmstadt, 7f.

OECD/NEA (1995) 'The environmental and ethical basis of geological disposal of long-lived radioactive waste', a collective opinion of the Radioactive Waste Management Committee of the OECD Nuclear Energy Agency.

Rawls J. A. (1999) *Theory of Justice.* Revised Edition, Cambridge, MA.

Roeser S. (2011) 'Nuclear energy, risk, and emotions', *Philos. Technol. 24*, 197–201.

Shrader-Frechette K. (2000) 'Duties to future generations, proxy consent, intra- and inter-generational equity: the case of nuclear waste', *Risk Analysis 20(6)*, 771–78.

Streffer C. (2009) 'Radiological protection: challenges and fascination of biological research', *Strahlenschutzpraxis, 2009(2)*, 35–45.

Streffer C., Bolt H., Follesdal D., Hall P., Hengstler J. G., Jacob P., Oughton D., Prieß K., Rehbinder E. and Swaton E. (2004) *Low Dose Exposures in the Environment.* Springer, Berlin.

Streffer C., Gethmann C. F., Kamp G., Kröger W., Rehbinder E., Renn O. and Röhlig K.-J. (2011) *Radioactive Waste – Technical and Normative Aspects of its Disposal.* Springer-Verlag, Berlin.

Taebi B. (2011) 'The morally desirable option for nuclear power production', *Philos. Technol. 24*, 169–92.

Tremmel J. (2009) *A Theory of Intergenerational Justice.* Routledge, London.

UNSCEAR (2006) *Sources and Effects of Ionizing Radiation.* United Nations, New York.

Index

For Product Safety Concerns and Information please contact our EU
representative GPSR@taylorandfrancis.com
Taylor & Francis Verlag GmbH, Kaufingerstraße 24, 80331 München, Germany